Decoding Anorexia

Decoding Anorexia is the first and only book to explain anorexia nervosa from a biological point of view. Its clear, user-friendly descriptions of the genetics and neuroscience behind the disorder are paired with first person descriptions and personal narratives of what biological differences mean to sufferers. Author Carrie Arnold, a trained scientist, science writer, and past sufferer of anorexia, speaks with clinicians, researchers, parents, other family members, and sufferers about the factors that make one vulnerable to anorexia, the neurochemistry behind the call of starvation, and why it's so hard to leave anorexia behind. She also addresses:

- How environment is still important and influences behaviors
- The characteristics of people at high risk for developing anorexia nervosa
- Why anorexics find starvation "rewarding"
- Why denial is such a salient feature, and how sufferers can overcome it

Carrie also includes interviews with key figures in the field who explain their work and how it contributes to our understanding of anorexia. Long thought to be a psychosocial disease of fickle teens, this book alters the way anorexia is understood and treated and gives patients, their doctors, and their family members hope.

Carrie Arnold is a freelance science writer and blogs daily at EDBites.com. She is an advisor to the advocacy organization FEAST (Families Empowered And Supporting the Treatment of Eating Disorders) and regularly appears at national and international eating disorder conferences.

Decoding Anorexia

How Breakthroughs in Science
Offer Hope for Eating Disorders

Carrie Arnold

Routledge
Taylor & Francis Group

NEW YORK AND LONDON

First published 2013
by Routledge
711 Third Avenue, New York, NY 10017

Simultaneously published in the UK
by Routledge
27 Church Road, Hove, East Sussex BN3 2FA

Routledge is an imprint of the Taylor & Francis Group, an informa business

Library of Congress Cataloging-in-Publication Data
Arnold, Carrie, 1980–Decoding anorexia : how breakthroughs in science offer hope
for eating disorders / Carrie Arnold. p. cm. Includes bibliographical references and index.
ISBN 978–0–415–89866–9 (hardback) – ISBN 978–0–415–89867–6 (paperback)
1. Anorexia nervosa. 2. Eating disorders–Psychological aspects. I. Title.
RC552.A5A75 2012616.85'262–dc23
2012015294

ISBN: 978–0–415–89866–9 (hbk)
ISBN: 978–0–415–89867–6 (pbk)
ISBN: 978–0–203–08817–3 (ebk)

Typeset in Minion
by Swales & Willis Ltd, Exeter, Devon

To Stephanie Milstein, Ph.D.

Contents

Foreword

My first thought when I heard the title "Decoding Anorexia" was "What a great title!" Anorexia nervosa is such an enigma—to clinicians, researchers, parents, partners, and sufferers themselves. If only we had a decoder ring or an Enigma machine to decrypt the mysterious language of anorexia nervosa that can perplex us all.

Carrie Arnold has provided us with a masterful code cracker that triangulates three perspectives in a unique way. As someone who has suffered from anorexia nervosa, as a trained scientist, and as a science writer, Carrie brings together her three perspectives to present a digestible chronicle of anorexia nervosa from the inside out, emphasizing the biological perspective.

When some readers see the term "biology" they may think about running for the hills; but don't! Carrie provides us with a clear and user-friendly description of all facets of the biology of anorexia nervosa, from genetics to neurobiology. She then pairs the biological explanations with her own, rich, first-person description of what those biological differences feel like to someone with the disorder. She also weaves in the personal narratives of several women and men who have either survived or succumbed to the illness. Finally, she incorporates rich interviews with many of the key figures in the field. But these are not canned interviews. Sometimes speaking to doctors and researchers can be supremely frustrating. You want to just stop them, rewind, or take some sort of Rosetta Stone course to be able to translate what they are saying. In her inimitable way, Carrie got them to talk in real terms, offering rich analogies, telling stories, and providing vivid illustrations of the work they do and how it contributes to our collective understanding of anorexia nervosa. Whether she's talking to Walter Kaye about neuroimaging, to me about genetics, to Jim Lock about set-shifting, or Kelly Klump about hormones—reading her capture of the scientists' words is like having them all sit around in your living room talking to your grandparents, in terms they can understand, about the science of anorexia nervosa.

Decoding Anorexia doesn't shy away from the difficult topics and it does not sugar-coat the reality that is anorexia nervosa. Carrie takes on the complicated topics, such as what is recovery, psychiatric commitment, and the fact that there might be something different about the brains of individuals with anorexia nervosa that influences how they experience starvation.

Her anthropomorphizing of brain parts provides a clever mnemonic to understand how different parts of the brain work together to do something as simple as choosing what to eat. She illustrates the total breakdown of the orchestra when the conductor is too hungry to lead the various brain sections in their respective roles in that decision-making process.

Carrie's frank accounts of her own relapses serve as warnings to others about how treacherous the food deprivation and excessive exercise trap can be and how you can slip back into destructive patterns before you are even aware of what is happening.

Most importantly, Carrie underscores in so many ways the critical role that anxiety plays in vulnerability to anorexia nervosa. Well over half of individuals with anorexia nervosa suffer from anxiety disorders and, of those who do, the majority report that the anxiety disorder predated the eating disorder, suggesting (and vividly illustrated in *Decoding Anorexia*) that anxiety is a pathway into the disorder ... and finding alternative ways to manage anxiety is a pathway out.

In the end, Carrie offers hope. Understanding biological differences and how hard-wiring might make your experience of the world different from others' provides a comforting explanatory model for many individuals with anorexia and their families who have struggled to decode this perplexing illness.

If you happen to be a little biology-phobic, take the book one chapter at a time. But in so doing allow Carrie to enlighten you about the biology, take time to integrate what she discusses into your own experience of the world, and benefit from her ability to expertly unite her three unique traits as a sufferer, a scientist, and a writer to provide one of the more lucid descriptions of the experience of anorexia nervosa ever chronicled. Once you are done, you too will have cracked the anorexia code and have greater compassion for yourself or for someone you care about who has the disorder.

Cynthia M. Bulik, Ph.D., FAED
Director, University of North Carolina Eating Disorders Program
Author of *The Woman in the Mirror: How to Stop
Confusing What You Look Like with Who You Are*

Introduction
Off the Couch and Into the Brain

Why won't you just *eat*?

My mom practically wailed this question as she pleaded with me to take another bite, just one more bite of fat-free yogurt, of a lettuce leaf, of anything. I'm full, I told my mother. I ate earlier. I'm not hungry. I don't feel good. I do eat, you just don't believe me. I had been diagnosed with anorexia nervosa only three months previously, and I hovered dangerously near death as my illness stripped the flesh from my bones with the ruthless efficiency of a piranha. But I didn't see this—I just saw the same scrubby redhead I always saw when I looked in the mirror.

I couldn't understand why my friends and family were so worried. I felt fine. Sure, I was freezing all the time, even in the muggy summer heat. I had a nasty habit of blacking out almost every time I stood up. Tumbleweeds of hair rolled across the bathroom floor as I simultaneously sprouted a coating of fine, downy fur all over my face and stomach. Yet I could exercise for hours a day. I was acing my advanced science courses at college. I scribbled bizarre and macabre poetry late into the night. And I looked in the mirror and saw a completely normal-looking person. In fact, the person I saw could stand to lose about ten more pounds. So how could I be too thin? There was no way I was going to stop losing weight until I could see I was thin. My friends and family were clearly delusional. Didn't they see the disgusting quantities of food I ate each day—the spoonful of yogurt, the egg white drowned in mustard? They had the problem, not me.

Anorexia had essentially blinded me, both to my illness and to its consequences. I had lost over one-third of my body weight in six months. Even the idea of picking up a fork filled me with terror. I could no more eat a bite of lasagna than I could build a rocket ship. But back then, and for many years to come, I thought self-starvation was simply a choice I was making. Of course I wasn't choosing recovery—there was nothing to recover from. I didn't have a problem. Or if I did, it wasn't that serious. I liked not eating. It made sense when almost nothing else did.

On the outside, my eating disorder appeared to be little more than an obstinate refusal to eat anything but lettuce leaves and weigh more than 100 pounds.

Some people assumed I was a vain little girl whose diet had gone overboard in her attempt to look like the supermodel du jour. Relatives told me that I would get better when I accepted how much Jesus loved me just the way I was, and that a failure to do this would condemn me to hell. When I told a friend in graduate school, a young woman with her Ph.D. in psychology, about my eating disorder, she said, "So your mother must be pretty controlling, huh?"

These so-called answers seemed hollow and false. They didn't help me understand why I felt compelled to starve myself or to blaze a trail away from anorexia and towards life. Yes, I thought I was fat, but I wasn't consumed by these thoughts until after I started losing weight. Ditto for the allure of models and freakishly skinny women. And there's nothing like watching your youngest child starve herself into a nearly unrecognizable wraith, her quirky humor replaced by the death mask of an eating disorder, to make a mother over-controlling.

I was first diagnosed with anorexia nervosa in the spring of 2001, at the end of my junior year in college. I had begun exercising and trying to eat "healthier" as a freshman at a small liberal arts college in west Michigan, but these habits initially stayed well within the realm of normal eating behaviors. Even throughout my sophomore year, I remained far more concerned with the crushing depression and anxiety that continued to plague me than the size of my thighs.

I spent the fall semester of my junior year studying in Scotland and returned carrying wonderful memories, gifts for all, and yes, five extra pounds. Not much, but just enough to make my favorite jeans a smidge tighter around the waist. Away from exercise during this semester, I began the spring of my junior year with an innocent, earnest desire to workout regularly and shed those five pounds.

My restricting started slowly as I vowed to cut out "extras" from my diet. That meant skim milk instead of cream in my coffee, no late-night snacks, no calorie-laden beverages, and low-fat versions of everything. Baby carrots accompanied my sack lunch instead of pretzels or chips. Soon, however, more and more food seemed extraneous. I didn't need any milk in my coffee. Maybe I shouldn't eat any fat. I stopped eating meat and peanut butter. Then I cut out bread and pasta. Although my actual diet became limited and bland, I enjoyed how it "tasted" of virtue and superiority and calm and control. This taste, combined with vast quantities of black coffee and diet soda, rapidly drowned out any hunger pangs I may have had. Ten pounds came off before I even noticed.

I relished my weight loss success for about 30 seconds before a horrific fear clawed its way into my brain and refused to let go: I couldn't gain this weight back. That would be awful, terrible, a nightmare. The only solution that slowed the racing tattoo of my heart was a vow to keep losing weight. Then I wouldn't have to worry. Then things would be fine. Looking back, I realize that I can say: there. That's when I first became anorexic. I wasn't clinically underweight at that point, but I was unable to start eating on my own, I was terrified of gaining weight, and I was unable to see what the issue was.

The obsessive-compulsive behaviors I thought I had conquered in high school roared back to life as I starved myself, and the bottom rapidly fell out from under me. Even a prestigious internship working in the smallpox labs at the Centers for Disease Control in Atlanta couldn't override my terror of eating, and I soon landed in the hospital, the first of many stays that would come to demarcate my life. These treatments, at some of the nation's most well-known and well-respected eating disorder treatment centers, took on a harrowing pattern: I entered treatment, distressed and very ill, ate just enough to be discharged, and then immediately lost what little weight I had gained. The process seemed to repeat itself endlessly as I cycled in and out of hospitals and treatment centers.

I finally managed to cobble together several years of relative wellness, loosely defined as not living at death's door, only to relapse spectacularly as a stressful new job stretched me to the limit. This time, I began purging as well, abusing laxatives and diuretics in a frantic terror to rid myself of every unnecessary ounce. I became phobic of water and ChapStick, afraid that they might add a fraction of a pound or a single calorie to my meager intake. Five years of abusing my body began to add up, and I wound up back in the hospital and back in residential treatment, this time for seven months. By this point, I had long since accepted that I had a problem that could be called anorexia, although I didn't think I was thin enough to "qualify" for the diagnosis. I was also quite happy to recover from my eating disorder, just as long as I didn't have to eat and gain weight.

During my time in treatment, I begged therapists to help me understand why I had gotten sick, hoping that I could answer this question and get rid of the eating disorder. The answers I had unearthed as the key to my eating disorder, and the manner in which I found them (answers first, food second), were in line with traditional thinking on eating disorders. Perhaps anorexia was "about" my pathological need for control—when everything else felt out of control, at least I could control my food and my weight. But as time passed, it became patently obvious, even to me, that although I desperately yearned for control of these things, I never once really possessed them. Or perhaps my mother and I were enmeshed, and I was unable to grow up and individuate properly. Truth be told, my mother and I were quite close, and remain so to this day. My mom prepared the food in my family, so anorexia could be a way I could metaphorically reject her without actually breaking off our relationship. Maybe my over-zealous dieting was a feministic "up yours" to the patriarchy, but done in a nice, obedient, womanly way. Except these things never crossed my mind as my weight plunged. Eating terrified me, of this I was certain, and my life simply came to revolve around this fact.

In sessions with my psychologists and in group therapy and on the phone with my parents, I discussed these ideas over and over and over again. Still I remained entrenched in the eating disorder, and anorexia ruled my mind and filled my thoughts. As the months passed and the treatment bills mounted, I was filled with a nagging doubt that maybe anorexia wasn't really "about" anything at all. Discharged from treatment with plenty of insight but no real clue how to eat, I relapsed almost within hours. Disillusioned with traditional psychotherapy and desperate for some kind of answer, I took matters into my own hands. I returned to the medical research journals into which I had delved as an undergraduate biochemistry major in the hopes that science could provide the insight that therapy hadn't.

What I found astonished me. The biggest risk factor for developing an eating disorder was genetics—leading researchers estimated that up to 80 percent of your risk of developing anorexia was due to your genes and not what magazines you read or how much control you had. I learned that my history of obsessive-compulsive disorder (OCD) was more than just a difficult time in my teens but instead dramatically increased the probability that any attempt at weight loss would become a knot of fears and compulsions. I was far from alone; two-thirds of those with anorexia have a history of anxiety disorders. I learned of new treatments that might give me a fighting chance at recovery. A new treatment for adolescent anorexics, known as the Maudsley Approach, prioritized re-feeding and weight gain, which resulted in recovery rates of 75 percent, recovery rates that were maintained for five years. For anorexia treatment, this was nothing short of astounding.

Through my reading, I began to realize that my eating disorder was driven not by society or by some error in my psyche, but by something deeper and more primal. The core of my eating disorder, that "root cause" I had spent so many thousands of dollars searching for in therapy, was biology. Anorexia was a biologically based mental illness that I didn't choose and my parents (and society) didn't cause.

Up until just a few years ago, the idea that eating disorders, indeed any mental health issues, might have a biological basis was essentially anathema. Psychotherapy held the answers to my questions, not biology. Bad parenting caused eating disorders. Our thin-is-in culture caused eating disorders. Fears of growing up caused eating disorders. A need for control caused eating disorders. Low self-esteem caused eating disorders. Never once in my first seven years of treatment did someone mention biology or genetics. Never once did someone attempt to lift the shroud of blame that had enveloped both me and my parents.

Despite arming myself with the latest research, years of failed treatments and ongoing physical damage from chronic starvation and malnutrition left me with little hope. I gave therapy one last shot and began working with a therapist who lifted that shroud and I emerged, blinking into the sunlight. Dr Milstein was well-versed in the latest evidence-based treatment for eating disorders, and she didn't waste time on "why." Unlike previous therapists, she didn't give me the asinine advice that I just needed to get laid. No, she said, I needed to eat, and eat regularly. Many of our initial sessions focused on overcoming the obstacles I had to eating, which included moving home and putting my mom in charge of planning and preparing my meals. Our discussions then moved on to a wide array of topics, from childhood body image issues to how to recover in a toxic society. I stopped mulling over playground bullying from the second grade and started trying to understand how my brain fell under the powerful sway of starvation.

As my eating and weight normalized, I began to explore why I got sick and how these factors continued to leave me vulnerable to relapse. My brain, I learned, was wired differently. Tiny genetic differences in such intangibles as the HT2A serotonin receptor had me pre-wired for anorexia from birth. That innocent attempt at losing five pounds in my junior year of college had set off a series of events that tripped those neurochemical wires and ultimately snow-balled out of control.

Talking to other sufferers, ranging from a middle-aged woman who finally recovered from a 40-year battle with anorexia and bulimia, to a young man from Singapore still in the midst of his struggle, I learned that my experiences were hauntingly similar to theirs. We all shared the endorphin highs of star-vation and exercise. During our eating disorders, we showed almost identical phobias about food and weight and had developed odd rituals around eating and exercise that demanded almost every waking moment. That people of dif-ferent ages, races, cultures, and socioeconomic classes had all developed virtu-ally identical fears and phobias during their illnesses only confirmed that some-thing far deeper than culture was at work.

I also queried the college friends my eating disorder had left behind in its frenetic obsession with food, asking them what they thought of their bodies and food to bring a broader perspective to my own anorexia. Before the eating disorder, I was hardly the most body-obsessed of any of my friends, nor was I especially diet-savvy. Furthermore, several of my classmates who joined me on trips abroad gained weight and then set about losing it upon their return. Only I developed anorexia—why? What made me different from my classmates that drove me to eschew food and fat? What drove me to tether myself to the treadmill, to become a walking, calorie-counting manual? And how did my friends escape from their diets completely unscathed, while mine morphed into an eating disorder that followed me for a decade? What, if anything, did my personal history of anxiety and depression have to do with my rapid descent into anorexia? What part did coming of age in the late twentieth century play? This book is my answer to those questions.

Although the vast body of research clearly points to a genetic basis for eating disorders—close relatives of those with anorexia are twelve times more likely to develop an eating disorder—no one is discounting the importance of envi-ronment for a moment. Any illness is the combination of nature and nurture, genes and environment, culture and chemistry. Environment clearly has a role to play. Many eating disorders begin with a diet, and a culture that says thinness is next to godliness will almost certainly be more conducive to eating disorders than one that promotes a Venus of Willendorf ideal.

Harvard anthropologist Anne Becker found that the arrival of American tel-evision on the island of Fiji in the mid-1990s brought with it the body image woes so common to me and my peers. Traditional Fijian women admired fat-ness in themselves, and dieting was a foreign concept. In the early 1990s, most adolescent Fijian girls accepted their bodies and eating disorders were essen-tially non-existent. But three years after these girls began watching American television, over two-thirds had dieted to lose weight, and 11.3 percent had forced themselves to vomit in an attempt to lose weight.

But even cultures that embrace a much larger female body, such as the Caribbean island of Curacao, have rates of anorexia nervosa comparable to North America and Western Europe. In the 1980s, researcher Hans Hoek found that people on the island of Curacao suffered from anorexia about as much as those on Long Island or the British Isles. Biology might not be destiny, but it still matters, and it matters a lot.

Understanding anorexia requires knowledge of both the biological and the cultural factors driving this disease. Through my research, I have found it virtually impossible to completely separate the effects of nature and nurture. Rather, the interweave of biology and environment produces anorexia nervosa on a loom that has existed for thousands of years. This warp and weft produces a slightly different weave in every single person, and different patterns emerge in different places and cultures and eras. But the core of the illness—the fear of food, an inability to maintain a healthy weight—remains the same.

Anorexia nervosa is a baffling, cunning disease that plagues millions of people around the world, from every country and socioeconomic class. It is the most lethal of all psychiatric illnesses, claiming up to one-fifth of its chronic victims, mostly through cardiac arrest and suicide. Those who survive are not guaranteed a full recovery, and many continue to live in the shadow of anorexia, unable to fully extricate themselves from their eating disorder. Yet recent scientific advances have dramatically remodeled how we perceive and treat eating disorders. These scientific and clinical advances launched me on a journey to better understand anorexia within the context of my own life, and as an entity in and of itself. To better understand the illness that has haunted me for nearly a decade, I needed to answer three basic questions: Why do people develop anorexia? Why do people stay ill for so long? How can people get better and stay better? To answer these questions and understand anorexia, I needed to get off of my therapist's couch and start peering into my brain.

I am a scientist by training and a science writer by profession. On my search for answers, I dusted off my biochemistry and epidemiology training, as well as my journalism skills. I interviewed psychologists and sufferers, geneticists and anthropologists, parents and activists. I read thousands of scientific research reports and attended conferences. I began a blog and started to interact with the wider eating disorder community. As I did, I began to understand the factors that made me vulnerable to anorexia in the first place, the powerful neurochemistry behind the siren call of starvation, and why I, and so many other sufferers like me, have found it so difficult to leave anorexia behind.

1 From Starving Saints to Dieting Divas

Kate went on her first crash diet when she was 16. Although the diet—and the boyfriend dispute that sparked it—seemed to resolve itself, Kate's eating habits didn't remain normal for very long. That tiny taste of starvation and self-denial never really left her brain, and soon she found herself worrying that no food was really good enough to eat. Something was always wrong with what was being served. Soon Kate was living on little more than bread and water, and her weight plunged.

Family and friends began to comment about her unusual eating habits. They urged her to eat more, but Kate always had a reason why she didn't need to eat. Later, psychologists would say that Kate was just exerting a need for control or was using food to express her fears about leaving her parents' home. But Kate never elaborated much on her underlying motives. All she ever said, with her usual tight-lipped manner, was that she didn't need to eat and, besides, she was just fine as she was. Nothing was wrong with her eating habits, so would everyone please leave her alone?

Always religious, Kate attended her usual services with a renewed vigor. She always allowed herself to take communion—the bread was *holy*, blessed by God, so how could anything be wrong with it? Despite being urged to eat more by those at church, Kate quietly persisted in her self-starvation. Not eating, she said, made her feel pure and closer to God. How could that be a bad thing? It wasn't, her church friends said, but neither was eating to sustain basic bodily functions. Kate was growing facial hair, a sure sign of her body's beleaguered reserves and futile attempts to keep itself warm.

As the years passed, even Kate herself began to understand that her self-starvation had spiraled out of her control. Consuming even the smallest amounts of food caused her great pain. If she did eat more than the daily crumbs she allowed herself, she forced herself to vomit. She wrote pages about what a vile person she was, about how she deserved this torment since she was such an awful person. Kate begged for forgiveness, to be relieved of the burden of starving herself. But these prayers weren't answered.

At the age of 33, after 17 years of anorexia nervosa, Kate died of starvation.

So who was Kate? To many readers, her story seems so familiar: a teenage dieter whose life was ultimately lost to the clutches of an eating disorder. Her story is, in fact, familiar as one of the countless tragedies of anorexia, but Kate's anorexia had nothing to do with supermodels or a diet-obsessed culture. It couldn't have. "Kate" is really Saint Catherine of Siena, who died in 1380 (Reda and Sacco, 2001).

When I first read Saint Catherine's story, I was struck by how similar our stories were. True, I didn't use religious language to explain my eating disorder, but the core symptoms—a fear of food, an inability to maintain a normal weight—were the same. Some psychologists have hypothesized that Catherine wasn't suffering from anorexia nervosa. They called her illness *anorexia mirabilis* because it was supposedly motivated by faith and the extreme starvation was considered miraculous. Modern anorexia, they say, is different because it is motivated by a thin-is-in culture, rather than a holy-is-in culture.

This difference, however, assumes that anorexia is a sociocultural disease. It's true, I live in a very different world than Catherine of Siena. I experienced a profound cultural pressure to be thin; Catherine did not. On the other hand, I have a world of opportunities at my fingertips, something that Catherine would have found foreign, even frightening. Catherine lived in a convent, and her day-to-day living was ruled by the dictates of religion. I'm probably at the opposite end of the religious spectrum.

Miraculous Starvation

Our contemporaries also had very different understandings of anorexia. Catherine's starvation made her a saint in some eyes, a sinner in others. Either way, such power to deny yourself food had to come from somewhere beyond this world. Nowhere did people call Catherine's self-starvation an illness. Nor did Catherine mention the profound body dysmorphia that affects many modern people with anorexia. She never mentioned wanting to lose weight to look better in a nun's habit, or to eat more "healthfully," or to "get in shape." Her motivations—what we know of them, anyway—were almost purely religious. Catherine feared that eating would make her impure or unholy, not fat.

When my parents began to worry that I was eating too little and losing too much weight, they had me talk to a psychologist, not a priest. I was diagnosed with an illness and spent time in several different hospitals and treatment centers. I saw my thighs expand if I ate an extra mouthful and feared weight gain above all else. The mere thought of putting on a few pounds was enough to send me into a tailspin. I used my common cultural language to justify my bizarre behaviors: I was trying to get fit, to eat better, to lose a few pounds. In reality, my behaviors were driven by an irrational fear of food and fatness.

So yes, from a cultural standpoint, mine and Catherine's experiences were very different. If anorexia really were a sociocultural illness, then I would agree that our afflictions were probably not the same. After all, Catherine's food refusal made her a saint. All it got me were threats of a feeding tube and never-ending requests for diet tips. Then again, people in Catherine's time thought that epilepsy and other seizure disorders were evidence of demonic possession. Now we know that seizures occur when massive neuron activity floods the brain. Not surprisingly, the experiences of patients with epilepsy have also changed over the years. Instead of being ostracized or undergoing ineffective exorcisms, current epilepsy patients receive medication and support. Despite these massively different theories of causation and different patient experiences, no one proposes that the medieval epileptic had a different disorder than those today.

The difference between anorexia nervosa and epilepsy is that most people accept biology as a cause for epilepsy, but not anorexia. If anorexia nervosa is a disease of Western culture, then we shouldn't see it in areas without strong Western influences. Yet we do. Recent studies in both China (Lee *et al.*, 1993) and Ghana (Bennett *et al.*, 2004) found rates of anorexia nervosa equivalent to those found in Western countries. Cases of anorexia have also been reported among the Amish (Husni *et al.*, 2001), which isn't a group of people that has access to television or magazines. Clearly, cultural mandates for extreme thinness are not required for anorexia.

Look at the case of Mollie Fancher, one of the famous "fasting girls" of the nineteenth century. Just as current tabloids and magazines speculate about whether certain starlets are anorexic or bulimic, newspapers in the nineteenth century shared lurid stories about girls who claimed they hadn't eaten a single bite of food for years (Brumberg, 2000). Rumored to have survived over a decade without food, the bedridden Fancher became the equivalent of a modern-day reality television star when the media caught wind of her alleged exploits (Stacey, 2002). In the first description of her case, a reporter in *The Brooklyn Daily Eagle* wrote this:

> Her books were her delight; like many another she neglected all for them, and would arise late in the morning as a consequence of weakness, hasten away to school without a breakfast, fearful of being tardy, and then at evening, in her anxiety to learn her lessons, again neglect a meal for which she felt little inclination.

(Dailey, 1894)

Although Fancher never spoke of wanting to be thin, she certainly displayed many of the personality characteristics of someone with anorexia: studious, obsessive, perfectionistic. In fact, this newspaper clipping written over a century before I developed anorexia fits me perfectly. Despite differences in location, time, and culture, Mollie and I shared a similar predisposition to anorexia.

It's something shared by June Alexander as well. When June first developed anorexia at the age of 11 in the 1960s, she was living on her family's dairy farm in a remote area in southeastern Australia. She had never watched television, read a fashion magazine, or even had running water. She grew up in a town where there was no processed food, no advertisements for it, and no advertisements for diets and diet products. Everything she ate was made from scratch by June's mother, and she remembers the food as being nutritious and wholesome. If exposure to popular culture were the only thing that caused anorexia, June would never have gotten sick. But she did, and she remained ill for more than 40 years before finally recovering in her fifties.

June was a happy but anxious child, a tomboy who loved helping out her father on the farm. When June was well-behaved, her mother called her "Tim." It made her heart leap to know she had been a good girl and was appreciated by her parents. Eventually, however, puberty caught up with June. The beginnings of breasts and the start of her periods made it obvious that her days as a tomboy were over. Bras and maxi pads meant being a woman, and that was something that June didn't want. She was desperate for these signs of femininity to disappear.

This realization coincided with a doctor's visit to the school to weigh and measure all of the students. June worried intensely that she would be the only girl with breasts, and that her teacher might be able to see the students when they were only in their underwear. Her mom and older sister laughed at her worries, which left June to try and figure out a solution on her own. "I remember the moment very clearly when I was in the schoolyard playing a ball game, and it was like something went *bing* in my brain. After that I seemed to know exactly what to do," June said. Not eating would eliminate any burgeoning signs of womanhood.

"It wasn't a conscious thought. It wasn't 'I'm going to do this.' I felt compelled to do it. It was as if I had a force in my mind telling me this was how I was going to survive this thing, and this was how I was going to cope," June said. Just a few days after this compulsion emerged, June had a lesson in school where she learned the meaning of the word "calorie." Her brain latched on to every word in the booklet she received. Counting calories and burning them through exercise was the answer she had been looking for.

"I controlled my anxiety by restricting my food," June said. Eating anything at all made June extremely uncomfortable and anxious. "I had this intense fear of eating. And if I did eat, the guilt would be totally enormous, and I would have to go and do some physical activity to compensate," she said.

The one time June did eat without guilt that year was when her mother burned a batch of "fairy cakes" (I would call it angel food cake). "I felt really sorry for her, and I said I'd eat them," June told me. Their wrecked, worthless state matched June's feelings about herself, which made them appropriate fodder for her.

Although June did start eating again after a year of undiagnosed but intense anorexia, her eating disorder hadn't gone away. She transitioned into bulimia, where she would binge on massive amounts of food and then attempt to undo her binge by fasting and over-exercising. On the outside, June looked normal. Inside, she was miserable. Her difficult behaviors and emotions, brought on by depression, anxiety, and an untreated eating disorder, alienated her family, who blamed June for her disorders.

June married and had four children by the time she was 26, and all the while her eating disorder raged. She had been suffering from the disorder for more than 20 years by the time she finally received a diagnosis. June shared her story of more than four decades of torment at the hands of an eating disorder in a two-hour phone conversation that left me simultaneously heartbroken and hopeful. Nowhere in this conversation did June mention cultural pressures to be thin or how she compared herself to models, nor did she mention bad parenting as the cause of her disorder. "What happened to me was that my anxiety just got so intense that I retreated into the illness. It was the way I coped and survived a very stressful time," June said.

I nodded in agreement. I had grown up immersed in a diet culture, but most of the time I didn't give a hoot about being thin. I wanted to lose weight because I thought it would make me happy. I found that anorexia not only alleviated my depression but it also gave my anxiety a focus. Channeling my anxiety into food, weight, and exercise gave me something concrete against which to take action. I could measure my progress in neat numbers. Obsessive worrying and other compulsions didn't provide the same relief as anorexia. It had nothing to do with fashion magazines.

So if it's not culture, what causes anorexia?

"No issue of sexuality, parental conflict, or separation can cause such a distortion of perception and priority. What is going on in the anorexic is a physiological dynamic. The patient is literally starving herself to death," writes Dr James Greenblatt in his 2010 book *Answers to Anorexia*. "The pieces of the puzzle are diverse. Yes, there is a powerful psychological component to anorexia. But there is also a profound physiological one" (p. ix).

The research is clear: anorexia nervosa is fundamentally based in biology. Cases of anorexia exist across time, culture, gender, and socioeconomic class. Anorexia is as biological as schizophrenia and bipolar disorder, all of which are referred to as biologically based mental illnesses. Up to 86 percent of your risk for developing anorexia is genetic.

Researchers haven't found a single gene that causes anorexia, and it's unlikely they will. Most illnesses aren't caused by a malfunction in a single gene. Rather, genes generally increase or decrease your risk of developing the disease. This risk is subsequently influenced by the environment in which a person lives. Anorexia arises from a complex interaction between malfunctioning hunger signals, anxiety, depression, and difficulties with decision making.

Someone isn't born anorexic. The disease generally begins around adolescence, although reports of anorexia in young children and older adults are becoming more common. Sufferers and even clinicians often refer to the coming together of the factors that set off an eating disorder as "the perfect storm." Changes due to puberty, life stress, a period of inadequate nutrition, bullying, and even illness can all work together in concert with someone's genetic predisposition to set off anorexia.

New genetic studies say that relatives of anorexia sufferers are 12 times more likely to have an eating disorder than those in the general population. Other genetic studies have found that genetic risk for anorexia seems to be shared with anxiety and mood disorders. People who suffer from anorexia also share a unique personality profile: they tend to avoid anything they consider "danger-ous," they prefer sameness to novelty, they like objects to be symmetrical, and they have extraordinarily high levels of obsessionality and perfectionism. Brain scans have shown that anorexia sufferers process social information differently, as do their unaffected siblings. Even after recovery, the brains of anorexia suf-ferers function differently than the brains of those who have never had an eating disorder. These differences, combined with thousands of other studies, provide convincing evidence that anorexia is a biologically based mental illness.

Not everyone agrees with me. In fact, in some of the circles I travel in, this statement is controversial, even heretical. "Popular magazines made me feel I had to be thin," they tell me. Or that bad parents and a traumatic past caused their eating disorder. If anorexia were biological, they say, it would invalidate all of their years of suffering. That's not my goal. What I'm saying is that, without a biological predisposition, no amount of crappy parenting, horrific abuse, and beauty magazines that only make you feel ugly would cause an eating disorder. Someone's biological predisposition is affected by their environment—what their parents were like, the culture in which they were raised, and even the sea-son in which they were born.

Even some scientists remain unconvinced that someone will be able to identify genetic markers for psychiatric illness. Specific types of studies, known as genome-wide association studies, look at a person's entire genome and then compare dif-ferences in gene sequences and even in the single DNA building blocks called nucleotides. Many of these genes come in different variations, known as poly-morphisms, that vary in just one DNA building block, known formally as single nucleotide polymorphisms (SNPs, pronounced "snips"). The goal is to identify SNPs that are found significantly more frequently in people with an illness than in the general population. To do this, you need lots of people to participate, which is difficult in a disease that is as relatively rare as anorexia nervosa.

Even if you can get enough people to participate to identify meaningful genetic differences between a group of people with anorexia and those without, some scientists think that looking for genetic causes for psychiatric disorders like anorexia is pointless (Latham and Wilson, 2010). These genome-wide asso-ciation studies will work for diseases like diabetes, Crohn's disease, and even cancer, but they will never work for anorexia, depression, or OCD.

Cynthia Bulik, director of the Eating Disorders Program at the University of North Carolina, Chapel Hill, chalks some of this prejudice up to the centuries-old idea that the mind and body are separate entities—a theory known in academic circles as "dualism." "I have this sense that even scientists out there still have a mind/body split, and they still think that psychiatric disorders are somehow dif-ferent than biological disorders. And that dualism underlies a lot of their resist-ance to viewing psychiatric disorders as biologically based," she said.

The other piece of this resistance stems from the fact that "once an idea is out there, it's so much harder to erase it by science than to introduce a new idea," Bulik said. "They've got to be hit over the head with really dramatic data before they believe it."

Advances in genetic technologies, neuroimaging, and brain development have demolished the idea that mental disorders aren't based in the brain. Over the last ten years, our understanding of mental illnesses in general and anorexia in particular have undergone a revolution. We can now confidently say that anorexia is a brain-based mental illness. No, we don't know everything about anorexia, not by a long shot, but we are moving out of the Dark Ages and into the light.

So what does "brain-based mental illness" even mean? Let me start with what it doesn't mean. It does not mean that:

- environment does not play a role in its development
- environment does not play a role in recovery
- it is 100 percent biologically based
- it is 100 percent genetically inherited
- it can only be treated by physician or with a pill
- psychological interventions won't help
- the patient can't do anything to influence the outcome.

These different thoughts (Ravin, 2011) on what anorexia actually is can dramatically affect how sufferers think of their own illness. As much as I was told to look for causes of my illness in my family and culture, I ultimately blamed myself for my eating disorder. I was the idiot who bought into the ideals presented by digitally altered models. I was the one unable to let go of my disorder. My chronic anorexia meant I was ultimately choosing to stay ill. It was my fault I still struggled after a decade because I didn't work hard enough in therapy and I didn't uncover the roots of my disorder. I felt lost in a morass of despair and self-hatred.

"The idea of anorexia as a choice is laughable," June said. Many people told me that they wanted "just a little anorexia." In common belief, anorexia can be both chosen and un-chosen. Anorexia for a week or so would help them lose weight. Once they can zip their skinny jeans, they can start eating again. Except if anorexia is a choice, it can't really be an illness. Nor, I like to tell people who tell me this, would anyone really want anorexia if they really knew what it was like. Anorexia isn't skinny models and weight loss. It's despair, loneliness, osteoporosis, and death.

In a 2011 paper in *European Archives of Psychiatry and Clinical Neuroscience*, Herpertz-Dahlmann *et al.* write that:

> assumptions regarding the aetiology of eating disorders and, in particular, anorexia nervosa (AN) have built the foundation for a stigmatization of patients and their parents. In a recent investigation, many adolescents with AN were found to hold themselves responsible for their disease; approximately one-third of the patients agreed with the statement that young women or girls with AN were to blame for their condition.

(n.p.)

Learning about the biology of anorexia helped me reframe my struggle. It absolved me of the guilt for causing so much pain in my family. It freed me from looking towards the past for potential causes and helped me look towards the future, towards what I needed to do in recovery. This knowledge didn't cure me, but it did steer me towards effective treatment.

My friend Katie, a 27-year-old psychology student from England and a fellow blogger, knows exactly how a science-based understanding of anorexia can change the course of illness. Katie's eating disorder started when she was 12, with a combination of food restriction, binge eating, and over-exercising. Her weight dropped some—not dramatically, but Katie admits that at age 18, when she went off to university, her weight "wasn't where it needed to be." While away, Katie was the victim of a violent crime and developed post-traumatic stress disorder, along with severe digestive problems, which dramatically increased both her anxiety and her weight loss.

"For about three months, I basically stopped eating. My weight got lower and lower and lower, and I ended up at a day patient program in Dorset [England]," Katie said.

Although Katie completed the day program, she relapsed when she moved across England. After several months of escalating behaviors, she moved back home to Dorset and was sent back to the same day patient program. "They told me it was over-ambitious to recover fully and all sorts of this rubbish," Katie said.

While Katie, who was 24 at that time, was on a waiting list to start the day program, she started a blog to chronicle her recovery from anorexia. "I decided I was sick and tired of having anorexia ruin my life. I don't know how I made that decision, seeing as my physical state was so bad I shouldn't have been able to be that rational," she said.

Through her blog, Katie said, she began to learn about the wider world of eating disorder science that was not available through the local eating disorders service. "I just started reading and realized I'd gotten it all backwards," she said. "One of the first things I came across was the revolutionary idea that I needed to be at a healthy weight before my eating disorder thoughts would disappear."

I could relate to this, I told Katie. Much of my treatment consisted of lots of therapy and much less food. The idea was to figure out why I'd developed anorexia and gain back a sense of control in my life, and then we could tackle the food aspect. Except, as Katie said, this was all backwards. Eating properly and gaining weight wouldn't cure the anorexia, but it would enable me to tackle the obsessive thoughts, fears, and worries with a healthy, functioning brain.

"No one had told me that before," Katie continued. "I was told that if I worked on my issues, I would find it easier to eat and gain weight. It was the biggest load of rubbish ever."

When Katie turned to the research literature, one of the first things she learned was that people recovering from anorexia who maintained a higher body weight had lower rates of relapse (Mayer *et al.*, 2007). She had been studying psychology, and so she went back over her textbooks and notes and started to ask herself questions. "I wondered how much of this was biological, how much was just habit, and how much was psychological," she said. "But I had never thought of it in biological terms because it was so much easier just to blame everything on your issues. Then you don't have to gain weight."

This switch is ideal for someone who is deathly afraid of eating because it prolongs actually having to face the fears of food. Issues? Let me tell you about my issues, I thought, since as long as we're discussing mother issues, and teasing, and roommates, I don't have to put the fork in my mouth and coax that number on the scale upwards.

"This approach let me feel like I was doing something to tackle the eating disorder without actually having to do any scary stuff," I told Katie. "It wasn't until I started eating properly that it occurred to me that food and weight gain could be therapeutic in and of themselves."

The other important thing that Katie learned through science was that she could stop blaming herself for her eating disorder and ongoing struggles. "My therapist tried to use tough love as motivation, and we all know how well that works with people with eating disorders," she said, rather sarcastically. "You're blaming me? Oh, great! That's wonderful! Now I can blame myself more! Thank you for backing me up there!"

So without any professional support, armed only with science, a blog, and supportive friends and family, Katie went about the arduous task of gaining weight and recovering from anorexia. Despite the lack of professional help (or maybe because of it), Katie's anorexia has been in complete remission for nearly two years. She maintains a healthy weight, eats freely and without fear, and has returned to her university studies to become an eating disorders psychologist.

"My theories on what caused eating disorders changed dramatically between the ages of 15 and 25," she said. "I realize now that I had a lot of the traits that predisposed me to anorexia—I've always been a bit obsessive and sensitive. Whereas before, I would have said that being bullied at school caused it, now I realize that being bullied made me anxious, which made me lose my appetite, which led to the discovery that restricting made me feel better."

Mothers, Models, and Other Myths

For people like June, Katie, and me, the discovery of anorexia's biology was an individual act. Doctors and therapists didn't inform us of these facts. We stumbled upon them almost completely on our own. But formal eating disorder programs are beginning to integrate biology into their treatment approaches for anorexia and other eating disorders.

"Science can provide people who are suffering from eating disorders help in developing their own explanatory model [of their illness]," Bulik said. "If we're all grasping for 'why'—why me, why now, why my family?—then I think having an evidence-informed explanatory model can be really helpful. I think people come up with non-evidence informed explanatory models and that can just be detrimental. It can't give you that sense of 'aha!' or 'I get it.'" Instead, sufferers may try to force their experiences into a sociocultural model, or what Bulik calls the "I wanted to look like a thin model" model.

The cold, hard facts about anorexia are certainly important in getting people to understand what causes this eating disorder and what it's like to actually have anorexia, but science can also help build compassion for those who suffer. "Science moves away from finger-pointing and blaming. And with higher understanding, we can be more compassionate," Bulik pointed out.

A 2008 study led by Bulik herself found that college students had more sympathy towards anorexia sufferers after reading information that indicated a biological and genetic explanation for the disorder versus a sociocultural explanation (Crisafulli *et al.*, 2008). This is why Bulik and other therapists often begin treatment with psychoeducation, providing information on the condition, how it's treated, and what patients and families can expect from treatment.

It's something that psychotherapist Sarah Ravin thinks is one of the most crucial parts of treatment. "The science makes a huge difference in my practice. It's something I share with patients and their families from the very first initial evaluation. I think it makes a tremendous amount of difference at first for the patient's parents because it's very confusing and frightening for them to see their kid acting like an alien. Often times they'll think 'What am I doing wrong?' or 'What have I done to cause this?' By having the biological explanation, it makes everything easier to swallow, so to speak," Ravin said.

"I would say the biological explanation makes the biggest difference for the patients who have already been through traditional treatment multiple times and have never recovered or who have relapsed," she said. "For them, it's a breath of fresh air. If it's a newly diagnosed 13- or 14-year-old girl, and the parents learn about the biology right away, it definitely speeds up the recovery. But for the people who have been sick for a very long time, learning to approach the illness in a whole new way—as an illness rather than a choice—it really enables people to recover."

This is almost identical to what happened to me, I told Ravin. "Therapists used to make comments to me that 'I really can't help you because you're not ready to recover.' And I really blamed myself for not being able to get better," I said.

"Waiting until the patient has the insight and motivation to recover is one of the worst things that professionals can do," Ravin said. "Insight and motivation are not going to come until you're already well into recovery. So it's really delaying the treatment process."

Ravin, who received her Ph.D. in clinical psychology in 2008, specializes in the treatment of eating disorders in adolescents and young adults. In her busy practice outside of Miami, she uses scientific evidence in every aspect of treatment, from intake to final discharge. Most of the families and patients she sees are ultimately receptive to the idea that anorexia is a biologically based mental illness. But she and I have both found that, ironically, some of the people most resistant to this idea are other eating disorder professionals.

"What I find interesting is that despite so many good scientific explanations of what causes anorexia—or at least, what *doesn't* cause anorexia—people still persist in thinking that, if we could get rid of all the Photoshopped models, then we wouldn't have eating disorders," I said. Or that many psychologists hold dear the idea that errors in parenting lead to the seeming need for control that is expressed through the eating disorder.

Holding onto ideas that have been shown to be false is known as belief perseverance, Ravin told me, and she sees it all the time. "Belief perseverance is the idea that people tend to cling to their beliefs, even in the absence of data confirming their beliefs," she said.

"When a person has a belief, they will absorb and pay attention to any information that supports that belief. Information that refutes that belief, they will discount or ignore. It's sort of like a filter. People cling to that belief because it serves some sort of important function for them."

So if a treatment provider believes that intrusive parents play a causal role in anorexia, they will discount the studies that show family-based treatment (FBT, more commonly known as the Maudsley Method or the Maudsley Approach) is effective for treating adolescents with anorexia. They might say that FBT isn't appropriate for all families, or that the evidence isn't all that convincing. Perhaps they believe that saying "parents don't cause eating disorders" means letting parents off the hook (Lyster-Mensh, 2011). Or they might say that someone with anorexia is really "starving for love" and needs to work through her issues first (Goulston, 2010).

True, Ravin concedes, FBT isn't perfect. Not all families can successfully re-feed their ill child, nor do all people with anorexia respond to FBT. However, she pointed out, FBT has been shown to be the most effective treatment for adolescents with anorexia in numerous clinical trials. Ignoring that data, Ravin says, is irresponsible. In the complex world of eating disorders treatment, replete with its acronymed treatment modalities (CBT, DBT, ACT, FBT—to which many of us have said "WTF?!?") and array of spa-like treatment facilities, accurate, evidence-based information is nearly impossible to find.

"You know as well as I do that the first place people go for information now is places like WebMD and the like," Bulik told me. Websites can have lots of good information about many different illnesses, but there's just not much really good information to give people about how to treat anorexia, especially in adults.

"I don't know why we're so bad at that, Carrie, but we're still all lured into rocking chairs and horses when we would never think of a rocking chair for something like an ingrown toenail," Bulik said. Part of the problem is finding ways to explain the science of eating disorders to people without any science background. It's not uncommon for health reporters to have no background in biology or medicine. This, combined with the greater accessibility of sociocultural models and the ease with which they make sensational copy, means that science is the focus of relatively few articles on eating disorders in the general media.

"The bias of the media is obvious even just in the way that the information is presented. I mean, it's usually in the 'Style' section, rather than the 'Health' section, where it belongs. And the media has a huge influence in the way society at large perceives eating disorders. *That's* the media influence on eating disorders—not pressuring people to be thin, but by affecting how many people, even clinicians, view eating disorders," Ravin said.

The benefits of science don't end at improving how people understand anorexia. It also improves how we treat anorexia.

"You need to make sure that when you embark on a treatment path that you all have a shared sense of what this disorder is all about. That's really the first place that science comes in. Let's get our terms correct. Let's make sure we understand what we know and what we don't know about causality. Let's understand what we do and don't know about the recovery process and the recovery trajectory. And we use all of these 'knows' to help people understand," Bulik said

In the UCAN (Uniting Couples against Anorexia Nervosa) study she's conducting at the University of North Carolina, Bulik pointed out that many of the partners are engineers. "They expect recovery to be linear," she said.

"My dad's an engineer. He's the same way," I laughed.

"Exactly. They're thinking she's getting better, she's going to keep getting better, she's on an upward trajectory, it's all good. And we're having to say whoa—let's look at the data, let's discuss what's going on here, and what this recovery process is going to look like. It's going to go up and down. We're hoping that it's going to be overall a positive trend, but it's not going to be a straight line. We use the data to help them develop realistic expectations," Bulik said.

"When I started to learn more about the neuroscience of anorexia, it helped me stop blaming myself for not being able to get better by just talking about my issues and hoping I would magically start to love cheesecake—which was how I was treated for the first six or so years of my disorder," I said. "Science let me focus more on how to move forward."

"The point you make is a very interesting one, and it's a hard one for people to grasp. The reason it's hard for people to grasp is that they don't think of eating in terms of social and cognitive variations. To a person without an eating disorder, you pick up the spoon and put the food in your mouth. What's the problem?" Bulik said. "To try and get people to understand, sometimes you have to change your approach. If I don't understand Russian, screaming louder and louder at me in Russian isn't going to get me to understand."

It occurred to me that much of my initial eating disorder treatment consisted of being yelled at in Russian. I knew that photographs of models were digitally altered—that didn't change my body dysmorphia. I knew that one piece of cake wouldn't make me fat—that didn't change my fear of eating it. The louder everyone yelled, the more I dug in my heels. I was scared and confused and nothing was helping.

Sarah Ravin used a different analogy in an essay she wrote for the advocacy organization FEAST (Families Empowered and Supporting the Treatment of Eating Disorders):

Here's the way I see it. A person with active anorexia nervosa or bulimia nervosa is drowning in a freezing ocean. School A (the psychodynamic school of thought) proposes that you talk with the drowning person about how she is feeling and help her to explore the issues in her past that have gotten her into the water or interfered with her ability to swim. Once she develops this insight, she will swim safely to shore and avoid the water in the future. School B (the cognitive-behavioral school of thought) proposes that you send a swimming instructor into the water to teach her how to swim. School C (The Maudsley approach) sends a lifeboat to the drowning person, pulls her aboard as she is thrashing about (despite her protest and resistance), and rows her safely to shore. After she has been medically cleared and has recovered from the effects of hypothermia and near-drowning, she begins to take swimming lessons with a certified instructor. Once she has mastered the skill of swimming and can keep her head safely above water, she begins to process the experience of near-drowning, she explores the factors that brought her into the water, and she learns ways of avoiding a similar predicament in the future.

(Ravin, 2009)

Changing Minds and Hearts

It would be too easy, at this point, to portray science as a knight in shining armor that galloped in and saved my bony self from the clutches of anorexia. That isn't quite true. For one, I probably would have tried to kick the knight off his horse. For another, science doesn't account for the months and years of hard, impossible work that I needed to do in order to get better. I didn't have a magic pill or potion. No wand or study or data set made it all better. But science pointed me in the right direction.

"I think that, a hundred years from now, the biological explanation of eating disorders will be completely obvious to the average person on the street, but it's going to take some time to sink in, and for people to be born into a culture where it's understood," Ravin said.

Despite the fact that many other anorexia sufferers, as well as treatment providers, have begun to recognize the value of science in understanding and treating all eating disorders, most people continue to view anorexia through a sociocultural lens. "Maybe more than any other disorder, we have this false sociocultural model that has an enormous amount of face validity. The world likes simple explanations, and this simple explanation makes sense to people. It seems to fit," Bulik said.

The most common response when people learn I had anorexia was a solicitation for diet tips. The second most common response is that people tell me they know exactly how I feel due to their own eating problems, which usually consisted of a few crash diets in college and the fact that they regularly ask their husbands if their jeans make their butts look fat.

This is, perhaps, the most dangerous and most unrecognized aspect to viewing anorexia as a sociocultural construct. It means that lots of people (usually women) think they know what it's like to have an eating disorder because they dieted a few times and they hate their thighs. It's like saying you know what it's like to have been decapitated because you've had a paper cut. But with this way of looking at eating disorders, paper cuts and guillotines are considered the same.

"Not a lot of people think they've had a little bit of a hallucination because they've asked their husband if they heard something. The perceived continuum doesn't necessarily exist. We don't know whether the dieting and my-butt-looks-fat lies along the same biological continuum as anorexia nervosa," Bulik told me. "We perceive it as the same continuum, and I don't know about you, but I'm not convinced."

"Me, neither," I said.

So what will it take to change minds, I asked Bulik. Why do the sociocultural and parental causes of anorexia—the models and moms explanation—still persist as the dominant explanation for why someone gets sick?

"We're going to need lots of accurate media, strong research findings that we can hit people between the eyes with, and a concentrated effort to debunk myths. Those seem to have been the only things that have worked for other disorders," she said. "We also have to educate practitioners, because some of the biggest biases are still out there among physicians and dietitians and all sorts of people who those with eating disorders present to. And if they go and see these people for help and they get met with all sorts of crazy myths ... Not every anorexic person is strong enough to go 'Excuse me, sir or ma'am, your understanding of my condition is inaccurate and outdated.'"

Nor should someone with anorexia be expected to do this. If I visit an oncologist, I would expect them to have read the latest research journals and devise a treatment plan for me that is based on the studies appearing in these journals and that is deemed most appropriate for my particular case. For reasons that remain unclear, this same expectation doesn't exist for psychotherapy.

A biological explanation for anorexia also doesn't mean that psychotherapy has no place in treatment. "I don't understand where people get the idea that if something is psychological, it can be changed, but if it's biological, it can't be changed," Ravin said. Look at illnesses like diabetes, she pointed out. They're very biological, and yet they can be managed with medication and dietary changes. The fact that diabetes involves a biological inability to maintain proper blood sugar levels doesn't mean that you throw up your hands and die of high blood sugar on the bathroom floor. It means you take aggressive steps to manage the disease and keep it in remission.

Psychotherapy changes the brain, as neuroimaging studies in both spider phobia (Paquette *et al.*, 2003) and OCD (Schwartz *et al.*, 1996) have shown. These studies show a very real change in a sufferer's neurobiology, an idea that is gaining more traction in psychological circles. The spider phobia study is especially relevant to the treatment of anorexia, especially if you consider a phobia of food and weight gain to be one of the central features of the disorder (Strober, 2004).

"What the study shows is that their brains still react the same way after treatment," Bulik said about the spider phobia study, "but their response to that reaction is different. Even if you don't change the biology, you change the way you respond to the biology. And I think that's really important, because we're not out there to change the biology. It's bio feedback, in a way. If you can keep yourself from freaking out when you feel your heart rate going up, that's an important thing."

"It's sort of like how I'll sometimes still feel an internal flutter of fear when I see a rich piece of chocolate cake, but I can say, 'Oh, but that's just cake and I've eaten it before and I've been just fine and it looks good and my pants will still fit when I finish,'" I said.

"Right. Your brain might have the same pattern that it had back when cake was terrifying," Bulik said. The difference is that I've learned better ways to respond to my fears now, and so cake-o-phobia no longer dictates whether or not I have a slice.

Of course, not being controlled by food fears is one of the first steps, but decision making around food is still a complicated and difficult task, even for someone without an eating disorder.

2 Interoception and the Insula

Where do you want to go for dinner?

It's a simple enough question: find a mutually agreeable place and time, and then show up. Yet answering this question requires an enormous amount of information that the brain must process. What types of food does everyone like? Where are some good restaurants? Are they open? Can you park your car easily? Is it too pricey or too casual? What if no one likes the selection? Should you meet at a bar for drinks before or head out for dessert after?

When the brain is healthy and working properly, it's relatively straightforward to come to a decision. You weigh the pros of that new pizza place (good reviews in the newspaper, great atmosphere, big selection) and the cons (no parking, a little expensive), and conclude whether it's worth a try. Different parts of the brain process different aspects of the decision. If one part isn't functioning right, making a decision becomes much more difficult. For someone with anorexia, deciding on where to go for dinner can be simply impossible.

At the 2011 International Conference on Eating Disorders in Miami, I attended a talk given by Bryan Lask, an eating disorder expert at the Ellern Meade Centre for Eating Disorders in London, and Kenneth Nunn, a child and adolescent psychiatrist at the University of New South Wales in Australia, who had us divide into groups and try and figure out where to meet for dinner. But there was a catch. Each of us had to play the role of a different region of the brain that had been implicated in anorexia nervosa.

I got to play the role of the basal ganglia, which is involved in movement/exercise, precision, and also malfunctions during OCD. Seeing as I've struggled with an exercise addiction, I'm known to be ludicrously precise, and I also had OCD as a teen and young adult, I'm pretty tight with my basal ganglia. Other people in our group played the role of the prefrontal cortex (which functions as a sort of chief executive in the brain, as it often has the final say on what we do), the nucleus accumbens (the brain's pleasure center), the insula (which acts as a relay station, helping the different parts of the brain communicate with one another), and others.

During the first selection, we were told to operate to the best of our abilities. As the basal ganglia, I made sure that everyone had the restaurant's GPS coordinates and knew exactly what time we should meet. I double-checked to make sure that the restaurant didn't have any major food safety violations and that they could handle someone with a food allergy. The other parts of the brain did their jobs as well and, within a few minutes, we had decided to meet our friends at the hip Asian joint down the block for drinks and sushi at 6:45 that night.

Then, we had to make the same decision in a malfunctioning anorexic brain. As the basal ganglia, I couldn't find the "perfect" restaurant or be sure that everyone else in the group would agree. The prefrontal cortex was also malfunctioning, and pretty much left the five brain parts to rule in anarchy. The insula was simply missing in action and none of the brain parts could talk to anyone else. Our decision? Skip dinner.

All around the room, other groups like ours returned with the same verdict: no dinner. With a malfunctioning brain, the decision was just too complicated, and so the "brains" defaulted on not eating. Our group decided we'd get tattoos instead, and maybe head to the casino. Another group went to the gym. Mostly, people retreated to their rooms and spent a socially isolated evening on their own.

Sound familiar?

Lask and Nunn referred to this conundrum—an endless shouting by the various parts of the brain while the prefrontal cortex merely shrugged its shoulders and the insula had long since left the building—as analysis paralysis. Analysis paralysis is over thinking things, constantly tweaking details, getting bogged down and unable to move because you just can't figure out what's important. It's waiting to tackle a problem until you find the "perfect" solution. Since no perfect solution exists, the problem never gets solved. You are essentially paralyzed by your over-thinking.

Figuring out where to go for dinner seems like a pretty simple decision. It's not like figuring out where to move or whether to take that job or how much to invest in your 401(k). It's just dinner. Yet the decision-making process, though it can happen lightning fast, is also very complicated. If the brain can't share and process information—if the insula isn't working properly—the brain gets stuck on the simplest of decisions, like a scratched record or CD.

The insula is known to malfunction in anorexia. Starvation reduces blood flow to the brain, which makes other areas of the brain malfunction as well. Soon, the simplest questions cause paralysis and the brain defaults to a simple answer: no. I already ate. I'm not hungry. I'm busy. No, thanks. I'd rather not. No. No. No.

It's our way of avoiding analysis paralysis. Our brains, Nunn said, are rather like Congress. Lots of bickering, lots of going back and forth, and without strong leadership, nothing gets done. Even if the insula alone isn't working properly, the entire brain is affected, and it gets stuck in analysis paralysis. We can't find the "right" food to eat, so we don't eat. We can't break our rigid eating and exercise routines. It's too complicated, and our brains are simply stuck.

Who's Who of the Brain

Since I'm going to be talking quite a bit about many of these brain regions throughout this book, I thought I would arrange a short meet-and-greet with our new "friends." In their book, *Who's Who of the Brain*, which I relied upon heavily for this section, Nunn, Lask, and Tanya Hanstock assigned each brain region a name and personality, as well as assigning it some neurological real estate in the town of Cephalton-upon-Ridge. I'm only including the characters that play a major role in anorexia for simplicity and brevity. Although in later sections I will refer to these characters by their formal anatomical names, I found that the authors' naming scheme helped me better remember what everyone did.

Frederick Foresight (prefrontal cortex)

Frederick Foresight is the mayor of Cephalton. Although he is rather young, he has a good knack for anticipating what is going to happen next. Frederick listens to what the other citizens of Cephalton have to say before he makes a decision about what everyone is going to do. His particular talent is looking at the big picture—seeing the forest for the trees. He also reins in some of the more unruly characters in the brain with his ability to understand the long-term consequences of an action. When a particularly complex problem stumps the rest of the team, Frederick generates new options and ideas, as well as figuring out a logical, flexible plan for executing the solution.

If Frederick becomes unwell, the effects radiate throughout Cephalton. Sometimes, Frederick becomes lackadaisical, uninspired, and frankly rather immobile, especially when it comes to making even the simplest of decisions. Without its mayor, the town of Cephalton lacks initiative, planning, and long-term outlook. Cephalton becomes rude and unruly as normal social behavior disintegrates. Other times, Frederick's illness can make him angry and impulsive. He lacks a sense of purpose and direction.

Rochelle Ringbond (cingulate gyrus)

Rochelle lives with her partner, Frederick Foresight. She has an extraordinary ability to focus on details and detect errors. Despite her superior error detection ability, Rochelle is highly attuned to others' pain and loves to spend time around children. The ultimate modern woman, Rochelle can utilize her large network throughout Cephalton to gather information and coordinate exclusive literary salons. Her emotionality helps counterbalance Frederick's cool rationalism.

Of course, even modern women become unwell. When Rochelle becomes ill, she loses her sensitivity and compassion, becoming almost blind to others' feelings. She often can't leave the house because of her need to check that all the doors and windows are locked, and the stove, coffee pot, and curling iron are turned off. She holds grudges and lives in the past. If her illness gets worse, she shuts down entirely and stops communicating.

Melissa Mirrorwood (somatosensory cortex)

Melissa is a fit and trim athlete who helps to run Cephalton's fitness center. Although she is profoundly aware of her own body and those of the people around her, Melissa isn't vain. She knows exactly how her body moves through the world, and she is extraordinarily sensitive to heat and pain. Melissa is a kinesthetic learner, preferring to learn by touch and doing than by reading or listening.

Melissa's illness can cause her to believe she is fat and ugly. She becomes obsessed with the size and shape of her body, particularly her stomach, hips, and thighs. Sometimes, Melissa will research cosmetic surgery procedures to fix her perceived flaws. At other times, she loses feeling in various parts of her body.

Maurice Mapply (parietal lobes)

Maurice lives with his partner, Melissa Mirrorwood, and next door to Frederick and Rochelle. Given his last name, it's not surprising that Maurice's hobby is map collecting, something he shares with Melissa. He is always superbly aware of the world around him. Besides maps, Maurice also enjoys mathematics, and is usually tapped to figure out how to split the bill when he and his friends are out at restaurants. Like Frederick, Maurice has tremendous skill at seeing the big picture, but Maurice can also zero in on the fine details.

Like all the citizens of Cephalton, Maurice can and does become ill. Typically, Maurice loses touch with the big picture and instead focuses exclusively on minutiae. Once, Maurice was seen wandering around town, unsure of how much money he had in his pocket, where he was, or how to get home. One of the most frustrating aspects of Maurice's illness for the other residents of Cephalton is that Maurice typically has no idea that he's not functioning at his best, and how his illness impacts others.

Sage Seahorse (hippocampus)

Sage is Cephalton's resident historian. His ability to remember names, places, and dates gives him a huge advantage as the town historian. He records and remembers everything that happens in Cephalton, both good and bad. Like Frederick, Sage's specialty is focusing on the big picture. But Sage's focus is slightly different—he sees the big picture over time and helps to put it into context. This focus helps to keep Sage from panicking, and he works hard to make sure that everyone else stays calm, too, since Sage can remind them of the important issues.

When he gets sick, the Cephalton Historical Society suffers without Sage at its helm. The archives become disorganized, and Sage loses touch with the data he loves. He can forget even the most basic of facts and can't keep track of the new information he gathers. He can also become rather disoriented, easily spooked, and overly emotional. This increases the stress of everyone in Cephalton, making Sage even more disorganized.

Annie Almond (amygdala)

Perhaps the best way to understand Annie is to listen to her theme song: "Truly, Madly, Deeply." It's how she does everything in life. She's very emotional and usually acts on her passions before she thinks them through. The town of Cephalton relies on this emotionality because Annie can raise an alarm before the rest of the town has spotted any danger. Although Annie can make snap judgments about people and places, her vast experience makes her remarkably accurate. Her friends Frederick Foresight, Rochelle Ringbond, and Sage Seahorse help keep Annie from overreacting.

When Annie isn't feeling well, she becomes stuck on thoughts and images of past events and constantly relives times of danger and threats. These memories can feel so real Annie forgets the present and loses herself in the past. Sage can sometimes hear Annie as she wakes up screaming and thrashing from a nightmare. But when he asks her what she was dreaming about, Annie often can't remember. Sometimes, she'll send out the danger signal just because something reminds her of one of her past traumas. At her worst, she stops eating and ignores everyone in Cephalton to focus solely on the threat in front of her.

Priscilla Prizeman (nucleus accumbens)

Priscilla is the ultimate party girl. She loves good times, good food, and good people, and tries to reap all the rewards from life. Despite being one of the most powerful people in Cephalton, Priscilla prefers to work behind the scenes. She exerts her influence by her "feel good" presence. If someone in Cephalton does something good, she can make them feel like they have just won the lottery. And the citizens of Cephalton return the favor frequently.

But Priscilla has her dark side. Her drive and dependence on reward make it easy for her to slip into the world of illegal drugs, alcohol, gambling, shopping, eating, and exercise. When she's well, she can keep this dark world at bay. But at just the slightest tip of the scales, Priscilla slides back into addiction. Once these behaviors become entrenched, Priscilla loses touch with her friends in Cephalton and ignores their advice. At her worst, she becomes irrational, confused, and out-of-touch with reality.

Corrie O'Graphie (basal ganglia)

If you're looking for Corrie at one of Priscilla's famous parties, look no further than the dance floor. Her dance training gives her a remarkable physical grace and elegant posture. She also finds part-time work as a professional choreographer. One of the older residents of Cephalton, Corrie's knack at choreography also gives her the skills to get things done when otherwise they might stall. All of her moves, whether strategic or on the dance floor, are well planned, as Corrie has a procedure and protocol for everything.

Corrie's illness tends to lower her drive and energy. Paradoxically, her perfectionism and obsession with minor details dramatically increase. She cannot seem to shift her thinking away from these unimportant facts, no matter how hard she tries. Nor can she stray from previous procedures, even when new evidence suggests that the old way of doing things might not be effective. Like a scratched compact disc, Corrie becomes stuck on a tiny snippet of a larger album.

Brenda Bridgehead (insula)

Of all of Cephalton's citizens, we will probably spend the most time getting to know Brenda. After all, she's the town's social networker. Without Brenda, the citizens wouldn't know when Mayor Frederick has called a meeting or when Annie is sounding an alarm. Frederick wouldn't be able to gather information effectively from the citizens of Cephalton without Brenda's accurate and timely reports on how the town, its residents, and the wider community are doing.

If Brenda becomes ill, the entire town essentially shuts down. Cephalton might have lots of activity, but nothing is getting done. No decisions are being made. Brenda's illness means she can't screen out information that is unimportant, and she can't keep the big picture in mind. She ignores status updates from the people in Cephalton. Her concentration deteriorates, as does her body image. Brenda withdraws socially because being with other people requires too many decisions and too much information, which she can't handle while ill. In short, when Brenda is ill, the entire community is affected.

The Insula Hypothesis

Reading a caricature of Brenda Bridgehead is one thing, but understanding what the insula actually does and how this relates to anorexia nervosa is quite another. The insula is a rather small bit of neurological real estate, buried deep within the brain (Nunn et al., 2008). Despite its small size, the insula plays a major role in our ability to navigate life, since it sends and receives messages from almost every part of the brain. Neuroscientist Hugo Critchley, now at the University of Sussex in the UK, first linked interoception to the insula in 2004. In a study published in the journal *Nature Neuroscience*, he showed that people with better interoceptive skills had larger insulae (Critchley et al., 2004).

The insula, Ken Nunn told me during an interview, is rather like an Internet server. Both an Internet server and the insula facilitate communication between different locations, and both connect to a wide array of different sources. If an Internet server goes down, the websites it hosts also go dark. Similarly, if the insula goes down, the parts of the brain to which it is connected (which is to say nearly all of them) also go offline. Insular dysfunction, then, is catastrophic.

"The insula helps regulate anxiety," Lask said. "If it malfunctions, anxiety goes sky high." It's exactly what researchers see in anorexia nervosa.

One of the insula's primary jobs is managing interoceptive awareness. Interoception is a little-known sense that monitors the internal state of our bodies. Just as external senses like sight, sound, taste, and touch help our brains understand the world around us, interoception allows us to understand our inner world. It includes things like hunger, thirst, body temperature, pain, disgust, and emotional state. In short, "mind and body are integrated in the insula" (Blakeslee, 2007).

Our interoceptive awareness tells us to raid the fridge when we're hungry or go to bed when we're tired. It tells us that our new wool sweater really itches and that our next-door neighbor is making us angry. It balances the need for change with the need to stay the same. Too hot? Take off your cardigan. Like the tea in your cup? Keep drinking.

But the insula does more than just monitor an interoceptive checklist of "thirsty, hungry, tired." Rather, the insula integrates this information into a single snapshot of who we are at any given moment. On top of interoceptive awareness, the insula also processes cognitive thoughts from the frontal lobes (the home of Frederick Foresight). We might feel the need to refill our coffee mugs, but our frontal lobes will tell us to put off this task while at a job interview or on an important phone call. Over time, this balance between thoughts and feelings, body and mind, becomes part of who we are. Our very "self" is centered in the insula (Damasio, 2003).

"The insula is the part of the brain that has been taking care of the body for hundreds of millions of years," said Bud Craig, a researcher at the Barrow Neurological Institute in Phoenix, Arizona. Most of this caretaking—like an adjustment of blood pressure or breathing—occurs without our knowledge. Other times, the insula makes us extremely conscious of an action we need to take in order to maintain the body's homeostasis, he explained. It might be a need to get some water, or a sudden spurt of fear to send us running from a potential attacker.

In patients with anorexia, however, the insula isn't functioning optimally. Similar to the fact that some Internet servers can process information much more quickly than others, the rates at which the insula can integrate information from around the brain can also vary widely from person to person. A group of neuroscientists at Cambridge University in the UK hypothesizes that these different processing rates in the insula and several other areas of the brain play an important role in mental illness (Ng *et al.*, 2001).

The insula in the brain of someone with anorexia processes information much more slowly than in the brain of someone without this eating disorder. In brain imaging studies, researchers found that areas of the brain directly connected to the insula had much lower blood flow than in control women (Chowdhury *et al.*, 2003; Lask *et al.*, 2005). In the brain, the amount of blood flow is directly related to how quickly information is processed. The firing of neurons requires energy and oxygen. Blood carries both of these necessities. Inadequate blood flow means neurons can't send messages to each other as quickly. Swedish researchers compared blood flow in the brains of 19 people with a history of anorexia, who were now at a normal weight, to healthy controls, and found that their insulae received significantly less blood even though they were currently not malnourished (Råstam *et al.*, 2001). Although the scientists couldn't rule out the possibility that this was the result of anorexia and not a contributing factor, the results seem to support Lask and Nunn's hypothesis. If the insula doesn't get enough blood in patients with anorexia, Nunn, Lask, and colleagues (2008) hypothesize, then this could mean that their insulae simply do not process information quickly enough.

Anyone who has ever tried to load a website over a slow Internet connection knows that the page can take much longer to load. Nor does the arriving information arrive at the same rate. Simpler elements like text generally arrive sooner and with fewer problems than data-rich elements, like slideshows and embedded YouTube videos. You only get a partial picture of the information contained in that website. An insula with restricted blood flow is like a slow Internet connection. Visual and auditory signals are ancient and have been honed by hundreds of millions of years of natural selection. Although sight and hearing are still extraordinarily complex, they are relatively simple and straightforward compared to interoception.

Although the World Wide Web is a relatively recent invention, not all elements were present at the beginning. In the early days of the Internet, most web pages consisted mainly of text elements, with an occasional image thrown in for variety. Only in the past few years, with the advent of much faster Internet connections, have websites regularly been using large audio and video files. When compared to sight, sound, and smell, interoception is a relatively new and data-rich sense. Just as websites often have difficulty loading large files over a slow Internet connection, the brains of people with anorexia have trouble processing interoceptive information. The slow information processing in the insulae of anorexia sufferers means that they can only get a partial snapshot of what is going on with their bodies and feelings.

Not surprisingly, people with anorexia have trouble sensing and responding to hunger appropriately. The body's hunger signals are blunted via abnormal levels of the hunger and satiety hormones leptin and ghrelin (Zigman and Elmquist, 2003), which become especially significant as the body begins to starve. Nor does the insula respond to hunger signals by making food seem extra tasty. When someone eats a food they really enjoy, blood flow dramatically increases to the insula as the pleasant taste is registered (Rolls, 2005). But brain imaging studies show that this spike is blunted in women with a history of anorexia. A group of recovered anorexic women was asked to sip sugar water after an overnight fast while they lay in a functional MRI machine. The control women generally considered the sugar water pleasant and, as expected, signals from the insula spiked. Not so in the women recovered from anorexia. Their insulae responded at a much lower rate than the control women (Wagner *et al.*, 2008).

Difficulties responding to hunger cues in someone with an eating disorder, however, doesn't tell researchers whether this is related to a problem with interoception or some other problem with hunger cues (the name "eating disorder" does provide a pretty big hint that there just might be problems with hunger and satiety signals). So researchers have assessed the interoceptive abilities unrelated to food and eating in those with anorexia. To formally measure a person's interoceptive skills, researchers use what's known as the heartbeat test. Study participants attempt to count how many times their heart beats in a minute without taking their pulse. Researchers then simultaneously measure their pulse electronically. Good interoceptive skills, researchers hypothesized, meant that a person is better able to sense the subtle *lub-dub* as their heart pumps blood and will report a pulse that is closer to the actual recorded value. When Critchley and his co-workers compared the results of 17 people on the heartbeat test to other measures of interoception, they found that, indeed, better interoceptive abilities meant the estimated heartbeat was significantly closer to the measured value (2003).

When a group of 28 women with anorexia nervosa were asked to complete the heartbeat task, they scored significantly worse than the group of 28 control women (Pollatos *et al.*, 2008). Since the heartbeat test doesn't measure anything related to food, weight, or eating that could be affected by the symptoms of anorexia, the researchers concluded that the interoceptive deficits seen in anorexia nervosa were global and not limited to hunger cues.

These two "I"s of anorexia—interoception and the insula—help to explain the wide range of seemingly unrelated symptoms frequently seen in people with the illness. For one, a wide range of studies have found that people with anorexia have difficulties recognizing and identifying their own emotions, a trait known as alexithymia (Bourke *et al.*, 1992; Harrison *et al.*, 2010). And the more problems an anorexia patient had identifying their emotions, the more prolonged their illness, according to researchers (Speranza *et al.*, 2007). Psychologists have found that alexithymia is directly related to interoceptive difficulties, in patients with anorexia (Greenberg, 1997), in those with other psychiatric disorders (Dunn *et al.*, 2010), and in non-clinical populations (Herbert *et al.*, 2011).

As well, a weakness in interoceptive skills may help explain why so many people with anorexia have difficulties understanding that they're ill. Known formally as anosognosia (pronounced ay-nose-ug-NOSE-ee-uh), this inability to recognize signs of their own illness is seen in schizophrenia (Pia and Tamietto, 2006), bipolar disorder (Gazalle *et al.*, 2007), and some stroke patients (Jenkinson *et al.*, 2011), as well as anorexia nervosa (Uher *et al.*, 2003). Lask and Nunn believe that deficits in interoception mean people with anorexia are just less aware of the physical signs of illness. This gap, combined with the ego-syntonic nature of anorexia, means that even deathly ill people can seem indifferent to their state.

"The function of the insula explains many different things about anorexia nervosa," Nunn said. "Anosognosia, the denial of illness, the inability to communicate feelings in a clear way and recognize feelings accurately, are all roles of the insula."

The insula, Nunn noted, also plays a role in feelings of disgust. It's a primal emotion, usually reserved for things that might kill us, like bodily waste, spoiled food, and (depending on your culture) cannibalism, pornography, and incest (Herz, 2012). Anorexia, some researchers hypothesized, might be related to disgust gone awry (Troop *et al.*, 2000). Instead of revulsion at spoiled food, someone with anorexia may be disgusted by any food. Indeed, when researchers compared 62 people with anorexia to 62 healthy controls, they found that those with anorexia had a stronger sense of disgust, especially where food was concerned (Aharoni and Hertz, 2012).

Beautiful Inside and Out

Perhaps the strongest relationship between interoception and anorexia, however, lies in the realm of body dysmorphia. Although not everyone with anorexia has the body distortions and fears of becoming fat—known as "nonfatphobic anorexia nervosa" or "atypical anorexia" (Carter and Bewell-Weiss, 2011) and most frequently found in young children and non-Western populations (Becker *et al.*, 2009)—the great majority of anorexia patients do suffer from body dysmorphia.

Plenty of women in Western cultures have body image issues, the kind where someone cranes their neck in the mirror wondering if their jeans make their butt look fat. This isn't the kind of body dysmorphia typically seen in anorexia. I've known acutely ill women with anorexia who didn't have an ounce of fat on their bodies but insisted they had a ginormous badonka-donk butt. For me, as long as I was following my eating and exercise rituals, I didn't really feel fat. My problem was that no amount of weight loss registered in my brain. I thought I looked the same at my lowest weight as I did at my normal, healthy weight. I would stop losing weight, I told myself, when I finally felt as thin as everyone was saying I already was. This type of body dysmorphia is less "I don't like my thighs" and more like a delusion.

Almost any book or popular article relates this body dysmorphia to the thin ideal and the cultural obsession with dieting. This view of cultural factors causing eating disorders is so prevalent that, in June 2011, the American Medical Association released the following statement:

> Advertisers commonly alter photographs to enhance the appearance of models' bodies, and such alterations can contribute to unrealistic expectations of appropriate body image—especially among impressionable children and adolescents. A large body of literature links exposure to media-propagated images of unrealistic body image to eating disorders and other child and adolescent health problems.
>
> The AMA adopted new policy to encourage advertising associations to work with public and private sector organizations concerned with child and adolescent health to develop guidelines for advertisements, especially those appearing in teen-oriented publications, that would discourage the

altering of photographs in a manner that could promote unrealistic expectations of appropriate body image.

(American Medical Association, 2011)

Cultural images of über-thin celebrities certainly doesn't act to prevent eating disorders, nor does it make it easier to recover, but it's also true that less than one percent of the population will develop anorexia during their lifetime, whereas virtually everyone is exposed to these media images (Hoek and van Hoeken, 2003). Clearly, another factor is at work here. A growing body of new research has begun to show a strong link between interoceptive difficulties and body image distortion in anorexia nervosa.

Neuroscientist Manos Tsakiris at Royal Holloway, University of London defines body image as "a conscious representation of what we look like." In non-scientists' terms, body image is how we picture ourselves in our heads. Most of the time, the image we have of our bodies in our heads is pretty close to what our body actually looks like. While body image includes the size and shape of your body, it involves much more than that. Closing my eyes and picturing myself at my desk writing, I see a redhead that's about average height and wearing a baggy gray hoodie. I can see my green eyes, the mole on my neck, and the delicate curve of my fingers clicking against the keyboard.

Ask me to picture my size and shape, however, and I can honestly tell you that I have no clue. Although I have separated my body image from my self-esteem, such that feeling unduly huge doesn't make me feel like a failure or wreck my day, I still can't picture myself accurately. I overestimate my body size. I often feel like the largest person in any room. I first remember feeling this way at my sixth birthday party. When I was four, I wore size 4 toddler. When I was five, I wore size 5. Now that I was six, I had skipped up to size 6X, a fact that horrified me. None of my friends wore clothes this big. Cultural ideals of thinness were not on my radar and, looking back almost 30 years, I had no real way to explain this until I learned of the connection between impaired interoception and body dysmorphia.

From the outside, it doesn't seem that having trouble telling if you're hungry or tired could cause body dysmorphia. After all, looking at yourself in the mirror is a visual act, not an interoceptive one. Yet seeing our own body is only one aspect of how body image is formed. When forming their body image, "someone with high interoception will place more weight on proprioception and inner feelings, while someone with low interoception might place more weight on visual cues," Tsakiris said.

If body image is a combination of interoceptive and external cues, then Tsakiris hypothesizes that people with anorexia and others with low interoception, such as those with body dysmorphic disorder, have a body image that is more dependent on external cues. Tsakiris tested this idea using the Rubber Hand Illusion (Tsakiris *et al.*, 2010). Although the Rubber Hand Illusion sounds like a cheap trick you'd see on a carnival midway, it actually allows neuroscientists to study the links between body and mind.

In 1998, psychologists Matthew Botvinick and Jonathan Cohen asked ten healthy subjects to place both hands on the table in front of them. Then, they placed a screen on the inside of the left arm, running parallel to the arm, to conceal the person's left hand from their sight. Immediately to the right of the screen, Botvinick and Cohen placed a realistic, life-sized rubber hand. Then, they began simultaneously gently stroking the subject's left hand and the rubber hand with a small paintbrush. After a minute or two of brushing, something unusual happened. The study subjects began to feel as if the rubber hand was their own. Their body image had spontaneously morphed to exclude their real left hand and to substitute a lifeless rubber hand in its place (Botvinick and Cohen, 1998).

To measure the relationship between interoception, body image, and the Rubber Hand Illusion, Tsakiris and colleagues asked a group of 46 neurologically healthy undergraduate women to complete the heartbeat test. Based on the results of this test, the women were split into high- and low-interoception groups, in which their average estimated heart rate was 81 percent and 49 percent accurate. The women were then given questionnaires to assess body image, as well as participating in the Rubber Hand Illusion. Women in the high-interoception group were less likely to report feeling that the rubber hand had become part of their body.

In 2006, a previous study had found that both males and females who reported more eating-disordered thoughts and behaviors (including body-image dissatisfaction) were more easily swayed by the Rubber Hand Illusion (Mussap and Salton, 2006). Researchers also found that the insulae of women with anorexia showed a different pattern of activation than control women while looking at images of slim women, indicating that aspects of interoception related to body image were different in anorexia nervosa (Friederich *et al.*, 2010).

For kicks, I did the heartbeat test on myself one evening as I was sitting and reading. Using a stopwatch, I tried to feel my heart beating for one minute. Then, I took my pulse for a minute. I waited for two minutes, then took my pulse again. I averaged these, and found the difference between my estimated heartbeat and my average pulse. I divided this difference by the average pulse, which gave me an error rate. Subtract the error rate from 1, and you have your accuracy rate. According to Tsakiris, an accuracy rate above 0.80 is high, between 0.60 and 0.79 is medium, and below 0.59 is low. Mine was 0.62.

For the more mathematically inclined of my readers, the formula is:

$$1 - \frac{|\ estimated\ hear\ beat - average\ pulse\ |}{average\ pulse}$$

Tsakiris concluded:

> the present study provides the first direct evidence for an active modulatory role of interoception on the experience of the body *from the outside* … Intriguingly, anorexic patients display decreased interoceptive

awareness, and their body image dissatisfaction is correlated with activity in the right insular lobe. The finding that interoceptive awareness can modulate exteroceptive representations of the body has important implications for impairments of body-awareness where the integration of the body as experienced from within and from the outside may be severely disrupted.

Humans are profoundly social animals, however, which means body image is more than just asking yourself "What do I look like?" It's also "What do other people think I look like?" Because of their difficulties with interoception, when people with body dysmorphic disorder were asked to recall early memories, they were significantly more likely to describe their own personal experience as if it was happening to someone else. Rather than focusing on the memory itself, the women with body dysmorphic disorder focused on what others must have been thinking of them (Osman *et al.*, 2004). Given the similarities between anorexia and body dysmorphic disorder (Sherman *et al.*, 2006)—similarities that extend far beyond the similar body image disturbance seen in both disorders—it's not unreasonable to think that those with anorexia have similar memories.

Looking Inward

We're not born with a pre-formed body image. Babies have neither a body image nor a sense of self. They exist in a confusing sea of sights and sounds, with no real sense that they can navigate this world or make things happen. As a caregiver responds to a baby's cries for food, burping, or a diaper change, the baby begins to develop an awareness of self, that they can make people respond. Psychologists call this a sense of agency. The growing child begins to see him- or herself as the narrator in their own life story. They are the subject of this particular plot. Everyone else around them are "objects," and are viewed as separate from the self.

Thinking of yourself from another's perspective is called "self-objectification." You're treating yourself as if you were an object in your own life. Researchers asked a group of 204 healthy undergraduate women a variety of questions about body shame, eating disorder symptoms, how much they tried to control their diets, and self-objectification. Those women that most frequently thought of themselves from other people's perspectives had the most eating disorder symptoms (Noll and Fredrickson, 1998).

Typically, these high rates of self-objectification in people with both disordered eating and eating disorders have been linked to cultural factors like models, advertising, and over-sexualization (Fredrickson and Roberts, 1997; Fredrickson *et al.*, 1998; Calogero *et al.*, 2005). But recent neuropsychological studies hint that the links between self-objectification and eating disorders—in particular, anorexia nervosa—may stem from something deeper than Photoshopped ads and sexy swimsuit models.

Italian researcher Giuseppe Riva calls this persistent self-objectification in eating disorders "allocentric lock" (Riva, 2012). Normally, the body provides plenty of information about its internal states so that people can break away from viewing their own body from a third party's perspective (known as allocentrism). When interoception is impaired like in anorexia, this information isn't there, leaving the person unable to perceive themselves from a first-person perspective. Without good internal cues, the person with anorexia can't accurately perceive the physical changes that accompany weight loss, leaving them locked into a state of perpetual body image dissatisfaction.

This allocentric lock is amplified by anxiety. If significant anxiety isn't present before the onset of anorexia (approximately two-thirds of people with anorexia have a history of anxiety disorders), then it almost always appears during the course of the illness (Kaye *et al.*, 2004). Researchers have found that anxiety increases the likelihood that a person remembers an event from an allocentric perspective, even in people without anorexia or any known interoceptive problems (Antonova *et al.*, 2011).

Allocentric lock is something captured somewhat clumsily in a sentiment from my cousin when he learned of my anorexia diagnosis. He said, "Really? Anorexia? *You?* Huh … I always remembered you as the chubby one." Inappropriateness of the comment aside (for the record, my cousin didn't mean to be hurtful), it illustrates how I could get so stuck in the allocentric lock during my eating disorder. I was never a small child. Though not overweight, I was significantly taller and stockier than my peers. My shyness and book smarts made me a magnet for bullies, and one of the (many) things they teased me about was my weight. Without strong interoceptive cues to counterbalance the taunts, I began to see myself as fat. I would have sworn up and down that I was one of the heaviest girls in my high-school class. Flipping through my yearbook now, such cognitions are almost laughable. I was no stick—I have always been muscular and athletic—but I wasn't as large as I thought, either.

I had no internal perception of my own body size. If kids said I was fat, then I was fat. It must be true. Therefore, I was fat. *Quad erat demonstratum.* As I started to lose weight in my initial descent into anorexia, I was stuck in viewing myself from the perspective of the middle-school bullies who had felt me up and called me a fat cow in front of the whole class. My ever-shrinking thighs and protruding ribs didn't feel any different. They didn't look any different. No matter how thin I got, I was stuck in Riva's allocentric lock. I couldn't help but view myself from the old perspective because my interoception was so blunted.

These differences in perspective can also be seen in brain imaging studies. In a study of ten women with anorexia and ten healthy controls, researchers found that the brains of both the anorexia patients and the healthy controls looked remarkably similar when they looked at images of other people. But when both groups of women looked at pictures of themselves, the brain functioning was remarkably different. The insulae of the anorexia patients showed almost no activation, whereas it did in control women (Sachdev *et al.*, 2008). This study validated the results of a 2003 study that found similar neural responses to digitally distorted photographs of others in both people with anorexia and control women. When they looked at altered images of themselves, however, those with anorexia had a global hypoactivation of their brain processing—which included the insula—compared to the healthy women (Wagner *et al.*, 2003).

If problems with interoception create many of the core features of anorexia nervosa, then treating the illness should also target these same factors. Besides improving nutrition and restoring weight, several interoceptive-focused therapies have also showed promise in treating eating disorders. The use of yoga as an eating disorder treatment has become popular in part because of its mind–body connection. Previous studies have found that those who regularly practice yoga have better body image and lower rates of disordered eating (Dittmann and Freedman, 2009), as well as subjective measures of improved interoception (Khalsa *et al.*, 2008).

In 2010, researchers at Seattle Children's Hospital found that yoga improved eating disorder psychopathology in a group of 54 adolescents with eating disorders (Carei *et al.*, 2010). After 12 weeks of weekly hour-long yoga sessions as an addition to treatment as usual (follow-up with a physician, therapist, and dietitian), the yoga group showed a significant decrease in negative body image and food preoccupation when compared with those teens who didn't participate.

At the start of the study, lead researcher and clinical psychologist Tiffany Rain Carei said that many of the teens were so out of touch with their own bodies and internal perceptions that they couldn't balance properly on their own two feet. "They would always lean one way or the other. They just weren't checked in," Carei said. "But yoga let the kids connect with their bodies in a positive way."

By the end of treatment, the study participants could center their bodies and stay upright. "Before, their life was really out of balance, and yoga helped bring them back into balance," Carei said.

Giuseppe Riva tried a more high-tech approach to improving body perception. He found that immersive virtual reality helped reduce body dysmorphia in anorexia sufferers. Riva used two different tasks to help the patients more realistically evaluate their body size. The first involved selecting two different full-body avatars: one that represented how they would like to look and one that represented their actual appearance. Then, using the patient's own measurements, they created a virtual model to match her real-life proportions. In their virtual world, the patients could compare all three "versions" of themselves. Often, Riva said, the patients found that they were actually smaller than their "ideal" bodies. Being able to see this, he noted, provided solid visual evidence that their perception was actually off.

The second task that Riva gave his patients was to pick out a virtual chair to sit in that would perfectly cradle their derrières. Then, the patients had their based-on-real-life virtual figure sit in the chair. Almost always, the virtual chair was far too big for their virtual behinds. Since so many people with anorexia have a significant distortion of their stomach, hips, butt, and/or thighs, this chair exercise targets their most noteworthy body disturbances.

"Immersive virtual reality forces you into an egocentric viewpoint," Riva said. It forces the person to think about how they actually experience their body. The task doesn't ask someone to think about what other people think about their body, but to learn for themselves the actual size of their body. The emphasis on this viewpoint might be why Riva and other psychologists testing virtual reality can get good results in just a few sessions, rather than several months (Riva, 2011).

Perhaps, too, the virtual reality therapies work more quickly in anorexia because the digitized avatars can skirt the distortions specific to viewing pictures of one's self. A college friend told me she could no longer deny her unhealthy weight loss after viewing her high-school prom pictures. "I almost didn't recognize myself," she said. Although I scrutinize photos of myself just as I scrutinize my body in the mirror, other people have told me something similar. The virtual reality might trick the brain into combining a first-person body image with the standard anorexic stance of perceiving themselves from an outsider's perspective. With the merger of these two perspectives, someone with anorexia can begin to develop a perception of their inner states and feelings.

"The sense of self is built up from a representation of internal states," Critchley told me in a January 2011 piece I wrote on interoception and body image for *Scientific American Mind* (Arnold, 2012). Part of what results from this sense of self is body image, an ability to form an accurate mental image of ourselves. Building this sense of self requires recognition of internal states, which consequently requires interoceptive awareness. The neurological root of the body dysmorphia seen in anorexia might be related to a lack of a sense of self, stemming ultimately from difficulties with interoception.

The question that remains for researchers is how these interoceptive difficulties arose. Were they inherited? Did they arise from parenting or cultural issues? And why do they tend to emerge most profoundly during adolescence? Questions like this are best answered with genetic studies.

3 Climbing the Family Tree

My anorexia diagnosis initially looked like a statistical aberration on the family tree. Sure, we had more than the usual array of nutcases and addicts, but not eating disorders. As the years passed and I observed my relatives' behavior with an eye that was more attuned to the behaviors peculiar to eating disorders, I began to find more and more evidence that I was not alone in my anorexia diagnosis.

I discovered my great-grandmother's precipitous midlife weight loss, for which doctors had no real explanation. My maternal grandmother enjoyed daily walks, but these turned into multiple hours of daily treks at the local shopping mall during a stressful time in her life. She told my mom it was probably excessive, but she didn't know another way to make it through the day. For a woman in her late sixties, this sounded like compulsive exercise. My mother's sister was always slight and told us she had to watch every morsel that passed her lips because she was diabetic. A day didn't begin until she had put in a session on her elliptical trainer in the basement. Any deviation in her daily eating and exercise routines sent her into a tailspin.

In contrast, both my parents had a very relaxed attitude about food and exercise—perhaps even too relaxed at times. Exercise specifically to burn calories was looked upon as crazy, bordering on torturous. My dad's idea of a diet was eating three cookies after dinner instead of four. If you asked either of them how many calories were in something, they would shrug their shoulders with blissful abandon. They were of average-ish weight, though never particularly slender. (My family hails from Eastern Europe, and one did not survive the raiding hordes of Cossacks without being at least somewhat sturdy.)

Although the eating disorder genetics may have bypassed my parents, other predisposing traits didn't. When I was younger, my mom struggled with serious depression. The depression abated as I finished elementary school, but her anxiety didn't. A stereotypical worrywart, my mother always assumed the worst would happen. Everything had to be done just so, and she organized her life to avoid as many anxieties as possible. Both my parents were notorious perfectionists and developed an array of mostly internal rules about how things were to be done. I managed to inherit all of these traits: depression, anxiety, and perfectionism.

These personality traits in combination with the quiet emergence of anorexic traits in many of my relatives made me particularly vulnerable to anorexia. I didn't know that as a freshman in college, when I started avoiding dessert and exercising more. I didn't know that as a sophomore, when I became dependent on exercise as a way to relieve stress. And I didn't know that as a junior, when I thought I would lose the five pounds I had gained while studying in Scotland. My DNA turned my innocent-sounding decisions into a perfect storm that would occupy the next 12 years of my life.

Chopping Down the Family Tree

Clinicians noted many years ago that eating disorders could run in families. Initially, psychologists attributed this to factors in the family environment, things like controlling mothers, absent fathers, and an over-emphasis on appearance (Bruch, 1979; Minuchin *et al.*, 1978). The role of genetics in human behavior and psychiatric disorders was essentially non-existent at the time. Researchers believed that humans were like a blank slate at birth, shaped and molded not by DNA but by parents and culture (Pinker, 2003).

Certainly familial and cultural environments play an important role in shaping who we become and the potential emergence of any number of medical conditions, psychiatric illnesses included. Starting in the 1990s, however, a series of studies comparing the rates of eating disorders in identical and fraternal twins began to shift this line of thinking. Environment wasn't irrelevant, but it wasn't the only or even the most important factor in determining who developed anorexia and who didn't. More than 100 recent studies have shown that anorexia is driven by genes, not culture.

Except if anorexia is a biologically based illness, people ask me, *then where is the anorexia gene?* It's a good question with a very complicated answer. To start, researchers will never discover an "anorexia gene" because anorexia and eating disorders are complicated illnesses that are influenced by a large number of genes. Most other illnesses, even things like cancer, diabetes, and heart disease, have a similar genetic pattern: lots of small genetic influences add up to increase or decrease the chances that someone will develop that illness. These small influences mean that researchers aren't going to find a single gene that determines whether or not you will develop anorexia. Rather, a number of genes have small effects that add together to make it more or less likely that a person will develop anorexia nervosa.

Before the completion of the Human Genome Project in 2003 and the simultaneous advances in DNA sequencing technology, studying large numbers of twins was a convenient way to figure out the role genetics played in different disorders. Identical twins (also known as monozygotic twins) share 100 percent of their DNA, giving them the same DNA sequence. Fraternal twins (aka dizygotic twins) share only 50 percent of their genes, just like normal siblings.

Genes Meet Environment

If anorexia nervosa was completely determined by genes—if a person's risk for developing anorexia was 100 percent genetic—then if one identical twin had anorexia, then the other twin would always develop anorexia. In fraternal twins, if one twin had anorexia, then the other twin would develop anorexia about half the time, since fraternal twins only share half of their DNA. If anorexia was a socially constructed illness, then the probability of the other twin developing anorexia would be no different in identical and fraternal twins, since the distribution of genes would be irrelevant.

Thus far, researchers haven't found any illness that is completely determined by genes or by environment. Instead, genes can increase or decrease the likelihood that you will develop a particular condition, as can environment. The chances of anyone developing anorexia is a complex push and pull of nature and nurture. Twin studies helped scientists figure out the relative contributions of genes and environment in the tug-of-war that ultimately resulted in anorexia.

One of the first formal genetic studies, published in 1988, looked at 45 different twin pairs (25 of these twin pairs were identical twins) in the UK in which at least one twin had been diagnosed with anorexia. The researchers found that, in 55 percent of the identical twins, both twins had anorexia. In the fraternal twins, five percent of them both had anorexia. A detailed family history of the twins also showed that five percent of close female relatives also had anorexia. These results showed that "genetic factors are very significant in the aetiology of anorexia nervosa"(p. 561), and the researchers estimated that up to 80 percent of the risk for developing anorexia is genetic (Holland *et al.*, 1988).

Other twin studies confirmed these findings. A 1985 study done by Michael Strober and colleagues at the University of California, Los Angeles found higher than expected rates of anorexia, sub-clinical anorexia, and bulimia in the close relatives of patients with anorexia nervosa (Strober *et al.*, 1985). Another study found that having a twin with anorexia nervosa increases the co-twin's chances of developing not only anorexia, but also bulimia, major depression, and low body weight (Walters and Kendler, 1995).

Scientists have also used twin studies to look at whether risk factors for anorexia can be inherited alongside other mental disorders like anxiety, depression, and substance abuse. It turns out they can. When researchers studied over 1,000 twin pairs that participated in the Virginia Twin Study, they found that some of the same genetic factors that predisposed a person to major depression also made them more likely to develop anorexia (Wade *et al.*, 2000). Similar studies found that generalized anxiety disorder shares a similar relationship with anorexia (Dellava *et al.*, 2011). Close relatives of anorexia patients were also more likely to have both major depression and obsessive-compulsive disorder (Lilenfeld *et al.*, 1998). Two specific aspects of perfectionism—an unusual worry or concern about making mistakes and doubting that their actions are correct—were also more common in people with anorexia and bulimia and appeared to confer some genetic risk to the development of an eating disorder (Bulik *et al.*, 2003).

Together, these studies indicate that genetics create 60 to 85 percent of a person's risk for developing anorexia nervosa (Wade *et al.*, 2000). Considering that the genetic risks for developing schizophrenia and bipolar disorder are similar to anorexia, and that psychologists accept both bipolar disorder and schizophrenia as being biologically based, researchers conclude that the biological basis for anorexia is just as strong. Statements about the proportion of genetic risk for a particular illness have a very specific definition to population geneticists that isn't immediately obvious to those outside this particular field, said Kelly Klump, a psychologist specializing in behavioral genetics at Michigan State University.

When a researcher says that 60 to 85 percent of someone's risk of developing anorexia is genetic, they mean that 60 to 85 percent of the reason that I developed anorexia and, say, my best friend from high school didn't has to do with differences in genetics. I carried different versions of genes than she did, and these specific genetic variations increased the chances of my developing anorexia. It doesn't mean that 60 to 85 percent of anorexia cases are caused by genetics and the rest by environment. Nor does it mean that 60 to 85 percent of the reason one particular person develops anorexia is genetic. What it does explain is the proportion of the reason one person has anorexia while another does not.

If 60 to 85 percent of anorexia risk is genetic, that still means that between 15 and 40 percent of someone's risk is caused by environmental factors. Scientists divide these environmental influences into two types: shared and non-shared. Shared environmental influences include broad factors like culture and traditional gender roles, as well as factors specific to individual families and peer groups. Non-shared environmental influences are unique to each individual person, and include pre- and peri-natal events, infections with bacteria and viruses, and teasing or bullying. When researchers looked at a large number of published studies examining the different environmental and genetic factors that influenced anorexia nervosa, known as a meta-analysis, they concluded that non-shared environmental factors seemed to play a much larger role than shared environment in the development of anorexia nervosa (Bulik *et al.*, 2000). A study of a large population of Swedish twins confirmed that genetics, non-shared environment, and shared environment influenced the development of anorexia in that order of importance (Bulik *et al.*, 2006).

"Twin studies have shown that anorexia, like other major mental illnesses, is heritable," Klump said.

Finding the Rosetta Stone

Although twin studies still have lots of uses, improvements in DNA sequencing technologies mean that researchers can look directly at the genes themselves to see what exactly is inherited in anorexia. So far, attempts to conclusively identify genes and gene variants with anorexia nervosa have been mixed. Researchers have thus far focused mainly on genes and proteins in the serotonin, dopamine, and noradrenaline neurotransmitter systems, as dysfunctions in all three of these systems have been seen in anorexia.

The serotonin system has received the most attention, as it has some of the strongest ties to anorexia. Other studies have linked abnormal levels of serotonin to depression (Kupfer *et al.*, 2012), anxiety (Durant *et al.*, 2010), and unusual feeding and eating behaviors (Leibowitz and Alexander, 1998). This, combined with findings that people with anorexia have unusually high levels of serotonin in their brains even after recovery (Kaye *et al.*, 1991), made scientists think that genetic variations in the serotonin system might account for some of anorexia's heritability. In the brain, levels of serotonin and other neurotransmitters are controlled both by proteins that release the chemical into the small space between neurons known as the synapse, protein receptors that recognize the neurotransmitter and receive its signal, and by reuptake proteins that act like a sponge and sop up specific neurotransmitters.

The proteins that control neurotransmitters are encoded by a variety of genes. Since genes are on chromosomes and chromosomes come in pairs, every person has two copies of each gene—one from their mother and one from their father. Many genes, like those that control neurotransmitter levels, have many different small variations that exist in a population. Some of these variants may only be different in one or two DNA bases. Each variant results in a slightly different protein that has a tiny but measurable difference in function. Researchers thought that specific variants of genes might be linked to anorexia.

Initial results looked promising. In just a few years, scientists quickly identified several gene variants in the serotonin system that were found much more frequently in people with anorexia than people without eating disorders (Kaye *et al.*, 2000; Ozaki *et al.*, 2003; Matsushita *et al.*, 2004; Klump and Gobrogge, 2005). Researchers had even identified an area on chromosome 1 where they thought some of the susceptibility genes were located (Grice *et al.*, 2002). These studies had scientists thinking they were close to cracking some of the genetic mystery behind anorexia. Except when researchers repeated these studies in different populations or with larger samples, their hopes were tempered somewhat (Klump and Gobrogge, 2005). Although recent reviews of other research studies have indicated many promising targets from other neurotransmitter systems to proteins regulating appetite (Helder and Collier, 2011; Clarke *et al.*, 2012), no specific gene variants have yet been conclusively linked to anorexia.

"There are a number of widely studied candidate [genes] in anorexia in the dopamine pathway, the serotonin pathway, and GABA [gamma-aminobutyric acid] genes, but I'm not aware of any real strong hits," said Ashley van Zeeland, a neuropsychologist and geneticist at the Scripps Research Institute in San Diego, California.

"One of the issues in regards to not only anorexia but neuropsychiatric genetics in general is that we haven't found any strong genetic links," she said. "It gets to this issue that people call the missing heritability. You have these psychiatric conditions that are known to be highly heritable, but a variety of genetic studies aren't really finding the variants that have been shown to account for the heritability that we know exists in twin studies."

The work of van Zeeland and her colleague Cinnamon Bloss has looked at another neurotransmitter known as gamma-aminobutyric acid (GABA), previously overlooked in genetic studies of anorexia nervosa. GABA is one of several major neurotransmitters whose dysfunctions have been noted in people with anxiety disorders (Lydiard, 2003), and it acts as the brakes for the brain, stopping the transmission of signals from neuron to neuron, which calms down brain activity. "In the absence of GABA, anxiety can increase," van Zeeland said.

Seeing as nearly two-thirds of anorexia patients also have history of an anxiety disorder (Kaye *et al.*, 2004), the idea of a GABA dysfunction in anorexia seemed like a reasonable hypothesis. When Bloss and van Zeeland searched the research literature, they didn't find any previous studies looking at GABA genes and anorexia. Bloss, van Zeeland, and their colleagues looked at over 5,000 variations in more than 350 genes in 1878 women with a current or past eating disorder. In these variants, the researchers identified one single variant in a GABA receptor gene that increased the chronicity of anorexia and decreased the likelihood of recovery (Bloss *et al.*, 2011). The same variant also increased the women's average anxiety levels, which could be how the variant affects anorexia outcome, the researchers noted.

One of the reasons it's been so hard to conclusively link gene variants to anorexia is the large number of study participants needed to show such an association. Anorexia is a relatively rare condition, and including thousands of people in a study is often too expensive, Bloss said. Many good results have come out of projects like the privately funded Price Foundation collaboration and publically funded studies from the National Institutes of Health, even if the results weren't quite what researchers had hoped for.

Another problem is the wide range of symptoms that can accompany anorexia. Someone with anorexia can engage in any variety of behaviors, including restrictive food intake, excessive exercise, vomiting, laxative or diuretic abuse, binge eating, anxiety, depression, and more. This range of behaviors—what researchers call "phenotypes"—means that researchers need to subdivide an already rare disorder into smaller categories. "To get a well-defined group of individuals, you're going to have a much smaller number than you started out with, and this makes it harder to find out which genes are associated with a pure presentation of anorexia," van Zeeland said.

Despite the rarity of strictly defined anorexia nervosa, certain aspects of the illness, such as anxiety, depression, and perfectionism, are common to a number of different psychiatric conditions. Perhaps these illnesses are the result of overlapping dysfunctions in the different neural systems. It could be that the neurological basis for both OCD and anorexia, or autism and anorexia, involves some of the same brain functions. It could be that different genes affect different brain pathways, and the combination of dysfunctional brain pathways determines what disorder you have and how it looks from a clinical perspective. Looking for the genetic basis of these overlapping dysfunctions could provide that increase in study subjects that psychiatric geneticists so desperately need.

"There's no one pathway to anorexia," Tracey Wade, an eating disorders researcher at Flinders University in Adelaide, Australia, said. Certain elements, like anxiety, depression, and perfectionism, appear to be common to many of the pathways leading to anorexia. Researchers have found that parents of anorexia patients have higher levels of perfectionism and greater concerns about weight and body size than parents of people without anorexia (Woodside *et al.*, 2002). Because this perfectionism helps explain someone's commitment to self-starvation and excessive exercise during anorexia nervosa (McLaren *et al.*, 2001), researchers believe that looking at the heritability of different aspects of anorexia might yield better genetic markers for the illness.

Like Mother, Like Daughter

Jen, a woman in her sixties living in the southwestern United States, knows all too well how damaging perfectionism can be. It's something she's seen in the form of her own eating disorder, and her daughter's. Jennifer lived all over the world while growing up, from the jungles of South America, to India, to the Philippines, moving every two to three years. Although Jennifer loved her childhood, the constant need to pack her bags and make new friends soon grew tiring.

Added to Jen's social difficulties were her fears of never being good enough or measuring up. Her parents described her as high-strung, intelligent, and driven—three adjectives that could just as easily have described me. "My family's early focus when I was growing up was on my grades," Jen told me. "All A's meant I was good and any other grade meant that I wasn't doing well—at least, that's how I perceived it. If I didn't make the grade, I was restricted from other activities."

What finally threw Jen's precarious world off balance was a growth spurt at age 14 and the resulting weight gain. Teasing, which was already a common occurrence, increased as her height and weight increased. "I guess one day I decided I needed to purge," Jen said. "It just ... happened."

Although Jen, then 15 and a freshman in high school, tried to stop purging, her eating disorder quickly escalated and took on a life of its own. Jen briefly lost a lot of weight—she never knew exactly how much, but looking at photos of herself at the time, Jen is horrified by how she looked—but then her eating disorder morphed from anorexia into bulimia. The binge/purge cycle stayed with her for almost 20 years. Jen finally sought help for her eating disorder in her thirties, shortly after her children were born.

Jen's eating disorder history was fertile ground for laying blame when her daughter, Emily, developed anorexia and bulimia, also at age 15. For a number of years, Jen absorbed this blame. "I carried it around like a wet blanket," she said.

No wonder the daughter has an eating disorder, the thinking went. *The mother taught her to value her appearance over anything else, and didn't allow her to mature into her own person. The mother is living vicariously through her daughter.*

The more Jen thought about this theory, the more she began to realize that it just wasn't true. Jen placed an emphasis on being healthy, true, but this emphasis was about taking care of yourself, not starving and purging or wearing a size 4. Jen prepared nourishing meals for her family, who had sit-down dinners, always. Emily had always been a finicky eater, even as a baby. It seemed that, even then, her anxiety and discomfort interfered with her ability to feed herself properly.

"Genetics definitely played a role in both our disorders," Jen said, noting several siblings, aunts, and cousins with their own eating disorders, as well as countless others who suffered from depression and addiction. "All the pieces were around there floating, and personally, I think that points to a genetic basis for everything that is going on with her and me."

Anorexia Takes Root

Jennifer's story illustrates another important factor in anorexia: the disorder usually develops around adolescence. Researcher Johannes Hebebrand believes that some of the increased risk for anorexia during adolescence has to do with the developing body. In early adolescence, he said, the body is at its leanest point. A female in early adolescence has much of her adult height but is lacking a large portion of her adult weight, most of which is fat stores to support pregnancy and lactation. This places her body mass index at a lifetime minimum, giving her little protective buffer if she gets sick, starts eating more healthfully, or trains harder at a sport.

Klump, however, believes that adolescence is such a high-risk period for the development of an eating disorder because that's when genes that increase a person's anorexia predisposition start getting expressed. "We know from other areas of psychology and psychiatry that the influence of genes does not have to stay constant across development. Genes can become more or less important in leading to behavior across development," Klump said. An example of this, she pointed out, is IQ. Genes influencing overall intelligence have much less significance in early childhood, where environmental factors predominate, than in adolescence and adulthood. Klump and other researchers have found a similar pattern in disordered eating thoughts and actions that can potentially lead to clinical eating disorders.

Klump believed that one of the reasons for the differences in genetic influences on disordered eating before and after puberty has to do with the body's production of the sex hormone estrogen. To test her hypothesis, Klump turned to the Minnesota Twin Study, which was comprised of 530 11-year-old and 603 17-year-old female twins. Klump and her colleagues gave all of the twins the Eating Disorder Inventory (EDI), a questionnaire that gathers information about disordered eating thoughts and behaviors, such as weight preoccupation, body image satisfaction, and binge eating. The EDI scores of the 11-year-old twins who had started puberty more closely matched those of the 17-year-olds than those of the 11-year-olds who were pre-pubescent. As well, when Klump analyzed the genetic data, she found that genetics had much less to do with the development of disordered eating in the pre-pubescent twins, but explained about 55 percent of the development of disordered eating in both the 11-year-old twins who had started puberty and the 17-year-old twins (Klump *et al.*, 2003).

These data, however, were just snapshots of one point in time. To more accurately see how puberty affected the onset of eating disorders, Klump decided to follow a group of twins over a period of seven years. The 772 female twin pairs completed questionnaires assessing factors of disordered eating at 11, 14, and 18 years of age. Similar to the other study, Klump and colleagues found that genetics played a much smaller role than environmental factors in disordered eating among pre-pubescent females, but that influence dramatically increased to about 50 percent post-puberty (Klump *et al.*, 2007). The results of both of these studies told researchers that puberty was a key time during which a person's genetic risk for developing an eating disorder dramatically increased.

The key factor that occurs during adolescence is an increase in the production of sex hormones like estrogen and testosterone. As many pop-culture portrayals would have it, the mere presence of estrogen magically makes women sob at greeting card commercials and moody at that time of the month. Instead, estrogen works by affecting whether a gene can function. Estrogen drives breast development during puberty by turning genes on and off in the brain, which causes certain proteins to be produced or not. The particular cocktail of proteins produced during puberty then drives an increase in breast tissue and other sexual characteristics.

Sex hormones do much more than just spur the development of breasts in females and facial hair in males, however. "Estrogen and progesterone are very potent regulators of neurotransmitter systems like serotonin and dopamine, which are systems that we know are disrupted in eating disorders," Klump said.

The rapid influx of sex hormones during puberty may wreak havoc upon these neurotransmitters, which can leave a person even more vulnerable to the development of an eating disorder. "Many of us have started to look at the pubertal period as a time of high risk for the development of genetic influences on eating disorders. We've known for a long time that puberty exhibits psychological and psychosocial risk for eating disorders, but now it really looks like it's a period of biological and genetic risk as well," Klump said.

Before adolescence, Klump says, young children's bodies produce similar amounts of estrogen. The start of puberty ratchets up estrogen production in females and testosterone in males. In young children, rates of eating disorders are almost evenly split between boys and girls—very different from post-puberty when females comprise a majority of eating disorder diagnoses. The presence of estrogen, and the genes it regulates, may help explain why eating disorders are more common in females than males.

"The picture that's starting to emerge is a picture of potentially different gene expression across sex. You have ovarian hormones coming on line in girls, and you start to get differential regulation of risk genes for eating disorders, causing greater individual differences in risk for eating disorders. This could be due to effects on the serotinergic, dopaminergic, and noradrenergic neurotransmitter systems that, in a downstream way, lead to the phenotypes that we see with anorexia and bulimia nervosa," Klump said. "All of this is speculative at this point, but when you put together the findings of the puberty studies, it definitely looks like sex hormones are doing something to increase genetic risk for eating disorders, even if we're not quite sure yet what they're doing."

Klump has traced the role of estrogen and testosterone in anorexia development to life in the womb. In fraternal twins where one sibling was male and one was female, Klump noticed something peculiar about their anorexia risk. Girls with a male fraternal twin had much lower rates compared to girls with a female fraternal twin. Conversely, males with a female co-twin had much higher rates of disordered eating thoughts and behaviors. When the researchers looked at both opposite- and same-sex twins, they found the highest rates of disordered eating in female same-sex twins, followed by females with a male co-twin and then males with a female co-twin, with the lowest rates of disordered eating seen in male same-sex twins (Culbert *et al.*, 2008). The researchers concluded that these differences in rates of disordered eating were "unlikely to be due to socialization effects alone" (p. 329).

A more recent study (released as I was finishing up this book) looked at a large population of over 20,000 twins from Sweden, Norway, and North America and found that prenatal hormone exposure had different effects depending on whether the person had anorexia, bulimia, or another type of eating disorder. As well, the researchers found that the effects of hormones might not have been as strong as researchers originally thought (Lydecker *et al.*, 2012). Still, this early hormone exposure probably has an effect on subsequent eating disorder diagnosis.

An Orchid By Any Other Name

Discussions of hormones and genes don't mean that environment is unimportant in the development of anorexia—far from it. We are all products of nature *and* nurture. Our genes affect which environments we seek out, and our environments affect which genes are expressed. The onset of puberty not only activates many of the genes that put a person at risk for developing anorexia, but puberty also brings a host of environmental changes. The complexity of the social and emotional issues with which teens must grapple increases, as do the effects of peer pressure. Adolescents begin to actively participate in mainstream culture, which can open a person's eyes to appearance and health concerns that they may have previously been blind to.

"Peer pressure to be thin seems to be quite significant, and it can be from the larger culture or the peer environment," said Wade. "People aren't very comfortable with their bodies, and certainly that type of environment is yet another trigger in people who have that genetic vulnerability."

And Photoshop-perfect supermodels aren't the only source of body discomfort. "I'm also very concerned about the anti-obesity environment. We get this message that obese people are bad, that it's going to be a strain on the health system, so much so that it's now okay to be fat-ist. In our prevention work, we get a lot of concern that we don't want kids to be too satisfied with their bodies, otherwise they might get fat," Wade said.

"Environment can be toxic. We know in Australia in the last ten years, obesity has started to level out," Wade said. "But what has doubled in the last ten years is disordered eating. You can't necessarily draw cause and effect there, but when people are trying not to put on weight, then they can resort to disordered eating."

In some people, what might look like healthful eating or just another teenage diet is really the beginnings of an eating disorder. Heightened fears about obesity, combined with a general assumption that people are unhappy with their appearance and that weight loss is the answer to these concerns, allow an eating disorder to hide in plain sight, sometimes for years. An eating disorder looks and sounds so familiar that patients, parents, and loved ones often don't recognize the initial signs.

For some patients I spoke with, the healthy-eating messages they received in health class, combined with their genetic predisposition to anorexia, ultimately resulted in an eating disorder. This type of gene–environment interaction happens in a large number of traits, from anorexia to cancer. Researchers generally define the gene–environment interaction as a measure of how sensitive someone is to different factors in their environment (Tsuang *et al.*, 2004). Some people are inherently less sensitive to their environment, others more so. Writer David Dobbs calls these people dandelions and orchids, respectively (Dobbs, 2009).

"Most of us have genes that make us as hardy as dandelions: able to take root and survive almost anywhere," writes Dobbs. "A few of us, however, are more like the orchid: fragile and fickle, but capable of blooming spectacularly if given greenhouse care. So holds a provocative new theory of genetics, which asserts that the very genes that give us the most trouble as a species, causing behaviors that are self-destructive and antisocial, also underlie humankind's phenomenal adaptability and evolutionary success" (n.p.).

A genetic vulnerability to an eating disorder doesn't automatically make you a card-carrying member of the Orchid Club, but many children who go on to develop eating disorders would probably be described as orchids by researchers, myself included. Anxious, moody, and hypersensitive even before you add the eating disorder into the equation, I felt like society was trying to jam my square-peg self into a round hole. I freaked out at the tiniest things and needed almost unfathomable amounts of alone time. I had a hard time figuring life out.

Typically, the gene–environment explanation in eating disorders goes something like this. My high-school friend, with a lesser genetic risk for developing anorexia, had tried weight loss diets in college but found them too difficult to keep up. She would occasionally go on fitness kicks and start running several miles a day, only to stop a week later because it was too much work. Then there was me. I loved restricting my food and losing weight. It was exciting, exhilarating. And exercise? Why go to the gym once a day when you can go twice?! My genes gave me a (skinny) leg up on the obsessiveness needed to maintain chronic starvation in the face of plenty, and even made the never-ending quest to eat less and exercise more soothing, if not outright pleasant.

Some researchers might hypothesize that living in a culture that touts weight loss as the key to social acceptance and personal fulfillment might have led to my eating disorder. Or that seeing digitally altered models in advertisements and magazines triggered a perfectionistic drive to look the same. These factors didn't help, but I didn't find them a fulfilling answer to why I had gotten sick. These definitions of environment seemed overly simplistic—shouldn't an environment include much more than this?

Historically, the "environment" in relation to eating disorders has typically been winnowed down to either "the culture" (Garner and Garfinkel, 1980) or "the family" (Minuchin *et al.*, 1978), which have been held responsible for the development of anorexia and bulimia. Although these two factors are certainly environmental and definitely important influences on everyone, they aren't the sole environmental factors that can interact with someone's biological predisposition to anorexia. Environment can include exposure to hormones in the womb, any number of pathogens and microbes, and even the time of year you were born.

Researchers have begun to expand their search into environmental triggers of anorexia into other, more varied areas. One particularly interesting area has proposed a mechanism by which genes and environment interact to perpetuate anorexia through the generations. "They might have been protected from developing anorexia if they hadn't been in that environment," Wade said.

From Nurture to Nature

Our life experiences—everything from that nasty cold we had when we were five to being bullied at school—can also be reflected in our genes. The new, rapidly expanding field of epigenetics studies how our environment can cause the subtle changes to the genome that affect which genes are expressed. Each human has between 20,000 and 30,000 genes spread over 23 pairs of chromosomes. DNA is a long, thread-like molecule; if the DNA in each chromosome was unraveled and placed end-to-end, it would be several feet long. In order to pack all of this DNA into the tiny nucleus of a cell, it folds and packs itself very precisely, depending on the type of cell. Those genes that are on the outside of the chromosome are active and turned into proteins. Genes in the inner portions of the chromosome are generally very quiet. Epigenetics has told researchers that environment doesn't affect gene expression by changing the actual DNA molecule. Instead, it affects how the genes are folded.

Think of the unraveled molecule of DNA like a blank sheet of paper. To decrease the amount of space it takes up in the cell, it folds itself up, much like an origami master can take that blank sheet of paper and turn it into a crane. The origami master can also transform that same piece of paper into a boat or a flower. These different origami shapes are like our cells—the same DNA is folded very differently, which leads to very different final characteristics. Epigenetics doesn't turn a crane into a tulip or a brain cell into a liver cell. Instead, it might crimp the crane's wing or smooth out the beak. These small changes in folding can alter which genes are easily accessible to the cell's machinery and can be expressed.

The origami master folds his or her figurines with their fingers. The cell folds its DNA using small chemicals called methyl and acetyl groups. The exact location of these groups smoothes out a fold or crimps the DNA even more tightly. Although researchers still aren't sure exactly how it happens, our environments help to direct the placement of methyl and acetyl groups. This placement and the subsequent changes in gene expression can affect everything from risk of heart disease and cancer to the likelihood of developing a mental illness like anorexia.

The field of behavioral epigenetics has found that difficult early life experiences in rats can decrease their production of a small molecule called BDNF as adults (Roth et al., 2009). Lower levels of BDNF have been linked to both depression and anxiety (Martinowich et al., 2007). Studies like this have given research a better understanding about how life events can affect a person's chances of developing a serious mental illness like schizophrenia or bipolar disorder (Fumagalli et al., 2007; McEwen, 2007). Some scientists think that dysfunctions in epigenetic regulation in the brain could be an unrecognized cause of psychiatric disorders (Tsankova et al., 2007).

The study of epigenetics in anorexia nervosa is still in its infancy, but researchers have found several important epigenetic differences in people with eating disorders. German researcher Helge Frieling of the Hannover Medical School found that women with anorexia and bulimia had an unusually high expression of a dopamine transporter gene, which removes dopamine from the synapse, the small space between neurons across which chemical messages are passed. As well, the women with anorexia had epigenetic changes to a dopamine receptor gene that decreased the production of that protein (Frieling et al., 2010). Although the researchers still don't know exactly what triggers these epigenetic changes that adjust levels of dopamine in the brain, they believe that an energy imbalance (eating too little for your metabolic needs) "may serve as a molecular switch in some adolescents, or may contribute to progression and persistence of the disorder, by changing the expression of different pathophysiologically relevant genes" (p. 581).

Still, considering that anorexia has been identified in cultures without the Western thin ideal, such as rural Africa (Binitie et al., 2000) and even among the Amish and Mennonite communities in North America (Husni et al., 2001), sociocultural factors don't actually cause anorexia. Disorders and illnesses that only exist in specific cultures are known as culture-bound syndromes. While these syndromes might be very familiar to the culture in which they exist, they are essentially unknown in other societies. Most culture-bound syndromes have psychiatric and/or religious overtones.

Given an eating disorder's surface similarity to common behaviors like dieting, frequent weighing, and obsession with shape and weight, many people initially assumed that anorexia was culture-bound. And at that point, no data suggested otherwise. Even with strong data from subsequent genetic studies that showed anorexia had a strong genetic cause, many clinicians and researchers still viewed anorexia and bulimia as exclusively sociocultural illnesses.

"Even at the end of the 1990s, people still weren't convinced that anorexia had any genetic influences, and I would present data at conferences to a lot of skeptics. I was presenting and someone raised their hand and said 'How can eating disorders have genetic influences if they're culture-bound?'" Klump said. "Everyone assumes [eating disorders] are culture-bound, so I decided to look at the data."

If a disorder is completely culture-bound, then the prevalence of the disorder would increase or decrease based on the culture in which you were looking. Rates of anorexia would be higher in cultures with an increased emphasis on thin females as the ideal of beauty, and much lower in those cultures that promote a fleshier female body type. Although data on the rates of anorexia in any culture are sketchy, studies have found only a minimal increase in incidence (the number of newly diagnosed cases of a disease in a particular population) of anorexia in the US since the 1950s (Owen and Laurel-Seller, 2000; Rubinstein and Caballero, 2000). If anorexia was culture-bound, the recent emphasis on a lean body type should have resulted in a significant uptick in anorexia cases. Strike one for the culture-bound hypothesis of anorexia.

As well, anorexia shouldn't be found in time periods or modern cultures that don't stress the importance of a svelte body, if the disorder is truly culture-bound. Except historical (Bell, 1987) and cross-cultural data (Rieger *et al.*, 2001) clearly indicate that anorexia exists across almost all time periods and cultures. Strikes two and three for the hypothesis that anorexia is a culture-bound syndrome.

"We uncategorically found that anorexia isn't a culture-bound syndrome," Klump said. What does seem to be tied to culture is the phobia of fatness, seen in many modern cases of anorexia in the Western world. Case descriptions of anorexia from the Middle Ages (Bell, 1987) into the mid-twentieth century (Habermas, 1989) would not infrequently fail to mention a desire to be thin or a fear of fat as a motivating factor for self-starvation, as do modern case reports from non-Western cultures.

Keel and Klump argue that:

> Although motivations for food refusal may have differed across periods (in many cases this information is simply lacking), purported motivations

may not represent the true causes of self-starvation. Instead, they may represent culturally meaningful attempts to understand an affliction that leaves women feeling unable and unwilling to eat. The extent to which fear of fat is viewed as causing AN may be, in part, an illusion. Thus, if the core feature of AN is taken to be an intentional yet nonvolitional self-starvation, then evidence of AN appears to trace back to early medieval times.

(2003, p. 754)

Culture doesn't cause anorexia, but it does provide the vocabulary with which sufferers make sense of their illnesses.

"We know little to nothing about which specific genes increase your risk for developing anorexia," Klump said. Generally, behavioral geneticists have focused their search for genes that may influence anorexia risk on those involved in the production of one of three major neurotransmitters: serotonin, dopamine, and noradrenaline (also referred to as norepinephrine).

Tantalizing clues have popped up in the research literature about certain genes involved in serotonin levels that can increase a person's risk for developing anorexia, but no specific genes have yet been identified.

"We're all at the same place in psychiatric genetics," Klump said. "We're trying to figure out a better way to model genetic risk, and the sample sizes that we need to see these effects, and we're just not there yet. We need a lot more time and new technology and new data."

"The field is exploding with new technology and new ways to look at this," Klump said. "We're hoping that with further refinement, we will get there."

4   Anorexia's Poster Children

Apartment 204 harbored a dirty little secret. My three friends and I managed to snag one of the much-coveted, college-owned Kraker apartments in the housing lottery as we entered our senior year of college. All four of us were consummate over-achievers, having accumulated enough college credits to catapult us to the top of the housing lottery and give us first pick of living arrangements. Kraker was a natural choice—the college had recently renovated the top two floors of a building over a downtown furniture store and had added amenities such as a dishwasher and full-size fridge, while covering the exposed brick walls with a fresh coat of white paint. The newness of the building, combined with the off-campus feel, made it perfect for four almost college graduates.

The peculiar personality dynamics of Kraker 204 didn't become apparent until shortly after we had all moved in. Three of the four of us were science majors, with a pre-law economics major rounding out the group. This we knew. What none of us really grasped was that by the time we began to haul our belongings to the apartment over the furniture store, three of the four of us would also have full-blown eating disorders. That past summer, I had transitioned from being neurotic and rigid about food and exercise to needing hospitalization for anorexia. I talked my way out of the hospital shortly before I had to pack my things and return to school. Sara, my roommate and fellow biochemistry major, had struggled with anorexia in high school, but had seemingly put her obsessions behind her. Although Sara remained cautious around food, she could eat normally—provided there was a bathroom nearby where she could throw up. Elizabeth, the pre-law student, had suffered from anorexia for years, and had started making some headway in her recovery as she moved through college. Her perfect 4.0 grade point average placed her first in our class, right in front of my 3.99. The past spring, however, she fell back into her old ways and was still in the process of pulling herself out.

I knew this on some level, but it never entered my conscious awareness until I took a long, hard look at the shiny new refrigerator in our apartment. My contribution to the fridge was simple: a jar of mustard, a jar of salsa, and a cucumber. I stacked my two cases of Diet Coke in the pantry and stashed a few cans in the back of the fridge. Elizabeth filled the crisper with fresh broccoli, green peppers, carrots, onions, and mushrooms that she steamed for dinner each night, along with a small poached chicken breast. Sara had skim milk and tortillas, some olive oil for her gourmet Italian specialties, a couple of cartons of light yogurt, and her own stash of Diet Coke.

The freezer, however, was Dana's domain (aside from Sara's container of fat-free frozen yogurt). Dana filled her space with frozen tacos and pizza rolls, pints of premium ice cream, and several sleeves of bagels. "I love good food," she said, "I just can't be bothered cooking it." She arrived in Kraker 204 with an armful of books, twirled around, and exclaimed, "Look everyone! I grew an ass last year! I actually grew myself an ass!" Dana, naturally thin as a rail, had vowed to acquire a booty she could shake on the dance floor during her junior year in Salamanca, Spain, which she did with the help of big bowls of paella with saffron, gazpacho, olive oil, and wine.

A math, chemistry, and Spanish triple major, Dana was far from an under-achiever. She worked as hard as the rest of us, and joined our collective worries over grades and grad school. Although Dana was disappointed when her test scores and grades weren't top notch, she wasn't devastated, either. She didn't lock herself in the closet and sob when faced with an A minus. She didn't obsess. She moved on. She laughed loudly, without apologies. When faced with life, Dana didn't hesitate and hold back. She didn't always jump in, feet-first, but she approached life on life's terms.

In this respect, she was the polar opposite of Sara, Elizabeth, and me. The three of us froze in fear when faced with life. This near-crippling anxiety invaded every aspect of our lives, whether related to eating, school, or not. Fun was a foreign language to us. If it was for Dana, she learned it as fluently as she did Spanish. Sara, Elizabeth, and I? We had yet to learn how to relax and enjoy life, how to roll with the punches, how not to flagellate ourselves with each perceived mistake.

Looking back, I can see that these differences between us and Dana—the anxiety, the obsessionality, the perfectionism—probably had as much to do with why we had eating disorders and why Dana never struggled with food and weight. All of us were naturally thin. All of us occasionally read fashion magazines and watched reality TV and probably wondered whether the Thigh Master might add some muscle tone. Our families were relatively similar—no one pressured us to diet or lose weight. But Dana's personality diverged in very important ways that dramatically altered her risk for developing anorexia.

The Best Little Girl in the World

Kim would have fit in quite well with the three of us in Kraker 204. I met Kim initially through her online blog, and we emailed each other for well over a year before I actually spoke with her on the phone. I called one blustery October afternoon.

We spoke for a while and Kim confirmed some of the details about her battle with anorexia that started when she was a senior in high school. Always a skinny kid, Kim had never previously worried about food and weight. "I remember this defining moment where a friend put her hands around my thigh and said 'You're so skinny—you're lucky,'" she told me. "And something clicked in my head where I thought this is something important, I should work to keep this."

Like a switch had been flipped, Kim began worrying about food and weight and calories, worries that soon occupied most of her waking hours. "I didn't have a reason to lose weight, I just suddenly became obsessed," she recalled. "I remember looking up things in my mom's cooking books, like how many calories were in an apple, and I would stress over whether it was 50 or 100. I started to pay attention to fat grams. I never had looked at nutrition labels before, but then I was strangely obsessed."

Even as Kim obsessed over food and weight, she was on track to attend Notre Dame University, halfway across the country. Anxieties about moving away from home only fueled her eating disorder. Unsure if she really wanted to go, but feeling that her scholarships almost obligated her to make the journey, and fearing that she would be a failure if she decided against Notre Dame, she accepted a spot and moved to Indiana in the fall of 1997.

Should. Failure. These were words that frequently appeared in my own vocabulary, I told Kim, and they affected many of the decisions I made and the journeys I took. Much of my own life revolved around things I thought I should do and a profound sense of guilt and failure if I didn't do these things exactly as I had hoped. And, just like Kim, the *should* related to my eating disorder always triumphed over the *should* related to school and life.

Shortly after Kim moved to Notre Dame, "everything kind of fell apart," she said. The eating disorder, which had managed to co-exist with academics during her senior year of high school, began to rage unchecked by worried friends and family. "I was on my own with my eating, and the dining hall ..." Kim hesitated for a moment and shuddered slightly. "I would start with a normal meal and then suddenly I was taking things out, and soon I was only eating baked potatoes."

Not long after whittling her diet down to little more than baked potatoes, Kim developed a high fever and passed out. The emergency room doctor questioned her about her gaunt appearance and eating habits, and told her, point blank, that she had been living on a starvation diet. Kim raised an eyebrow. Starvation diet? She told the doctor she had been doing a lot of walking lately, she was tired, and besides, she ate really healthful food. The doctor's concern fell on deaf ears—Kim was convinced she didn't have an eating problem.

But her convictions didn't last long. As she returned to California for the Christmas holidays, she broke down crying to her mother, telling her, "I don't know what it is but I'm just afraid to eat." Her mom's jaw dropped: could Kim have an eating disorder? She wasn't vain or into makeup and fashion magazines. Kim wasn't a girly girl—she hated clothes and shopping. Kim was the last person who cared what she looked like. At first, her mom regarded Kim as if she was a little crazy. But as her mom began researching Kim's eating problems and symptoms, she sat Kim down and told her, "I think you have anorexia." Kim shook her head—no, her fears of food didn't match the sensationalized stories of anorexia she had read in magazines. Yet the more she read, the more she had to admit to herself that this was exactly what she was dealing with.

"My mom said she always skipped the anorexia chapters in the *How to Raise Your Daughter* book because she thought that would never be an issue for me," Kim said. "She had no idea that it was an anxiety problem."

I had to laugh. I told Kim that, shortly after I was diagnosed with anorexia, my own mother told me, in a bizarre moment of completely blunt honesty, that she always thought I was too smart to develop an eating disorder. Like Kim's mother, my mom didn't understand the strong links between anxiety and anorexia, links that lay latent in my own family until that fateful day when I decided to lose five pounds. Neither of us had any idea that the obsessionality and perfectionism that enabled me to graduate high school as valedictorian and college as salutatorian would be the same traits that made me so profoundly vulnerable to anorexia. Kim, Sara, Elizabeth, and I all shared these anxieties, anxieties that existed long before the anorexia and would persist long after recovery.

Even as a baby, Kim's family noticed that she was always anxious and alert. "My grandma swears that the first day I was born, I was just looking around at everyone and analyzing everything," she said. "My mom always said to me, 'Your radar is always up—please put it down.'" This intensity, as Kim described it, translated naturally into perfectionism and high achievement in school. "I was just very punishing, very hard on myself, and very sensitive," she noted, three traits that reminded me of myself.

This raw determination and complete intolerance for mistakes permeated everything I did. In my childhood journals, I recorded events and thoughts and feelings, but mainly, I practiced my handwriting. I didn't think it was pretty enough or perfect enough—I wanted to rid myself of my childlike scrawl and obtain the elegant penmanship of a grown-up. So I wrote my name, my parents' names, my friends' names, over and over and over, determined to get it "right." Although this trait allowed me to excel in school and at music, it extracted a high emotional price. Like me, Kim found school to be a double-edged sword, bringing out both the best and the worst of her personality.

"When I got a C on a quiz once, I locked myself in a closet for the whole day to read the encyclopedia on the subject that I didn't do well on," Kim told me.

"That is precisely the sort of thing I could see myself doing," I said.

"I remember it like it happened yesterday—it was Mr Medina's seventh grade class on English literature," she said, "And the quiz was on Shakespeare, and I sat in the closet with the 'S' volume and read for hours." Kim laughed a little sheepishly at this. I joined in because I, too, had lived through these absurd episodes when the tiniest details could shred my self-esteem, episodes I thought no one else could ever understand.

Kim's parents, like mine, had no idea what to do with such a self-punishing child, no way to get her to lighten up and relax. "My parents used to say we'll give you money if you get a B in this class," Kim said, "And I just wouldn't do it. It didn't tempt me at all." It wouldn't have tempted me, either, I told her. Not in the slightest.

I took a deep breath and told Kim of my own perfectionism. I had been invited to perform at a special piano recital when I was about 12 or 13, and I had practiced my piece—a Beethoven sonata that I loved—for weeks, memorizing every note, making sure to articulate each phrase and each note. I made sure everything in my outfit matched, and my mom even allowed me to wear a little mascara. I took my place in the audience and continued to practice my piece on my lap. I tried to study surreptitiously while I waited for my turn to perform. After what seemed like an eternity, my turn finally came. I started playing, and everything went well until my finger slipped and I hit a wrong note. I shook my head slightly to try and clear the error from my mind and continue playing, but the spell I had cast upon myself was ruined. My fingers kept slipping and soon, the carefully memorized notes became a jumble of black dots. What comes next? I demanded of myself. Figure it out, you idiot. I couldn't. I had to stop playing entirely and start the piece over, from the beginning.

I made it through the sonata the second time, stood up to take my bow, and promptly fled the recital hall in tears. Out in the lobby, I sobbed, heartbroken at my miserable failure as a pianist. I had humiliated myself and my teacher. The tears became heaving sobs that just wouldn't stop. My mom ushered me out to the car, my carefully applied mascara giving me raccoon eyes, and I wailed that I sucked at piano, why did I bother, it wasn't worth it. I was devastated, and nothing my mother told me could convince me otherwise.

Never Good Enough

"Perfectionism is a pretty toxic trait," said Nancy Zucker, director of the Duke University Eating Disorders Program. Zucker (pronounced like sucker with a "z," she told me) said that, for folks who are profoundly perfectionistic, it's almost impossible to feel satisfied, like their efforts are enough to satisfy their cruel internal taskmaster. "It's like, they're hitting their head with a hammer, they're hitting their head with a hammer, and it hurts and it hurts and it hurts, but they said they were going to do it, so gosh darn it, they're going to make it work," she said. "There's a drivenness in their behavior, not for the joy of it, but avoiding the guilt of not doing it."

Was Dr Zucker peering inside my brain? Could she see not only what I was thinking but how I was thinking it? This was exactly how I experienced life. I performed for the camera, so to speak—I applied for the scholarships, I turned in the extra assignments, I accepted the piano recital invitations—not because I wanted to do these things, but because I would feel too guilty for not doing them. I was a finalist in a national essay contest that I entered because I didn't want to let down my high-school English teacher, not because I thought my essay, a character analysis in Ayn Rand's novel "The Fountainhead," was anything special. I never let go of the hope that one of these achievements would finally allow me to feel satisfied with myself.

When I decided to lose weight, I attacked my weight loss plan with the same perfectionistic zeal and verve that I gave to everything else in my life. I suddenly started paying attention to what I was told I "should" eat. I forced myself to go above and beyond recommended amounts of exercise. Rather predictably, my weight dropped. Also rather predictably, I kept on losing weight. I kept increasing the number of pounds I needed to lose in order to feel like I was "good enough." It wasn't enough just to be eating disordered or even anorexic. I had to be the best anorexic. Every time I went into the hospital, I wept that I would surely be the fattest one there and that I hadn't yet shown the world how good I could be at this anorexia thing. My eating disorder wasn't an extreme expression of perfectionism—I wasn't dying to be thin or starving to be perfect. But like many people with anorexia, my perfectionism was hopelessly intertwined with my eating disorder.

Perfectionism, says Dr Craig Johnson, Chief Clinical Director at the Eating Recovery Center in Denver, is defined as an inability to tolerate inexactness. "If somebody has a strong trait of perfectionism, it means that if they look at their bodies, they're going to have a tendency to want to control them," Johnson said. "And if they're benchmarking themselves against some particular standard out there, and they start deciding they are going to make themselves look a certain way, they are going to pursue it fairly relentlessly, and it will never be right. Because how much control do we really have over our bodies or appearance or our size and shape?"

Other researchers have described perfectionism as a "striving for flawlessness" (Flett and Hewitt, 2002). Despite the toxicity of perfectionism, many people who are perfectionists have other qualities that enable them to do well in life—qualities like work ethic, hard work, determination, and grit. Besides anxiety, perfectionism is probably the most notable pre-illness trait of people with anorexia. For someone with anorexia, these qualities are co-opted by the illness to demand ever more stringent rules about eating and exercise, as well as stellar grades and outstanding athletic or artistic abilities.

Researchers have identified two major types of perfectionism that can co-exist: others-oriented perfectionism, which is when a person expects perfection of others in his life, and self-oriented perfectionism, when a person expects perfection of himself. Although both depression and anxiety are linked to perfectionism, self-oriented perfectionism is particularly associated with extreme dieting and purging (Forbush *et al.*, 2007). Women who reported even just a single element of self-oriented perfectionism (high personal standards) had 3.5 times the risk of developing an eating disorder compared to women without this trait (Castro-Fornieles *et al.*, 2007).

A study of over 1,000 female twins between the ages of 25 and 65 found two other specific aspects of perfectionism that significantly increased the risk of developing an eating disorder: negative reactions to mistakes and the tendency to view mistakes as personal failures. As well, these perfectionistic traits only increased the women's risk of developing an eating disorder; they weren't related to other mental health problems like depression or anxiety (Bulik *et al.*, 2003). "Most patients and their parents say that perfectionism goes back to before they developed an eating disorder," said lead author Cynthia Bulik in a press release.

> Young girls who are highly perfectionistic and punish themselves unduly for perceived failures can be helped to learn how to give themselves a break and set more realistic goals. This could also help them develop more realistic body image standards as well and perhaps prevent them for developing such extreme weight-loss behaviors.
>
> (WebMD, 2003, n.p.)

I never judged my friends who got Bs and Cs, or who gained ten pounds during a difficult time in their lives. But when looking at myself, I applied a whole different set of standards, standards that were almost impossible to meet. If I did meet these standards, I immediately raised the bar and found myself in the same predicament as before. Furthermore, the thought of changing these standards never occurred to me. The problem wasn't my perfectionistic standards; it was my inability to ever meet them.

This perfectionism, says Zucker, is quite socially distancing. "One of the ways you bond with people is you say 'Well, I'm imperfect, here are my flaws, let me tell you about them' ... for hours," she laughs. But like most perfectionists, people with anorexia don't do this. "It's not because they want to be better than you, but because they're afraid of the exact opposite—that people won't like them as much if they knew they had these really genuine flaws," Zucker said. "The irony, of course, is that we all liked Martha Stewart better when she was arrested. Because that's the way it works, and now I like her very much."

Zucker's laughter and vivacious spirit caught me totally off guard. I had dealt with research scientists for years, most of whom were like me: driven, reserved, unemotional. Personality-wise, Zucker was almost the exact opposite. Her youth also surprised me. Usually, scientists with her pedigree are middle-aged or older; Zucker appeared to be in her mid-thirties, with dark brown hair that reached halfway to her waist. Within minutes of meeting her, I felt totally at ease, as if she could see straight through my perfectionistic façade into the interesting but messy person below and—most shocking to me—actually preferred that imperfect person.

To illustrate her points about perfectionism, Zucker tells the story of two Olympic athletes, both of whom are training for gold. One is very driven, always forging ahead, always practicing and improving her technique. Everything in her life is about getting this medal. The other is practicing, but also meeting new people and coaches, and learning from her mistakes. To this athlete, the gold medal is more about the journey than the actual event. "When the first girl gets the medal, she experiences the tragedy of perfectionism in this deflation: now what? My whole life was this, now it's over. When the other girl gets the gold, the gold is a symbol of a profound journey. It matters, of course, but it's kind of: what next?" Zucker paused for a moment. "The difference is not that there's always something next, it's the difference of whether you view what's next with this hopelessness or this anticipation."

Anticipation, I pointed out, was not usually a positive emotion for me. "Usually, all I can think about is what might go wrong, and my mind is overwhelmed by the sheer number of what ifs," I said. "My anxiety can get so high that I've been known to ditch friends for a fun night out because it's just easier to stay in, where everything—the people, the surroundings, the food—is familiar."

The Tortoise and the Hare

In clinical terms, the trait I have described above is known as harm avoidance. Zucker explained that harm avoidance is a heritable personality trait closely linked to anxiety disorders. People who have high harm avoidance are the stereotypical worrywarts of the world—they see danger where many people don't. They are hypervigilant for signs of punishment and respond strongly to changes in the environment they deem unpleasant. Not surprisingly, people with a history of eating disorders tend to score high on harm avoidance, and those who have an anxiety disorder and an eating disorder score even higher.

A friend on a trip to New Zealand described the adrenaline rush he got after bungee jumping and urged me to try it. "Tom," I said, "I get an adrenaline rush when I jaywalk. That much adrenaline all at once would probably kill me." I didn't realize it at the time, but I know now that this is classic harm avoidance. Not so much the not-gonna-throw-myself-off-a-bridge part, but how I detect danger in nearly everything I do. And so I stand back and observe from the sidelines, where it's safe.

People who are harm avoidant, says Zucker, tend to avoid people, but most of all, they avoid uncertainty (Ribases *et al.*, 2005). Even after weight restoration, anorexia sufferers remain "incredibly rigid," Zucker said. "They're better, but they're still living this restrictive existence." And this restrictive existence serves to decrease a fear of uncertainty and the unknown. Zucker describes many anorexia sufferers as the proverbial deer in the headlights, who freeze in fear at the slightest hint of danger. I think of Kim and how she described her anxiety radar, even as a young child. Kim, like me, was always on high alert for the slightest threat, and the more we looked for threats, the more we found them.

Craig Johnson describes harm avoidant people not as deer but as turtles. "They have a tendency to retreat fairly quickly in the face of anything unusual," he said. "And once they've retreated, it's kind of hard to coax them out." People with a so-called "turtle temperament" have a more fear-based relationship with the world.

"In the face of things that are new, they have a tendency to sort of rock back, if you will, in the face of new circumstances," Johnson said. "They don't throw themselves into new situations—that's not positively reinforcing for them." He described this feature as being restrained in the face of novelty, a temperament trait known formally as low novelty seeking. High harm avoidance and low novelty seeking tend to go hand in hand, and lead to a preference for the familiar. Anything new is frightening; even if it's a positive change, it's still different and therefore threatening.

These traits of anorexia sufferers—shyness, caution, perfectionism—make them the stereotypical "good girls," the ones people don't worry about, the ones who don't make trouble. "These are not traits that result in somebody being kind of wild and crazy," Johnson said. "They aren't doing high-risk behaviors, they're not oppositional and defiant, they're not pushing the outside of the envelope in experimental behaviors. It's a more anxious, fearful group." Like Elizabeth, Sara, Kim, and I, these fears and anxieties were obvious even from a young age.

The opposite of these turtles is what Johnson refers to as hares. Hares generally tend to suffer from bulimia or the binge/purge subtype of anorexia. They tend to be more impulsive and chaotic, more drawn to drama, and much more novelty seeking. They get bored with things easily. They are also, I've found, an awful lot of fun. That group generally shows their impulsivity through bulimic behaviors, although these impulsivities may extend into substance abuse, shoplifting, and sexual promiscuity (Fassino *et al.*, 2002). Although someone with a hare temperament may begin their eating disorder by restricting their food intake, "their temperament is going to prevail ultimately, and [the hares] might stay in that restricting defense for a bit, but they'll ultimately move back to the bingeing," Johnson said.

Several more formal studies have divided people with eating disorders into three major personality groups: high functioning/perfectionistic, overcontrolled, and undercontrolled. The scientists asked over 100 psychologists to recall an eating-disordered patient on their caseload with either anorexia or bulimia. Then, the psychologists were asked to indicate whether their patients had a wide array of personality characteristics. Eating disorder patients in the perfectionistic category were commonly described as conscientious, self-critical, and articulate. The overcontrolled category was described as passive, dysphoric, and inhibited, whereas the undercontrolled group was impulsive, emotional, and chaotic. Not surprisingly, people with the restricting subtype of anorexia were divided between the perfectionistic and the overcontrolled group; the binge/purge subtype was found most frequently in the perfectionistic and undercontrolled group (Westen and Harnden-Fischer, 2001). Further studies showed that separating eating disorder sufferers into these three categories predicted more about their response to treatment (Thompson-Brenner and Westen, 2005) and their co-occurring psychiatric disorders than their actual eating disorder diagnosis (Cassin and von Ranson, 2005).

Regardless of category, by early childhood, "very attuned mothers knew that these were kids that, despite being very competent and smart and capable in many ways, were slightly overwhelmed by the world out there," Johnson said. "So attuned mothers that knew this about their kids would do what attuned mothers often do; they become sort of more overprotective and controlling because they do understand that there is a fragility to the kid that other people may not see."

"For 30-plus years, in the literature in anorexia nervosa, we have accused mothers of anorexics of being over-protective, controlling, and intrusive. The truth of the matter is, these mothers actually had children who did probably require some overprotectiveness and helpful management from them of their interface as things got more complex developmentally for them. So we kind of apologize to mothers more for not getting it ourselves," he concluded.

This sounded a lot like my own childhood, I told him, how I was overwhelmed by the world around me, torn by a fierce need for independence and a fear of what I might find on my own. "My mom might not directly step in, but she was more of a mediator between me and the outside world," I said.

"Appropriately so, yes," Johnson said. He told me that one of the most powerful trends in treating anorexia nervosa was the re-empowerment of parents, to help them "more actively understand and manage the psychological vulnerabilities that their kids have." I did the majority of my recovery work at home with my parents, where I felt safe. And this sense of safety and security was crucial to my first tentative steps towards recovery.

"The important work that's going on now is looking at the fear-arousal system and really trying to understand if we've got a hyper-reactive brain to environmental stimuli that makes these kids really anxious," Johnson said. Someone who is extremely anxious—someone essentially like me—ends up with a fear-conditioned brain. Always on alert for danger, the brain becomes hypervigilant for anything unsafe in the environment and responds without conscious thought (LeDoux, 2003). Johnson gave the example of a combat veteran with post-traumatic stress disorder who hits the ground when the car down the street backfires. Although it serves the person well to be motivated into behavior that will ensure its safety—hitting the ground before you think about it—it can become maladaptive if they're always sensing danger when none is around.

"If we have a kid who has this turtle temperament and yet they're extremely capable and also have social skills to perhaps mask the extent that they are anxious or overwhelmed by the amount of things that's coming at them," Johnson said, "what you could be seeing is a kid who is continually put in more stressful situations than they really can tolerate, so that the fear-arousal system is being ramped up on a moment-to-moment basis by the amount of anxiety that they're experiencing with the complexity of their environment. So they go through childhood with more stress than this brain can potentially manage, but they're smart enough and capable enough that they more successfully hide it. And then they hit puberty and all hell breaks loose."

I chuckled. "That's actually my life in a nutshell," I told Johnson, "because my mom always said to me 'I never knew you were anxious.'"

"The tragedy is not even necessarily that the parents were wanting to accelerate their kid; it's the kid's competitiveness and ambitiousness and achievement orientation, as much as anything else," said Johnson. "And it can just be driven by the fear of failure. That's the kind of brain that's going to be dosed on a continuous basis with pretty high levels of stress, which means they become progressively anxious, vigilant, sort of fearful of failing or of things getting too complex. It's the complexity that I think actually, for a lot of our folks, winds up getting them eventually. There are just too many things going on."

In this over-stimulated fear-arousal system, one of the first things to go in terms of basics is sleep (Shin and Liberzon, 2010). When you're anxious and afraid and worried what's going to happen next, it's hard to sleep, which dramatically compromises your ability to cope, so the stress goes up even further. "All of a sudden you have the cascade of brain chemistry and behaviors that winds up with sort of a breakdown," Johnson said.

Which essentially describes my four years of college. Awash in seemingly never-ending waves of anxiety and depression, I tried to cope by devising a rather draconian study schedule, forcing myself to put in at least 40 hours of studying each week. If I was awake, I forced myself to be working or studying. Whether I was in the cafeteria, at chapel services, or climbing the Stair Master, I brought notes to study. I memorized entire pages of my biochemistry textbook. I copied and re-copied my notes from class into a sheaf of color-coded pages to study.

With all of this studying, combined with 16 hours in lectures, two five-hour-long weekly laboratory sessions, and a part-time job editing the college newspaper that easily sucked up 20 hours each week, I was left profoundly sleep-deprived. My days generally began at 7:30 in the morning and didn't end until 3:30 or 4:00 in the morning. I fell asleep walking to class one day, sliding head-first into a three-foot high snowdrift. I lay there, ensconced in snow, trying to wake myself up before I froze. After lurching back to my feet, though, I didn't head back to my dorm for a nap. Instead, I brushed myself off and headed to my physics lecture. More often then I cared to admit, I slept at my desk, too exhausted to haul myself into the top bunk. I forgot what it felt like to be well-rested.

I fueled my marathon study sessions with never-ending cups of strong black coffee. If it didn't have caffeine, it wasn't worth drinking. Interestingly, caffeine addiction is very common in eating disorders, as it is often used as a calorie-free source of energy. Once, when I was feeling particularly desperate, I dissolved several tablespoons of instant coffee in a can of Diet Coke. The resulting brew was almost undrinkably foul—it tasted like used motor oil, and it made my stomach churn in protest. But this drink kept me awake for one more night, and so I accepted it as the necessary price I had to pay to maintain my perfect 4.0 grade point average. I eventually got one A minus and locked myself in my room for a week, sobbing and distraught that my perfect grade record, dating back to the beginning of elementary school, was forever ruined.

By the end of my sophomore year, the anxiety, exhaustion and depression had pretty much unraveled me. I got into a horrific screaming match with my roommate at a coffee shop, and the two of us—hysterical and exhausted—shrieked at the top of our lungs, hurling insults and swear words as we unloaded our frustrations in front of an audience of 20. The next day, I left a physics exam in tears because I couldn't think of how to solve a particular problem. I knew

I could figure it out, but I was so tired and I couldn't think straight, and all I wanted to do was sleep. And once the semester was over, sleep I did. My first night back home, I fell asleep at 10:00 pm and didn't wake up until dinner time the next day.

I deconstructed the previous two years with a friend that summer, trying to figure out how I came so close to snapping. As I told Katie of my study regimen, my anxieties over never having good enough grades (despite having a straight A average), and my intense guilt if I slept more than four hours each night, she looked at me and said, "It sounds like you had sleep anorexia." I blinked. And nodded. Katie was right. I had yet to show any overt signs of anorexia at this point, but even then, I understood the parallels. My anxieties almost unilaterally led to deprivation, whether sleep or food or something else entirely. I didn't realize that this so-called sleep anorexia was only the beginning of my massive war with my impulses and desires.

But as torturous as these obsessions and rituals were, they dramatically simplified my world. All I had to do was stay awake and study. All I had to do was eat less and exercise more. No longer did I have to worry about friends and dating and whether my car was going to survive the brutal Michigan winter. It didn't matter. All that mattered was that next grade or that next pound. This singular focus seemed almost natural and comforting, and so I resisted any efforts to diversify my life.

Shifting Gears

Dealing with life's complexities requires your brain to do a function called set-shifting. Researchers test this ability with the Wisconsin Card Sort Test, a card game in which the researcher continually changes the rules of the game without telling the person being tested. If the person can adjust to the new rules—if they can adapt to the new way the game is being played—then they have a good ability to set-shift. Many people with anorexia, however, have difficulties with set-shifting. They can't seem to let go of the original set of rules they learned as they played the card game and have difficulties adjusting to the changing rules. Several experiments, done by both Dr Tim Walsh at the New York State Neuropsychiatric Institute and Dr Janet Treasure at the Maudsley Hospital in London, have confirmed that people with anorexia show a significantly lower ability to set-shift, both during acute illness and after recovery (Steinglass *et al.*, 2006; Tchanturia *et al.*, 2012). Increased rigidity and inflexibility in childhood were associated with increased difficulties in shifting sets in anorexia patients (Treasure, 2007).

This is echoed in the rigid and ritualistic behaviors of anorexia nervosa and what Craig Johnson sees as a difficulty in integrating complexity into life. Researchers call this type of thinking obsessionality, which is closely related to perfectionism (Halmi *et al.*, 2000). Not the same as obsessions as they are formally described in the Diagnostic and Statistical Manual (DSM; psychiatry's official criteria to determine whether or not you're officially off the rails), which states that obsessions are intrusive, unwanted thoughts that create anxiety (American Psychiatric Association, 2000), obsessionality is more like a scratched record or DVD. It tends to get stuck on just one thing, going over and over it, even after everyone else is ready to move on. Whereas an obsession is a discrete thought that tends to pop into someone's head and cause intense distress, obsessionality is more a pattern of thinking, in which someone focuses a lot on a particular subject or detail.

This propensity of thinking about something over and over is generally present before the eating disorder (Anderluh *et al.*, 2003) and remains after recovery (Holtkamp *et al.*, 2005). As a child, I would listen to a cassette or CD so much that I would wear out the album. I also read and re-read some of the same books, enjoying the familiarity and the ability to repeat the same text. This easily morphed into a constant thinking of calories, exercise, and body size when the anorexia set in. "With anorexia, this obsessionality could be something they think a lot about, but they don't actually mind thinking a lot about," said Harvard University eating and anxiety disorders expert Steven Tsao. "In fact, some patients are happy to focus on [their eating disorder] and think a lot about it. I have patients that say 'If I don't spend my day thinking about food, what else do I do with myself?'"

It's a thought process I know all too well. Not only did the anorexia mesh perfectly with my tendencies towards obsessionality (in fact, my eating disorder probably enhanced my obsessionality), it also helped make me feel the world was simpler and easier to manage. I didn't have to deal with the many facets of adolescence and young adulthood. All I had to do was count calories and weigh myself.

"As we're asking them to multi-task more, or shift from one perspective to another, this is a group whose stress level goes up with that, and they start falling behind," Johnson said. "It's not correlated with intelligence. It's not that they're not smart enough—it's the multi-tasking piece."

I mentioned an office move I had experienced a year ago. The building I currently worked at in downtown Washington, DC was being renovated, and everyone in my division was moved to a rented office approximately one subway stop away from our old building. This new building was much more conveniently located, and had both heat and functioning bathrooms, all of which I was looking forward to. But the move, even a small, positive move, caused me to come almost unhinged. I found the changes enormously stressful and found myself reverting to my old anorexic ways as the move approached.

Johnson nodded—my work experiences reflected difficulties in set-shifting. Kids who are at risk for difficulties in set-shifting often surface as they transition from the fifth grade to the sixth grade, transitioning from a single-class setting to a multiple-class setting that involves managing a locker and moving classes each hour. "It's not that they can't do the schoolwork from period three to period four, it's that shifting gears from period three to period four is challenging them," he said. "And then they have to switch from four to five, and from five to six, and they start worrying about all of those shifts."

When I started middle school, I told Johnson, I planned out every move in between classes—when I would go to my locker, when I would visit the drinking fountain, and when I might have the opportunity to use the restroom. "Everything had to be all planned out," I said.

"You got it. That was perfect. That's it," Johnson said. "The planning you had to do in your day, and the anxiety that this raised for you, was to the power of three compared to a single teacher just teaching all of these different subjects."

"When I would get into the eating disorder," I said, "it was also a way to rapidly decrease any complexity that I had because it didn't matter. It was totally extraneous to what am I going to eat, when am I going to exercise, and how much do I weigh."

"You made your world small by essentially organizing yourself around the rules of anorexia nervosa."

"Yes," I replied. "My first psychiatrist told me, 'When you have too much on your plate metaphorically, you make sure you have too little on your plate literally.'"

"Exactly," said Johnson. "I always say I wish I had a nickel for every anorexic that I sat across from and I ask, 'What happened? What do you think happened that led to you developing the eating disorder?' A million times, the answer I'll get is, 'Things just got too big.' 'Well, what do you mean by that?' 'I don't know—it just got too big.' And of course, anorexia nervosa is about making everything small again and reducing the complexity of everything."

Or at least you feel that you can do something about the thing that's causing you so much stress, I pointed out.

"You can assert a sense of order," Johnson concluded.

This need for order and control, as well as a rigid, inflexible thinking style, are common childhood traits in many anorexia sufferers. British researcher Janet Treasure asked a group of eating disorder sufferers what they were like as children, asking them about five key personality traits:

- Perfectionism: Did they spend a lot of time on their hair, making sure that there were no bumps? Did they struggle with school assignments, either spending an inordinate amount of time studying and revising papers, or turning assignments in late because things weren't done "right"?
- Inflexibility: Did they like to have extensive, detailed plans about an upcoming event? Did they have difficulties in dealing with change, whether small changes in a daily schedule or larger changes, like moving to a new school?
- Rule-bound: Did they feel they always had to follow the rules? How much did they bend or break the rules set by teachers and parents? Did they persistently follow internal rules, such as "I'm going to study two hours each day to prepare for my SATs next month"?
- Excessive doubt and cautiousness: Did they worry a lot about making a mistake? Did they ask for reassurance that they were doing things correctly?

- Drive for order and symmetry: Did they always straighten pictures hanging on the wall, sort their closets by color, and make sure things were "just so"? Were they fastidious about personal appearance?

Treasure found these traits were remarkably common in people with eating disorders—two-thirds of anorexia nervosa patients reported being either inflexible or rule-bound, with similar numbers reporting perfectionism—and remarkably uncommon in healthy control women. Furthermore, each trait increased a person's risk of developing an eating disorder seven times. Having all five traits raised this risk 35 times compared to women who had none of these traits (Anderluh *et al.*, 2003). Looking back, I recognize all five traits in myself. When I was in eighth grade, I skipped out on my brother's high-school graduation party in order to study for an upcoming test. My parents rarely told me "no," not because they were overly permissive but because it never occurred to me to ask to do anything even marginally objectionable. I was so stressed out starting both middle and high school that I had difficulty sleeping for weeks. I irritated more than one of my teachers by constantly pestering them to make sure I was doing my assignment right. I even once asked my chemistry teacher if I was boiling water in the proper manner, unsure if I was seeing enough bubbles to proceed with the next step of the experiment. I organized my books by Dewey decimal number (for that matter, I still do).

Obsessive-compulsive personality traits are different from both obsessive-compulsive disorder (OCD, which I have) and obsessive-compulsive personality disorder (OCPD, which I don't). OCPD is only diagnosed when these personality traits begin to infringe upon nearly every aspect of the person's life and greatly diminish their ability to live a full, happy life. Although I had plenty of obsessive-compulsive personality traits, they never reached the degree of full-blown OCPD. Most people thought I was anxious, a little neurotic, and really on top of life—all of which were true (except for that last one), but rarely did they find these characteristics bothersome. Not so in people with OCPD. Nor does OCPD involve the obsessive thoughts and exacting rituals found in OCD, although people can have both OCD and OCPD.

Researchers have started looking at these childhood obsessive-compulsive personality traits, known collectively as an endophenotype, as a potential harbinger of an eating disorder. A genotype is the full array of genes that you carry, although scientists frequently use the word to refer to the particular gene they are discussing. Genotype creates phenotype, which are your unique visual characteristics, such as hair and eye color. An endophenotype is just as identifiable as a phenotype, except an endophenotype cannot be detected visually, and is expressed along the long, winding road from genotype to disease. A disease endophenotype is heritable and can be also found in non-affected family members. Furthermore, an endophenotype is expressed whether or not a person is currently ill.

The obsessive-compulsive personality traits that Treasure identified serve as a good eating disorder endophenotype because sufferers report these traits before the onset of illness and they persist long after recovery. Even after long-term recovery, anorexia sufferers continue to report levels of perfectionism and a need for order and symmetry at higher levels than women who have never had an eating disorder. They also report more difficulties set-shifting and greater cognitive inflexibility (Tenconi *et al.*, 2010). And there is growing evidence to suggest that close family members of people with eating disorders also have higher levels of perfectionism and anxiety than the rest of the population (Bellodi *et al.*, 2001).

These endophenotypes, however, aren't clinical disorders. They are more like personality traits. But other psychological disorders frequently occur alongside anorexia, and understanding their relationship to the eating disorder is crucial in understanding both what causes anorexia and how best to treat the disorder.

5   When Anorexia Brings Friends

have distressing recollections of the event via flashbacks and nightmares and will often go to great lengths to avoid being reminded of the trauma. Their bodies are often in a chronic state of high arousal, usually experienced as irritability, being "jumpy," and having difficulties sleeping and concentrating.

Obsessive-compulsive disorder (OCD) is a pattern of repetitive, intrusive thoughts (obsessions) followed by ritualistic behaviors (compulsions) to "undo" or somehow fix the intrusive thoughts. Common obsessions include irrational worry about dirt and germs, fears of physically harming someone, a need for order and symmetry, feelings of being overly responsible for another person, and intrusive religious or sexual worries. Common compulsions include cleaning/washing, checking to ensure the door is locked, the stove is turned off, the window is shut, etc., repeating words or simple behaviors (flipping a light switch), counting, praying, and mentally replaying a situation over and over. OCD is the most common anxiety disorder in people with anorexia nervosa.

The thoughts seemed to come out of nowhere. As a teenager in the mid-1990s, my ninth grade health class was filled with fears over HIV and AIDS. During a video in the HIV prevention unit, when teens just like me were asking a physician all sorts of questions about AIDS transmission, my brain promptly and almost inexplicably went off the rails. With no explanation or rationale, I suddenly became consumed with frightening, intrusive *what if* thoughts. *What if the kid who sliced his lip open at camp had AIDS? What if a restaurant chef accidentally nicked his thumb and got blood in my meal? What if I had AIDS and gave it to the girls I baby-sat for?*

I fled the class in a panic and headed to the restroom. I couldn't calm myself down. I began hyperventilating. Finally, the anxiety built so high that I threw up in the second stall and then leaned against the stall door to catch my breath and wipe my eyes. I washed my hands twice. And then I returned to class.

The thoughts, however, were not flushed away as easily. They continued to haunt me. I spent hours wracking my brain for all the times when I had a cut and might have gotten even a speck of blood on someone else. I replayed the events in my mind, over and over and over again, to try and reassure myself that I hadn't given anyone a death sentence. No matter how hard I tried, I couldn't push the tormenting thoughts out of my head. I stopped sleeping at night. I was routinely so anxious that I threw up on a daily basis.

Still, the uncertainty persisted, so I began to wash my hands to ensure they were clean enough. A quick rinse with warm, soapy water turned into a prolonged ritual that ultimately involved scalding hot water and a bottle of bleach. I had to wash my hands five times in a row for 55 seconds each time. The number five seemed to have some sort of special power to make me feel better, and many of my rituals were repeated in units of five.

I had no idea that my symptoms were due to OCD. I thought they were a divine retribution to years of carelessness. I prayed each night to stop being tortured with these thoughts. The next day, they always returned. I wept in frustration and fear and grief, certain that these thoughts would haunt me for the rest of my life. Although I was well aware that my thoughts and actions were more than a little bizarre, I thought I had earned them. I found myself in a bind: either I really was dying of AIDS, or I was completely crazy. Afraid that someone would find out just how horrible a person I really was, I determined to keep my fears a secret. And so over six years passed between the time I first experienced symptoms of OCD and when I was finally diagnosed, ironically just as my anorexia was becoming obvious.

The relationship between OCD and anorexia was crystal clear in my mind. Many of my anorexic behaviors looked a lot like OCD compulsions, just about food and weight. I organized the pantry so that all of the nutrition labels faced outward. I checked and re-checked and re-re-checked my weight numerous times each day to make sure I hadn't gained any weight. Sit-ups and calisthenics were done in a certain order, and any interruptions meant I had to start all over again. I only let myself eat at certain times of the day. I kept track of my calorie, fat, cholesterol, sodium, and fiber intake in a little notebook, with rules surrounding how much of each item I allowed myself to eat at a certain time. My whole life became one giant OCD ritual—about food.

My irrational fears about fatness were almost exactly the same as my fears about contamination. Both fears were intense and frightening, and made absolutely no sense when I tried to explain them to others. Both were predicated on an intense doubt that I could be safe in this world (there's a reason OCD is referred to as "The Doubting Disease"). I was fairly certain I wasn't going to give someone AIDS, but I couldn't be sure. I was fairly certain this cracker wasn't going to make me fat, but I couldn't be sure. More so, these fears were omnipresent, and I couldn't put them out of my mind. All I cared about was making these fears stop, and I tried anything, whether it was washing with abrasive cleaners, or purging, or spending hours in the gym. Nothing else in life mattered. I just wanted to crawl out of my own skin.

The Doubting Disease

Before I was diagnosed with anorexia and before I began my research into my illness, I thought the biggest risk for developing an eating disorder was an obsession with fashion magazines and diet-obsessed, controlling parents. I never expected to uncover the strong links between eating disorders and anxiety—I found that over two-thirds of people diagnosed with eating disorders also have an anxiety disorder. The most common anxiety disorder found in people suffering from anorexia nervosa was obsessive-compulsive disorder, a disorder with which I had been diagnosed shortly before the start of my own eating disorder.

The overlap between anorexia and OCD has long been noted in the scientific literature. Several researchers have hypothesized that anorexia is actually more of an obsessive-compulsive spectrum disorder rather than an eating disorder. Psychiatrist and researcher Albert Rothenberg of Harvard University writes:

> Obsessive-compulsive manifestations of rumination, ritualistic behavior, excessive cleanliness, excessive orderliness, perfectionism, miserliness, rigidity, and scrupulousness and self-righteousness were all significantly associated with the eating disorder patient group. The current eating disorder picture, therefore, appears to be a modern form of obsessive-compulsive illness beginning during the adolescent period.
>
> (1999, p. 469)

"When I began to work with people with anorexia and I saw what they do, I was hit by many of the things I was taught in graduate school about anxiety disorders," said Dr Steven Tsao, an expert in eating disorders and OCD at Harvard University's McLean Hospital, who received his postdoctoral training at the Klarman Eating Disorders Center. "If somebody has something that makes them very anxious—for anorexia, that's usually the thought of gaining weight—they do something to make themselves feel better and less anxious. Someone with anorexia could restrict their intake, it could be obsessive exercise, all that kind of stuff."

The two disorders share a very distinct neurological profile. Researchers have found high levels of serotonin in the brains of both recovered anorexia sufferers and those with OCD. Brain imaging studies of people with either anorexia or OCD found specific abnormalities in the basal ganglia, which are crucial in learning and the formation of habits. The two disorders also seem to have a significant overlap in genetic risk factors. A study presented by Lynne Drummond at the 2009 Annual Meeting of the Royal College of Psychiatrists in Liverpool, England, found that one in five people with OCD showed signs of clinically significant disordered eating (Royal College of Psychiatrists, 2009). About ten percent of the close relatives of anorexia sufferers could be diagnosed with OCD, whereas none of the close relatives of a group of healthy women had OCD (Bellodi *et al.*, 2001). The overlap was so significant that the authors said anorexia should be "considered part of the obsessive-compulsive spectrum of disorders" (p. 563).

Over time, however, Tsao began to see distinct differences between OCD and anorexia. Despite a significant overlap in the genetic risk and cognitive-behavioral symptoms of anorexia and OCD, the disorders are not one and the same. For one, people with OCD often experience their thoughts as foreign and intrusive, and as originating somewhere outside themselves. "They don't know where these crazy thoughts are coming from. They tried to push these thoughts away and not think about them. Anorexia patients, although they might be scared, seemed almost okay about organizing their lives around this type of thinking," Tsao said. "There are some who consider anorexia just a variant of OCD about weight gain, but I see them as being distinct enough that I wouldn't be able to say that, even though there is a considerable amount of overlap, especially in the function of the behaviors."

The obsessions and compulsions of OCD are experienced as unpleasant and stressful; they are what psychologists call egodystonic. I knew my obsessions and compulsions were bizarre and irrational, and they frightened me greatly. On the other hand, many eating disorder symptoms are egosyntonic. They're not uncomfortable, nor do they cause any real distress. Especially early in my illness, I didn't get upset when I felt compelled to starve or purge or exercise. These compulsions felt good. They made me feel special. I saw other symptoms of anorexia, such as low weight, hypothermia, and general physical decline, as a good thing. The weight loss meant that I was accomplishing exactly what I set out to do. How could the eating disorder be a problem?

My episodes of OCD made me feel distinctly less like myself, I told Tsao. The "real" Carrie didn't scrub for hours in Clorox and Ajax. She wasn't so anxious that she could barely get out of bed. She wasn't waspish and miserable and helpless and hopeless. So I began to fight the OCD, however ineffectively, and I experienced the retreat of these symptoms as a return to who I really was. The anorexia was different—night and day different. My eating disorder made me feel more like myself, more driven and focused, and I often didn't notice when I was slipping back into my old habits. As I started to restrict, I felt better. This wasn't a mental illness. The OCD and depression? *That* was mental illness. Anorexia was a solution, not a problem.

As well, some of the obsessive-compulsive behaviors seen in anorexia patients may be partly a result of the starvation process rather than an independent disorder. A group of Minnesota researchers, led by Ancel Keys, placed a group of otherwise healthy young men on a calorie-restricted diet to study the effects of starvation on the human body at the end of World War II. As their body weight dropped, the men became obsessed with food. They could think of nothing besides eating and cooking. They developed elaborate mealtime rituals (Keys *et al.*, 1950). "Someone who is just malnourished can look a lot like someone with OCD," Tsao said.

Although I had OCD for several years before the eating disorder started, my OCD symptoms escalated as I lost more and more weight. If I wasn't exercising, I was cleaning. I scrubbed my apartment at least twice daily and nearly passed out from the cleaning product fumes. While at work, I fretted about imaginary dirt in my bathroom. My eating routines also became increasingly bizarre. I ate cottage cheese one curd at a time with a fork. If I had multiple foods, I had to eat them in alphabetical order. If I ate too much, I had rules about how to compensate with purging or exercise. "I didn't know how to stop these rituals," I told Tsao.

Tsao likes to think of the relationship between anorexia and OCD as two overlapping circles in a Venn diagram. The similarities between the two disorders arise from not only a similar biochemistry, but also the similar functions of behaviors. "In OCD, rituals like washing your hands if you have contamination fears serve to reduce your anxiety. That's the same as any eating disorder behavior does for the fear of weight gain, whether it's purging or restricting or over-exercising. There's a functional similarity, and that's very, very important," Tsao said. "The feelings are the same. The form of the behavior may be different, but the feelings are the same."

I spoke with Kellie, a 30-year-old mother of three living in southern California who also suffers from anorexia and OCD, and her experiences told of the often complicated relationship between the two disorders. Although she had a brief bout of anorexia at age 12, her OCD symptoms didn't start until age 20, shortly after the birth of her first child. The normally cheery young woman became consumed with thoughts that she had committed a horrible crime. For hours each day, all Kellie could do was obsess about the possibilities that she was a bad person and that she had hit someone with her car and not realized it. "I once called the cops on myself because I was just convinced I had hit someone and I wanted them to check the intersection," Kellie confessed.

After taking an abnormal psychology class in college, she realized that her obsessions and compulsions were OCD and not a character failing. She started medication and therapy for the OCD, although the medication would eventually stop working and she jumped from pill to pill, looking for something to help relieve her tormenting thoughts. Two additional children and all of her medication had left Kellie with a few extra pounds that she resolved to lose with the help of a friend who had found success with Weight Watchers.

Two years ago, Kellie lost weight rather quickly with the help of reduced calories and a new running regime. For a few months, she seemed to remain healthy, not overly preoccupied with food and exercise. "Then, all of a sudden, I increased my mileage, and started cutting back points—a little bit here, a little bit there—and it just became a full-blown eating disorder," Kellie said. "It's a control issue. It's something I can focus on. The eating disorder became my obsession. The hit-and-run fears and worries about going to jail and everything else, those went away with the eating disorder."

Many of Kellie's anorexic rules seem to come straight from an OCD handbook. Food must be weighed and measured. Every bite of food must be written down. The list of food must be checked and double-checked to ensure Kellie hadn't eaten a bite too much. Exercise was demanding and regimented. All of these Kellie saw as compulsions to quell her fears that she might be gaining weight.

Nonetheless, Kellie noticed subtle differences between the OCD and the anorexia (which she says is the "OCD manifested physically"). The OCD, she said, was uncomfortable and distressing; the anorexia, she said, really wasn't. "I prefer my anorexia to the OCD," she said. Kellie found the anorexia more soothing and reassuring than her OCD rituals. "With anorexia, people can see how I'm feeling on the inside," Kellie concluded.

As I reviewed the interview transcript, I noticed something interesting, a tiny piece of semantics that seemed to encapsulate the difference between OCD and anorexia. Kellie frequently referred to her eating disorder as "*my* anorexia," but the OCD was usually just referred to as "the OCD." Like me, Kellie felt possessive of her eating disorder. It was *hers*. It was special, and she thought she could control it. More than that, we both found anorexia very seductive and appealing in a way that OCD never was. I would have emptied my bank account to make the OCD go away; I also would have emptied my bank account to be able to keep hold of the anorexia.

Treating someone with both anorexia and OCD often means tackling the disorder that is leading to the most problems with daily functioning. More often than not, that disorder is the anorexia. "The one thing we know about anorexia is that it's the number one killer in all of mental health. More people with anorexia are dying because of suicide and malnutrition than depressed people are killing themselves or psychotic people are doing something really dangerous and getting themselves killed," Tsao said. "So that is something I keep fresh in my mind when I treat somebody with both disorders. The eating disorder is just much more dangerous."

Just as it's easier to write two essays while focusing 100 percent on one topic at a time, rather than switching back and forth between topics, Tsao says that he generally sees more success with his patients who first tackle one disorder, then the other. "We don't want someone to go into treatment and then tell them to put half of your energy into addressing your eating disorder. We want them to put 100 percent of their effort and focus into it. It's going to lead them to get better faster. It's going to let them see they can do this and increase their self-efficacy," Tsao said. "Also, because of the overlap between the disorders, when you work on one, either the eating disorder or the OCD, you're likely to see a change in the other. Remember, it's the same brain that is having both these problems."

Although sometimes tackling the eating disorder will improve OCD symptoms, it's not uncommon for OCD symptoms to escalate during eating disorder treatment. Kellie told me her anorexia seemed almost a welcome relief from the unrelenting torment of OCD thoughts. As she started to decrease exercise and regain weight, however, her old OCD worries roared back to life. Her anorexia recovery started to falter, and she has since resumed her disordered eating and exercise habits.

"The eating disorder has once again taken full front in my life," Kellie said, also admitting she had stopped her medication because of weight gain fears, as well as stopping appointments with her dietician and cutting back on her meal plan.

It's why Tsao tries to make sure that the disorder that's not being actively addressed during psychotherapy maintains at status quo. He's seen patients make great strides in overcoming anorexia—resisting the urge to restrict, following their meal plan—only to find themselves washing their hands ever more furiously as a way to channel their increasing anxiety. "If you're not careful, the functional similarities between the two behaviors—because they do the same thing and make people feel less anxious—means that you could ramp up the other disorder in severity by having the first one that you're targeting get better."

People like Kellie and I, who have both OCD and an eating disorder, generally find it harder to reach recovery. Several studies have found that, on average, women with both eating disorders and OCD have more severe eating disorders that last for significantly longer than in women who don't have OCD. "It's that double whammy problem. It's harder to treat them because they're just sicker, and it's harder to break through on both of them," Tsao said. "Having said that, it's certainly not destiny that you're going to struggle with both for the rest of your life."

Moody Blues

Of course, OCD is far from the only psychiatric disorder that can co-exist with anorexia. Other anxiety disorders, like social anxiety (Schulze *et al.*, 2009) and post-traumatic stress disorder (Reyes-Rodríguez *et al.*, 2011), as well as major depression (Giovanni *et al.*, 2011), bipolar disorder (Fornaro *et al.*, 2010), substance abuse (Bulik *et al.*, 2004), and certain personality disorders (Cassin and von Ranson, 2005), are also relatively common in people with anorexia. Several people I spoke with told me of how their anorexia behaviors initially made them feel better and seemed to help them cope more effectively with their other mood or anxiety disorders. Becca, a 22-year-old actress living in New York City, said that her eating disorder symptoms were things she used to cope with depression and bipolar disorder.

Her initial weight loss was unintentional, but that didn't stop anorexia from taking over. Soon, Becca found herself restricting food even more. Her periods stopped, she became underweight, and people at her school began to talk. The hook of anorexia, Becca told me, was that it initially made her feel less depressed. "My eating disorder was about my feelings," she said. "Learning about the science of anorexia, and that I'm not restricting just because I want to be skinny, helped me understand what was really going on."

Kristina, a 23-year-old college student from South Dakota, showed signs of anorexia, bipolar disorder, and OCD as a child. After her parents divorced when she was seven, she began to worry about family finances. "I felt that I didn't deserve to, and shouldn't, eat, and that my needs added to the financial burden," she said. "I thought that food was a waste of money on me, although it wasn't really a weight thing at the time." Over the years, Kristina was diagnosed with everything from major depression to attention-deficit disorder, as clinicians tried to puzzle out her escalating symptoms.

By the time Kristina turned 13, the anorexia had become increasingly obvious, although the disorder waxed and waned in severity through the rest of her adolescence. Waxing and waning in tandem with the anorexia was her as-yet undiagnosed mood and anxiety disorders.

"It's all mixed together in this big ball," Kristina said. After all this time, she told me, it's impossible to sort out one disorder from another.

"The OCD and eating disorder were affected by where I was on the bipolar scale. The OCD definitely increased as I swung up [into a manic phase]," she said. The effects on her eating disorder were more varied. "I either restricted more or I didn't. I would think 'I got this. I can eat anything I want to. I'm great. I'm fine. I'm perfect.' But I needed more outlets for anxiety when I was manic, and that seemed to increase the OCD and the eating disorder," Kristina said.

Two of the most effective outlets Kristina found were exercise and self-harm. "It was a massive endorphin rush," she said.

While in college, Kristina slid ever more deeply into the anorexia and eventually entered a treatment program in Denver, which helped her better understand the complicated links between all of her disorders. "They're all interconnected and function off of one another. It's a joint effort. I have to recover from everything—they're not separate entities," Kristina said.

Understanding and accepting her own thoughts has been the key to her recoveries. "Realizing that I was sick, that this was a disease, and that these things were happening to me—I wasn't doing it—this was huge," Kristina said. "I can take a step back and look at the thought and see whether it's coming from a healthy place or an eating-disordered place, or whether a thought is an OCD thought."

The ability and willingness to look at one's own thoughts and feelings is one of the first crucial steps towards learning how to better regulate emotions, says Michael Anestis, a clinical psychologist who also researches distress tolerance and emotion regulation. I first met Anestis several years ago through his blog, "Psychotherapy Brown Bag." People with eating disorders, especially those with bulimic symptoms, he said, often feel emotions more intensely than the average person and have fewer skills to deal with their overwhelming feelings. This can lead to maladaptive attempts to cope, such as binge eating, purging, and self-injury (Nock and Mendes, 2008).

Self-injury frequently occurs alongside eating disorders—studies have estimated that between 25 and 40 percent of people with eating disorders engage in regular self-injury, such as cutting, burning, and self-hitting (Sansone and Levitt, 2002; Peebles *et al.*, 2011). Generally, people who self-harm regularly show more signs of emotional dysregulation and bulimic symptoms (Stein *et al.*, 2004), as well as other impulsive behaviors, like substance abuse and shoplifting (Liang and Meg Tseng, 2011). Of course, I know plenty of people (myself included) with primarily restrictive behaviors who also self-injure. Anestis sees both eating disorder and self-harming behaviors as serving much of the same function: to relieve the pain of intolerable emotions.

"Some people have more than one behavior that they engage in. They have this deficit in figuring out healthy ways to change what they're feeling, and this inability to stay in contact with what they're feeling," Anestis said.

Psychologists who research self-injury have found that people engage in self-harming behavior for any combination of four major reasons (Nock and Prinstein, 2004). Someone may hurt themselves in an attempt to feel better (relieve anxiety, vent anger, as a punishment), which is known as an automatic negative reinforcement (i.e., the motivation for self-harm is primarily internal). A 2005 study among adolescents who regularly self-harmed found that this was the most common motivation for self-injury (Nock and Prinstein, 2005). Automatic positive reinforcement happens when someone self-harms in order to feel anything at all, even if it is pain. The motivation is still internal, but it's to add a feeling, rather than take it away. Then, some people report self-injury in the context of social negative reinforcement, which means they are cutting or hitting themselves to avoid a response from someone else. If someone said they burned themselves in order to get out of an overly demanding social or academic event, this would be social negative reinforcement. Lastly, there's social positive reinforcement, in which a person self-injures in order to get a response from another person.

"There's this misconception that self-injury is a manipulative thing, that they're doing it for attention. It's an attitude common in clinicians, but it's actually rather unscientific. In fact, every study out there shows that the vast majority of people who engage in self-injury do so to regulate their emotions," Anestis said. "Self-injury offers an immediate relief—not a full nor an adaptive relief, but an immediate one—from negative feelings. So normally, it works."

Clearly, self-injury serves a function. It provides a volume knob for otherwise deafening emotions. But self-harm isn't the only way to modulate these emotions. A cuddle with a puppy or a phone call to a friend can also be effective, yet many people with eating disorders persist in very unhealthy ways of controlling their emotions—why? Anestis believes that this has to do with emotional and behavioral cascades. Both people with eating disorders and those who self-harm have a tendency towards obsessionality and rumination. That is, they can't stop thinking about negative events. This only serves to increase the importance and significance of the negative event, and gives the person a sort of myopia of negativity. Eventually, the negativity becomes more than the person can tolerate, and they engage in eating-disordered or self-harming behaviors as a way to distract themselves from their emotional pain (Selby *et al.*, 2008).

Although self-injury is most commonly associated with bulimic symptoms, it's not uncommon for people with restrictive anorexia to self-harm, for many of the same reasons that other eating-disordered people self-harm. Anxiety gets overwhelming. They're angry but can't express it. They've been so numb for so long that they're desperate for any feeling. Regardless of the eating disorder diagnosis or diagnostic subtype, self-injury becomes a way to self-medicate anxiety, depression, shame, and guilt. One woman with a history of anorexia wrote that:

> When I started to emerge from my anorexia, I needed some other way of dealing with the pain and hurt, so I started cutting instead. It is a way of gaining temporary relief. As the blood flows down the sink, so does the anger and the anguish. It's a way of transferring the scars and wounds inside onto a visible object, in my case my arm (once my leg and once my chest). It's easier to deal with it on the outside and it's a way of communicating the pain within.

> (Harris, 2000, p. 167)

The people I interviewed told me again and again that one of their main fears about gaining weight is that their emotional pain will become invisible. In acute anorexia, emotional distress is writ large on protruding bones, blue fingernails, and stringy hair. But the recovery of physical health often happens much before the recovery of emotional health, which can leave an anorexia sufferer alone, afraid, and adrift. These feelings of alienation can lead to suicide attempts and other risky behaviors, such as substance abuse. Angela learned the hard way about the close links between anorexia, alcohol abuse, and addiction.

I first met Angela on an online support board when she mentioned a comment from her psychiatrist. Noticing that we both lived in the same general area at the time, I emailed her and asked if she saw my doctor. She did, and we started up an online correspondence as Angela began working her way through recovery. As I was working on this book, I gave Angela a call and asked her to tell me her story of anorexia and addiction. We ended up chatting for two and a half hours, until each of us was nearly hoarse from talking.

Although her issues with both food and alcohol extend back many years, Angela, now 45, only began treatment for these much more recently. She grew up as the youngest child in a working-class family that she describes as "very dysfunctional." Her mother was frequently depressed and had a history of suicide attempts and psychiatric hospitalizations. Angela's mother continues to deny any eating issues, but the signs of anorexia were obvious to someone who knew what they were looking for. "She always wore a size 0, and weighed under 100 pounds most of the time. She didn't eat anything all day but drank a pot of coffee and maybe had a little dinner, and that's it. My mother was always like this," Angela said.

Her father wasn't necessarily any more functional. Angela's father was an alcoholic, and he got mean when he drank. "When he was drunk, he would get in our faces and was very abusive, both physically and verbally," she said.

This family history of eating problems and alcoholism loaded both the environmental and the genetic chances that Angela would one day develop these issues herself. Initially, Angela coped with the chaos at home by focusing on school and books. "They were my world," she said. "I really excelled at school, but I was always described as moody. I struggled both with migraines and with depression from an early age."

In high school, her depression intensified, and Angela made her first suicide attempt at age 17 after breaking up with her boyfriend. She pulled herself together enough to start her freshman year at a large state university. The school, which has a reputation for pretty intense partying, was Angela's introduction to the regular consumption of alcohol. "I pretty much drank my way through my two years there," Angela said. "I lost a four-year scholarship and a bunch of grants, and eventually my grades dropped so low that they asked me to leave. I could have done well, but I was too drunk or hung over to care."

As Angela returned home, she began to worry about her weight for the first time. It didn't matter that she had always been thin—she felt that she weighed too much and needed to go on a diet. "I started cutting out foods. First I cut out McDonald's, then I cut out pretty much everything else. It felt safer this way—this was the early '80s, and they didn't have calorie counts on everything. People weren't as obsessed with it as they are now."

Angela's weight plunged, and she hid the physical and behavioral signs of her disorder from her family. Eventually, she pulled out of the anorexia and regained some weight, although she continued to drink, though not to the same extent as when she was at college. Her initial recovery from her eating disorder enabled her to return to school and earn a degree in social work. Eventually, she found a job working with homeless individuals who also had substance abuse problems—pretty ironic for someone who would go on to develop many of the same issues. Around this time, Angela also met her husband in a local writers' group, when she was 28. He might have been 17 years older than her, but he seemed perfect for her. The couple married one year later and moved to a small town several hours away.

Angela felt like her life was on an upward trajectory. She had switched careers and now worked as a journalist at her local paper, a job she really enjoyed. Her marriage seemed great, and her weight and drinking issues were largely absent. A medication change, however, caused her to gain a significant amount of weight, and in 2001, she began a low-carb diet to lose the extra weight. She followed the plan religiously, and the weight started to drop off. Unlike college, Angela was able to stop before her weight dropped too low. Still, she said, "the idea got stuck in my head that weight loss was a good thing."

As more adjustments were made to her medications, Angela developed a condition known as hyperparathyroidism that may have been a side effect of one of the drugs. Her weight dropped further, and Angela garnered even more compliments for her figure. The thyroid condition resolved itself when Angela stopped the medication, but she found she couldn't increase her weight. In fact, she felt more driven than ever to coax the number on the scale even lower. At the age of 40, she found herself purging and cutting more foods out of her diet.

Eventually, she found herself unable to hide her destructive behaviors any longer. Her therapist at the time encouraged her to seek hospitalization for her eating disorder. Angela signed herself into a facility in a neighboring state and signed herself out less than 24 hours later, convinced she wasn't sick enough. When Angela started seeing an eating disorders psychiatrist—the same one that I had seen for many years—his calm insistence on a higher level of care persuaded Angela to enter the hospital in the fall of 2008. "I realized I needed it," she said.

Her initial hospitalization was followed by several other short admissions for anxiety and other issues related to the eating disorder. Slowly, she gained some weight and started to improve mentally. On New Year's Day, a little over a year after her first hospital stay, her recovery came crashing down. "I just basically stopped eating," she said. Within a month, she was back in the hospital. Her relapse continued for several months and through a specialized eating disorders program. Angela's husband left her, which jolted Angela into trying to eat more. The pair started to reconcile, but her husband decided he had had enough of the eating disorder and left for good.

This triggered a return to Angela's destructive alcohol habits. In just a few weeks, Angela was guzzling bottles of wine and severely restricting her food intake to prevent weight gain. She began to mix prescription tranquilizers with her alcohol. When Angela confessed her behaviors to her psychiatrist, he told her she needed to go back into the hospital for detox and refeeding. The day after Christmas, she signed herself into the psychiatric hospital for the last time.

"Anorexia and addiction are definitely linked. I know not everyone in the eating disorder world would agree with me, but anorexia is addictive. At its core, there are addictive components to it, just like there are in alcoholism and prescription drug abuse," Angela said. "The seeds for the alcoholism were planted with the anorexia. They're different, obviously, because their manifestations are different. One works through starving, the other works through drinking."

The debate about whether eating disorders are addictions is anything but settled, but the overlap between the two types of disorders is significant. When researchers surveyed 371 women with current or previous anorexia, they found that one-third of these women had a family history of substance abuse. As well, approximately one in ten of the women with restricting anorexia currently met the diagnostic criteria for substance dependence, and one-third of those with the binge/purge type of anorexia and those who had transitioned from anorexia to bulimia also met these criteria (Krug *et al.*, 2009). An addiction was associated with a greater number of co-occurring conditions (Bulik *et al.*, 2004) and significantly worse outcome in eating disorders (Herzog *et al.*, 1996).

Researchers have known of the links between eating disorders and mood disorders, anxiety, and addiction for decades. The potential link with another co-occurring condition has only recently begun to interest a large number of psychologists—the link between anorexia and autism spectrum disorders, particularly Asperger's syndrome. Both disorders, psychologists have noted, have certain core features in common: an obsession with details, rigid behaviors, and difficulties with social relationships (Oldershaw *et al.*, 2011). When researcher Janet Treasure at King's College London surveyed 22 anorexia inpatients, she found that these women scored significantly higher on measures of autistic symptoms than healthy controls (Hambrook *et al.*, 2008). A pair of Scandinavian researchers found that between 18 and 23 percent of inpatients with anorexia met criteria for Asperger's syndrome (Gillberg and Billstedt, 2000).

These social difficulties are not only more common than researchers initially thought, but psychologists are also starting to think that they are key to understanding anorexia. In a review article looking at similarities in how people with anorexia and Asperger's syndrome understand social situations, researchers developed a theory as to how the two disorders might be linked. They write:

> In essence, an individual with AN is disconnected from her internal experiences and thus does not use internal signals of hunger, fatigue, or affective state to guide behavior effectively. This lack of integration is further

compounded by difficulties in interpreting internal emotional experiences, deficits often referred to as poor interoceptive awareness ... Social anxiety in individuals with AN indicates that fears in social settings are independent of concerns about body weight or eating and relate more to a fear of negative evaluation. Thus, there is growing evidence that social fears and related social withdrawal are frequent, pernicious symptoms in AN. However, unlike ASD, the desire for social acceptance is more discernible.

(Zucker *et al.*, 2007, pp. 977 and 985)

Other psychiatric disorders frequently occur alongside anorexia—in fact, an eating disorder without a co-morbid condition appears to be the exception, not the rule. Although these co-occurring disorders complicate recovery, they don't make recovery impossible. The common thread through the wide variety of presentations of anorexia is, in fact, self-starvation. The destructive mental effects of malnutrition make the restoration of body weight crucial to the recovery process.

6   Starvation Becomes Obsession

The first hint that I was descending into starvation came from my mother. She had seen me a few short weeks before, at Easter, anxious and exhausted, not eating entirely well but not starving, either. Now that exams were over, she and my father arrived at my college apartment the first weekend in May to help me pack for a summer internship at the Centers for Disease Control and Prevention in Atlanta, Georgia. I was ushering her into my ramshackle abode, staggering and yawning after pulling an all-nighter to put the finishing touches on an independent study research project, when she stopped dead in her tracks.

She grabbed my shoulders, encased in a thin, ratty t-shirt. Her eyes traveled down my body to the now oversized pair of old hospital scrub pants I had cinched around my waist. "What happened to you?" she gasped. "You're just skin and bone!"

I frowned. I generally lost a few pounds during exams, given my crazy schedule and almost complete lack of sleep. I was aware that this was probably the pattern. And yeah, maybe my pants did look a little baggy, but my laundry skills were never something to brag about. I had been hoping to lose a little weight that semester, having gained a few pounds during a first semester spent studying and carousing (mostly carousing) in Scotland. My new exercise routine and ostensibly "healthful" diet had lifted the fog of depression somewhat. In short, I felt great.

Not believing that my weight had changed, I found myself standing on my parents' old rickety scale in my childhood bathroom that evening. I looked and felt the same, and yet my parents were insisting I was thin, too thin. Clearly, a date with the scale was in order. I had a vague idea what I generally weighed, though I wasn't yet in the habit of a morning trip to the scale. I stripped down to my underwear, took a deep breath, and tentatively placed one foot on the scale, then the other. Heart racing, I slowly, slowly peered at the number. I was down about eight pounds from my all-time high, about five from my usual weight. I felt victorious—my healthy eating attempts had worked!

Just a split second later, all of that changed. I panicked. This feeling would disappear if I didn't keep losing weight. I had to keep starving. With less than ten pounds lost, I was already stuck. The only way out was starvation. The anorexia didn't develop overnight. I had descended into fairly disordered and restrictive eating two years previously, as I arrived at college. Even though my weight stayed fairly stable, my neuroticism about food, weight, and exercise only increased as the years passed. But with that moment on the scale, I had crossed the line into anorexia. I could no longer eat enough to maintain my weight. I couldn't see my body properly—I thought I looked just fine even as my bones began to emerge from my flesh. I didn't have another period for about a year after my reckoning on the scale.

To outsiders, most of the recognizable signs of starvation are on the body. Skin becomes sallow and taught. A fine, soft fur covers the face, trunk, and limbs. Cheeks and eyes sink backwards into the skull. Hair gets dry and brittle, and then falls out, first several strands at a time, and then in massive chunks. The head starts to look too big for the body, and the neck too weak to support such a large head.

As Ancel Keys and his team of researchers learned in the 1940s, however, these outward signs of emaciation are only a small aspect of the wreckage created by starvation. Most of the damage is mental, invisible at a quick glance but virtually unmistakable to friends and family. In starvation, the body is generally far stronger than the mind. It can withstand more damage before it, too, starts to seriously suffer.

Part of the reason for this has to do with the brain itself. If other organs are like petrol-sipping Smart cars and fuel-efficient hybrids, the brain is a gas-guzzling Hummer. The brain consumes about 500 calories each day, approximately one-quarter of an average person's daily energy consumption. Considering that the brain only weighs about two pounds and accounts for only a small fraction of overall body weight (Miller and Corsellis, 1977), it's one of nature's penultimate energy hogs.

Not only are the brain's energy demands enormous, it's also a tremendously picky eater. No matter what array of carbohydrates, proteins, and fats are available for use, the brain prefers glucose and lots of it (Beckmann *et al.*, 1991). If glucose is in short supply, the brain will reluctantly use ketones, which are produced as the body uses its fat stores for energy, but it's not as efficient as glucose. The brain's abnormally high energy needs and its finicky eating help explain why starvation hits the brain first.

Starvation Guinea Pigs

Psychologists initially thought that many of the psychological traits seen in anorexia—the obsession with food, the anxieties, the mood swings—caused the disease. But the rediscovery of a once-obscure 1940s study on human starvation made them shift their thinking. A group of more than 30 otherwise healthy conscientious objectors during World War II participated in a year-long experiment where they were voluntarily starved to an average of 75 percent of their normal body weight. Then, researchers re-fed the men on a variety of different diets, to identify the most effective way to help the starving people of Europe and Asia after the war ended.

I first saw the two-volume *magnum opus* titled "The Biology of Human Starvation" in the library at the School of Public Health as a graduate student. Curious, I tried to drag both volumes back to the cubby where I was working. I was so weakened from my own self-starvation that I had to make two treks to the bookshelf, one for each volume. As I flipped through the pages, I chuckled to myself. Surely the starved men in the study would have been too weak to grab both books, too.

Ancel Keys, a physiology researcher at the University of Minnesota, wasn't concerned with anorexia when he began the starvation study. Already working with the military to develop nutrient-rich yet portable meals for frontline troops (which became known as the "K Ration," after its developer), Keys was approached with solving another rather practical problem. As World War II began to wind down, the Allies were facing the knowledge that much of Europe and Asia were enduring massive food shortages. Famine was more common than not. With their fears of a worldwide, post-WWII Soviet domination, the US military wanted to be able to step in first and provide better aid to the ailing countries. To do that, they needed to know how to best help rehabilitate starving people. Enter Ancel Keys.

Hunger has stalked humanity since the beginning of time. Keys himself noted hundreds of famines throughout recorded human history in the first chapter of his book. But knowing about famine wasn't the same as figuring out how to help large numbers of starving people. For that, you would need data, and lots of it. Plenty of people were starving during World War II, but Keys—ever the precise data wonk—needed to track exactly how much people ate, how much weight they lost, and other changes that accompanied starvation in order to figure out exactly which diets would best reverse these effects. To do that, Keys and his colleagues at the University of Minnesota needed to start with otherwise healthy individuals.

Most eligible men had already been drafted into the military, but a small cadre of conscientious objectors remained stateside. Opposed to war, most of these pacifists instead served their country in a variety of civilian roles, from wilderness maintenance to caretakers in insane asylums. Appealing to the men's interest in humanitarian issues, Keys published a brochure that asked them, "Will you starve so that they be better fed?"

A surprising number of men agreed. After undergoing rigorous psychological screenings, 38 men were allowed into the study in October 1944. They called themselves the starvation guinea pigs. The first three months of the study, Keys placed the men on maintenance diets with foods similar to those found in Europe. Things like rutabagas, cabbage, and brown bread were frequently on the menus. Outside of logging 22 miles on walks over the course of the week, and some assistance in the physiology labs, the men were generally free to do what they liked. They dated, attended classes, performed their own theater productions, even worked in part-time jobs.

All of that abruptly ceased when the starvation phase of the experiment began. Keys slashed their diets in half, from around 3,000 calories per day during the maintenance phase to around 1,500 calories per day during the starvation phase, which would last six months. It's worth noting that 1,500 calories isn't much less than most commercial weight loss plans. It's also worth noting that many people with anorexia regularly consume less than the 1,500 daily calories during the Keys study, and for a longer period of time.

The men noticed the difference right away. Their weight began to plummet. Their testosterone levels decreased, as did their athletic ability and coordination. Keys expected this. What Keys didn't expect was the mental change in the men. Food became the only thing that could hold the men's interest. In the control phase, the men packed lectures on world issues; now, they couldn't get enough of dry talks from agriculturists on the benefits of soybeans. One man began to hoard cookbooks, stashing them under his mattress like he would a pile of porn. If Keys worried about the men accessing girlie magazines or pornography, his worries could have ceased as the starvation phase of the experiment began. As one man said, he "didn't have the sex drive of a clam," a comment that included a reference to food, something never far from the men's minds.

Other mental changes began to appear on the regular batteries of psychological tests administered by Keys and his colleagues. Most apparent was an increase in neuroticism. Defined by psychologists as the persistent experience of negative emotional states like depression and anxiety, neuroticism has been associated with depression, generalized anxiety disorder, panic disorder, and a variety of phobias (Hettema *et al.*, 2006). Violent mood swings became common among the starving men, as did anxiety, hostility, and isolation.

On May 8, 1945, the day the war in Europe ended, halfway through the starvation phase of the experiment, one man failed to note anything about this monumental world event. Instead, he noted his weight (down to the quarter pound), and complained about how long he had to wait in line at the cafeteria. In his 2008 history of the Minnesota Starvation Study, titled *The Great Starvation Experiment*, Todd Tucker wrote:

> The men who had volunteered to starve themselves to aid the victims of war found their interest in the war almost completely erased by hunger. Their world had shrunk to include only the stadium and the meal line at Shevlin Hall.

In short, the men were behaving a lot like people with anorexia. My world shrank to my dinner plate, my gym shoes, and my scale. Nothing else mattered. Given the symptoms of the men in the Keys study, a group of Swedish researchers have hypothesized that anorexia is nothing more than self-starvation. Anyone who starves themselves will become anorexic, they say (Zandian *et al.*, 2007). While it's true that many starving people show physical and psychological changes almost identical to those seen in anorexia patients, they do not develop anorexia nervosa.

For starters, the men couldn't wait until the starvation phase was over.

They rejoiced when their calories were increased. Compare this to the howling and plate-throwing to which calorie increases are greeted in eating disorder patients. The men wrote in their diaries of their dread of the physical treadmill tests administered by Keys and colleagues. I would have silently rejoiced at the chance to run as fast as I could on a treadmill.

Perhaps the main difference between the men in the Minnesota Starvation Study and those with anorexia was this: the men were able to stop starving. Their continued participation in the study was a choice, made of their own volition. Keys had to take plenty of precautions to keep the men from cheating, but the men were making a conscious decision to starve themselves by participating in the study. They could have easily walked away from the laboratory and into the vast farmland beyond Minneapolis.

Someone with anorexia doesn't have that choice. Not eating has long since ceased becoming a conscious decision and started becoming an involuntary compulsion. Someone with anorexia can't stop starving themselves. This is the aspect of anorexia that makes it an illness rather than a choice. They literally can't decide to pick up the fork and eat.

It's something Tom Cramer couldn't understand. His wife, Meg, had been diagnosed with anorexia and Tom felt powerless to stop the disease. He couldn't understand why she wouldn't just eat. To get inside his wife's head, Tom embarked upon his own starvation diet to figure out what had such a tenacious hold on his wife. What he figured out was that his assumption that Meg wouldn't eat was wrong. Instead, he learned that Meg couldn't eat. On day three, Tom wrote:

> I began hearing the voice too: "Come on, you can do it. Don't give in. You're better than that." When I refused food, I had a sense of victory. The longer I resisted, the more powerful I felt. When Meg was admitted to the hospital, I thought that she had failed and allowed this to happen. Now I understood the seduction of the words in her head, how they could override the most basic human survival instincts. And I saw her as a hero—who had to be incredibly strong in her fight to recover.
>
> (Cramer, 2008, n.p.)

The Starving Body

As starvation persists, the body begins to adapt to its new energy-poor state. It's something I remember my psychiatrist, Alexander Sackeyfio, explaining so well shortly after my initial diagnosis that I called him back and asked him to re-teach me. He chuckled at my request. "You mean you were actually listening the first time around?"

He took a deep breath and started talking. Starvation not only alters how people think, it also physically changes the structure of the brain. The cortex, that gray, folded outer layer of the brain responsible for consciousness, memory, and perception, shrinks. "Most people with eating disorders will try to argue you out of this fact, saying that they think much clearer when they are starving," he said. "But there is a difficulty with decision making and putting concepts together because of the cognitive effects of starvation."

Although the cortex and gray matter of the brain shrink (Gaudio *et al.*, 2011), the ventricles in the brain, which contain cerebrospinal fluid, actually get larger. Larger ventricles correspond to greater levels of malnutrition, and these changes do appear to be reversible with refeeding (Golden *et al.*, 1996). "This confirms that there is some amount of atrophy in the brain in anorexia," Sackeyfio said.

Hormone production also slows. "The endocrine system is considerably affected. We know that most of the female hormones need fat to be produced," he said. "The thyroid slows down because there isn't enough protein to bind to the various aspects of iodine and so on, so thyroid production is actually quite low." Although this looks like hypothyroidism in lab results, it's actually a very common sign of malnutrition.

"Not," I pointed out, "that this stops stupid emergency room doctors from giving a malnourished anorexic a prescription for thyroid pills."

Sackeyfio sighed. "It's actually quite common. We also still have doctors who try to give women birth control to improve hormone function," he said, even though studies have shown that oral contraceptives don't actually improve bone density.

Even the immune system is affected. The number of disease-fighting white blood cells drops, which leaves people with anorexia more vulnerable to bacterial infections (Cason *et al.*, 1986). Ironically, levels of virus-fighting T cells remain relatively normal, which helps explain why starving individuals remain resistant to viral infections (Golla *et al.*, 1981). During the refeeding process, however, this resistance seems to drop, and several people have commented to me that they were felled by one cold after another once they began eating again. Clinical reports confirm that this resurgence in infections with eating disorder treatment is common and real (Nova *et al.*, 2002).

The gastrointestinal system is also disproportionately affected in eating disorders. The stomach shrinks, and emptying of food into the small intestine is slowed, a condition known as gastroparesis. This can lead to early feelings of fullness and bloating after eating, although this generally resolves with the regular consumption of adequate meals. Another problem the GI system encounters in starvation is the lack of production of certain enzymes to break down milk sugars and fats. Known as lactases and lipases, respectively, these enzymes are produced on demand. Starvation means little to no demand for their production, and so the body essentially switches production off.

"That disturbs digestion, and there's a tendency for the villi in the small intestine to atrophy. The villi absorb nutrients and slow the rate at which food passes through the system. When they atrophy, this makes food flow through the system much faster, and you actually get a malabsorption syndrome," Sackeyfio said.

Entire books have been written on starvation's effects on brain and body, so any interview would naturally only skim the surface of the subject. "It's a huge area, and, for whatever reason, people tend to overlook it," Sackeyfio said.

Physicians unfamiliar with eating disorders tend to be some of the biggest offenders. Some of the most blatantly uneducated and boneheaded comments I've received about anorexia have been from medical professionals. One doctor told me, at age 20 and 75 percent ideal body weight, that I couldn't have anorexia because I was too old and just had a thyroid problem. Another person suggested that I really just needed to go get laid ("But be sure to use a condom!"). A nurse told me she liked doing ECGs on her anorexia patients because we were "nice and bony."

"Most people prefer not to actually look at it. If I sent you to the emergency room with one of these diseases that causes your body to waste away and you showed up starving, people will look at you very differently from the person who walks in with anorexia nervosa," Sackeyfio said. "I've had patients walk into the emergency room with a blood glucose level of 33, and the staff will sit them in the corner and say 'Wait here while we try and do some other things for you.' If anyone else walked in with a blood sugar below 50, people would be running around to figure out how they can bring their blood sugar up."

Part of this misunderstanding and unhelpful attitude comes from the fact that many people with anorexia don't see these potentially lethal signs as a problem. For most people who present to the hospital with low blood sugar, they are uncomfortable and will cooperate with medical personnel to get these levels back to normal. Not so with anorexia patients. "They will sit there and look you in the eye and say, 'Guess what, I don't care, I like what is going on with my body.' Most doctors are trained to believe that, because they said so, patients should do it, and they get very offended by this population of people who challenge them," Sackeyfio said. "Abnormal electrolytes, low white cell counts, all these things are the same for everybody, and we should respect it as an ill state for everybody," no matter whether or not the patient believes it's a problem.

"The person who has the disease will say to themselves that everything is okay," Sackeyfio said. "You know, some people say that this is a type of denial, but honestly, I think it is because the brain isn't working very well. Therefore, you see your status as something that isn't bothering you and is something you can live with. Some people will say that they felt cold, and they felt awful, but they were too afraid of eating."

Even when I was faced with the mental and physical deterioration that accompanied my eating disorder, I didn't really see these as being particularly problematic. Low pulse and blood pressure meant that I was doing well at starvation. I got used to the cardiac arrhythmias and figured that I had survived this long, so they couldn't be a problem. Besides, I told myself, I felt better when I was starving. In the end, I found the physical effects of anorexia far less frightening than a plate of food. And so the illness persisted for years as doctors and family members grew increasingly frustrated at my flippant replies to deteriorating health.

The Serotonin/Starvation Cycle

Eating disorders researcher Walter Kaye thinks that changes to levels in the neurotransmitter serotonin may help explain why anorexia is self-perpetuating. Women who have recovered from anorexia—both the binge/purge type and the restricting type—have unusually high levels of serotonin in their brains (Frank *et al.*, 2002). In one study, researchers found that serotonin levels in women recovered from the restricting type of anorexia correlated with their levels of harm avoidance. More serotonin meant more harm avoidance (Bailer *et al.*, 2005). A different study also found a link between levels of serotonin and drive for thinness (Bailer *et al.*, 2004).

High levels of serotonin have been linked to traits like obsessionality, perfectionism, harm avoidance, and a need for symmetry. As well, serotonin is crucial in the regulation of mood, appetite, feeding behaviors, and motor activity. This makes someone feel anxious, edgy, and distraught, desperate to find a way to calm down and self-soothe. Although there's no way to tell for sure whether these neuroimaging studies in recovered women paint an accurate picture of what their brains were like before their illness began, researchers believe that these alterations existed before the onset of anorexia and likely contributed to the development of the disease (Kaye *et al.*, 2005).

The body makes serotonin using the amino acid tryptophan, which the body needs to obtain from food. Without adequate food, the body doesn't have enough tryptophan and therefore can't make enough serotonin. Consequently, serotonin levels drop. It's why people with anorexia often report that starving makes them feel better. It lowers levels of distress, and they feel less anxious. They finally get relief from the unbearable anxiety that has dogged them for so long (Kaye and Weltzin, 1991).

People without anorexia don't have these pre-existing high serotonin levels, so the serotonin drop that comes from food deprivation or dieting doesn't feel pleasant. Instead, dieting makes them irritable and cranky. Dieting isn't pleasant, it's torture. It's one of the reasons many people find it so difficult to stay on a diet. Someone with anorexia, however, gets a bit of relief from anxiety, and finds this a bit of a reward for sticking to their rigid meal and exercise routines.

When I first started restricting my food, I found myself feeling more calm, more capable, and more competent to perform my daily tasks. I had blissful moments of quiet in my head, something I had never really experienced. It was if not eating had basically grabbed hold of the volume control on my anxiety and twisted it to the left. This relief, however, didn't last long. All too soon, the anxiety returned.

Kaye hypothesizes that this is because the brain reacts to the serotonin shortage by increasing the number of serotonin receptors. Just as a resourceful seamstress can turn fabric scraps into a quilt, the increase in serotonin receptors allows the brain to utilize every last molecule of the neurotransmitter (Bailer *et al.*, 2007). The increased receptors mean that the brain begins to function just as it did pre-starvation. The anxiety relief begins to dissipate.

I, and others with anorexia, generally responded to this rebound anxiety by further restricting what I ate. Instead of eliminating specific foods, I started cutting out whole food groups. Again, I felt better after I did this, but the benefits were very short-lived. If I did try to push myself and eat more, I was filled with an intolerable anxiety. I felt horribly fat. I felt like I was a failure in life. I couldn't sit still, I couldn't concentrate. Regardless of how ill the anorexia made me feel, it was preferable to feeling like I was being drowned in relentless waves of anxiety.

This, researchers have found, is exactly how sufferers get stuck in anorexia. Eating more provides the body with the building blocks with which to synthesize serotonin. Except the brain, noticing the relative serotonin shortage, has dramatically increased its sensitivity to serotonin. Eating creates a flood of serotonin with which the brain can't cope. It takes weeks or months for the number of serotonin receptors to reset to their pre-illness levels, which is why refeeding is so torturous. The brain is literally drowning in serotonin, which means the sufferer is drowning in anxiety without a life vest. Recovery means enduring this discomfort for days on end.

The spike in anxiety that accompanies eating is one of the things that kept Rachel, a British woman now in her mid-forties, trapped in anorexia for more than 30 years. Always an anxious child (later in life, Rachel was diagnosed with OCD and Asperger's syndrome, which is on the autism spectrum), Rachel began to show signs of anorexia when she turned 11 and started puberty. "The behaviors acted like a tranquilizer," she said, "and my weight just weight down and down and down."

When Rachel was diagnosed with anorexia in the late 1970s at age 12, she had never heard of the disorder, and nor had her parents. Rachel didn't have any body image distortions, but self-starvation and over-exercise were the only ways she could find to help manage her anxiety. "It became a pattern: whenever I became stressed, I would fall back into old behaviors. Without them, I just felt 'wrong,'" Rachel said. "I couldn't cope if I didn't have my behaviors. If I wasn't emaciated, I felt more vulnerable because I felt that people expected more of me. I didn't have any excuse if I messed up."

Rachel's disorder waxed and waned over the years. She had a period of relatively normal weight and eating habits after she completed her Ph.D. in biomedical science, but a job transfer left her feeling once again isolated, depressed, and vulnerable. Her weight dropped dangerously low as she returned to her limited diet and a punishing exercise regime. Rachel focused on keeping the number on the scale exactly the same from day to day. "If that number was constant, I felt my life was in order," she said.

Eventually, years of severe anorexia began to take their toll on her body, and Rachel was given an ultimatum: if you don't gain weight, you will die. "When I started to gain weight, it felt like everything was becoming chaos. And the more weight I gained, the more chaotic it felt," Rachel said. Years of starvation made her brain very sensitive to serotonin and other neurotransmitters. The chaos Rachel felt was very real in her brain—the flood of serotonin left her anxious and adrift. But with the help of family and a supportive psychiatrist, Rachel has returned to a healthy weight and is having regular periods for the first time in her life.

Hunger Hormones

Serotonin alone isn't the only difference between a starving person and someone with anorexia. When scientists looked at the hormone profile of someone with anorexia and compared it with those who are starving, they found some notable differences. Hunger and appetite are regulated by a complicated series of physiological and psychological feed backs. As well, feeling hunger doesn't necessarily lead to the decision to eat. Researchers have found differences both in the hormones that lead to the feeling of hunger and in the decisions that lead to eating.

Two of the most important hormones regulating hunger and satiety are leptin and ghrelin, both of which are relatively new to science. Leptin was discovered in 1994 by researchers at Rockefeller University in New York City (Zhang *et al.*, 1994) as they tried to identify the gene responsible for a strain of obese mice. The gene, creatively named *Obese*, coded for a small hormone known as leptin. The obese mice produced a faulty form of leptin, causing them to eat almost uncontrollably and gain large amounts of weight. This led researchers to conclude that leptin provided satiety signals to the brain (Kolata, 2007).

Besides providing information on satiety, leptin also provides feedback to the brain about the body's energy reserves. Levels of leptin in the blood, researchers found, were directly proportional to the amount of fat on the body (Margetic *et al.*, 2002). If a person's caloric intake didn't meet their energy output, fat would be metabolized and leptin levels would drop (Dubuc *et al.*, 1998). This drop in leptin is meant to spur an eating increase, which is one of the reasons why so many dieters find it hard to keep the weight off. The more weight they lose, the more their appetite increases, creating a vicious cycle (Chin-Chance *et al.*, 2000).

From this standpoint, someone's ability to starve themselves should be impossible. The weight loss caused by anorexia should lead to a drop in leptin, which increases their appetite. Except that doesn't happen, which has led some researchers to wonder whether people with anorexia have abnormalities in their leptin levels. Someone in acute starvation should have extremely low leptin levels. Indeed, when researchers looked at women currently ill with anorexia, their leptin was low and increased significantly as the women gained weight (Himmerich *et al.*, 2010).

Still, when other researchers from the University of Kentucky used a more sensitive test to measure leptin levels in patients with anorexia and bulimia, they found that the anorexia patients had leptin levels that were higher than expected for their body mass index (Frederich *et al.*, 2002). The researchers wrote that these findings "may contribute to a blunted physiologic response to underweight and consequent resistance to dietary treatment" (p. 72). Bulimia patients, on the other hand, had much lower leptin levels, which the researchers believe may have contributed to their binge eating.

Although leptin abnormalities in and of themselves didn't play as large of a role in anorexia as scientists had hoped, other studies have found evidence that leptin does contribute to anorexia in two different ways. During re-feeding, leptin levels in anorexia patients can become higher than would be expected. This leaves the person feeling overly full and thus makes them extra vulnerable to relapse (Müller *et al.*, 2009). Low leptin levels have also been linked to restlessness and high levels of physical activity.

According to Johannes Hebebrand, a researcher at the University of Duisburg-Essen in Germany who has authored many of the studies looking at the relationship between leptin and anorexia, leptin's effects on anorexia are best seen in the hyperactivity that frequently accompanies the disorder. In 2000, Hebebrand and colleagues set out to see how leptin affected activity levels in rats. The researchers placed the rats on a calorie-restricted diet for seven days, which caused leptin levels to decrease as expected. The rats also showed a 300 percent increase in activity from their pre-starvation levels. The administration of leptin, however, prevented the onset of hyperactivity in the rats and stopped the excessive activity after it had begun.

To link these animal studies to actual behaviors in those with anorexia, Hebebrand and colleagues measured leptin levels in patients upon admission to an inpatient ward, and periodically thereafter as the patients gained weight. Those patients who felt the most restless also had the lowest leptin levels, and this restlessness decreased as their weight increased (Exner *et al.*, 2000). Researchers also found that blocking the effects of leptin could induce hyperactivity even in rats that weren't starved, showing that it was the low leptin that triggered the excessive activity (Hebebrand *et al.*, 2003). Administration of the atypical antipsychotic olanzapine (brand name: Zyprexa) helped decrease hyperactivity in starving rats and anorexia patients (Hillebrand *et al.*, 2005).

Whereas levels of leptin decrease with hunger, ghrelin spikes before meals. Considered by researchers to be leptin's opposite, ghrelin tells the brain to seek out food and energy (Inui *et al.*, 2004). Discovered in 1999 by a group of Japanese researchers (Kojima *et al.*, 1999), ghrelin stimulates appetite by acting on the hypothalamus to increase food-seeking behaviors (Tschöp *et al.*, 2000). It also contributes to eating behaviors by decreasing the stomach's sensitivity to distention after eating (Page *et al.*, 2007).

"Anorexia is a complex genetic disease, which means there are potentially a number of genes that have modest effects on determining someone's susceptibility to developing the disorder. It's interesting to think about which genes and pathways may potentially contribute. I think these appetite pathways may be important," said endocrinologist Elizabeth Lawson of Massachusetts General Hospital, who specializes in the study of hormones and anorexia.

Just as eating disorder researchers immediately began to investigate leptin abnormalities in anorexia, they also have looked at how ghrelin (mal)functions in anorexia patients. When compared with healthy women, researchers found that, as expected, those with anorexia have higher ghrelin levels, indicating a negative energy balance. Ghrelin levels normalized with refeeding and weight gain (Tolle *et al.*, 2003; Germain *et al.*, 2007). In healthy adults, ghrelin levels fluctuate throughout the day according to food intake and activity levels. People with anorexia, however, have chronically elevated ghrelin levels. Over time, researchers believe, anorexia deafens the body to ghrelin's insistent demands for food (Broglio *et al.*, 2004).

Ghrelin works in close concert with several other hormones, including insulin. Rising ghrelin levels stimulate the release of insulin and improve the body's sensitivity to it (Dezaki *et al.*, 2006). In anorexia, however, insulin levels are chronically high. The starved body needs to be ready to process glucose immediately, and having lots of insulin around keeps the body primed to do so. Over time, the body adjusts to high insulin levels and responds less avidly to its chemical signal. In anorexia, researchers found, these long-term, high insulin levels can then circle back and decrease the body's sensitivity to ghrelin. These findings can help explain why so many people with anorexia report feeling full after only a small amount of food. They're not making it up—their brains really think they are full, which makes it hard to eat the amount required to return to a normal body weight (Karczewska-Kupczewska *et al.*, 2010).

I had plenty of times when I lied as I told people I was full after just a few bites of raw veggies. But, on plenty of other occasions, I really meant it. One or two bites and I seriously couldn't bear to eat any more. The sensation was physical. I had starved myself for a week before a colleague's goodbye party so I could participate in the farewell meal without a major meltdown. I went planning on having a "light" lunch but knowing that the previous week's sacrifices meant I could "afford" it. Except a few bites of steamed shrimp later, I found myself disturbingly, disgustingly full. Once I read the papers about ghrelin, I understood my experience in a new light. Those few bites of shrimp caused my ghrelin levels to plummet, making me feel full, and causing me to push back from the table and leave most of my food untouched on the plate.

Even after weight recovery, ghrelin levels may not fully normalize. "There's some evidence for abnormal ghrelin secretion, which raises the question of whether abnormalities in this pathway may contribute to the disorder," Lawson said.

"Could these abnormalities predate the onset of anorexia?" I asked.

Perhaps, Lawson said. "It's hard to get at that question because it's so hard to predict who will develop anorexia. We can look at it in women who have recovered, but it's hard to know for sure what is true recovery in anorexia nervosa. It's certainly not just weight recovery, and it's very hard to define. And even if you found a group that you felt was relatively recovered, you don't know whether these changes are due to going through the disorder. But it is interesting that the abnormalities are still there even after recovery."

A Bone of Contention

Lawson would like to study the question from a genetic standpoint and see if people who develop anorexia have certain variation in appetite hormones and their receptors that may increase their risk for developing the disease. This could help answer the question of whether these hormone abnormalities contribute to disease onset, while sidestepping the difficulties in determining whether these changes in recovered women are an artifact of disease or not.

Implications of these appetite hormone abnormalities have implications in other areas of anorexia as well. In research presented at the 2008 annual meeting of the Endocrine Society, Harvard University researcher Madhusmita Misra presented data that showed a connection between high ghrelin levels and a lack of regular menstrual periods (amenorrhea) in female teenage athletes. Although the athletes without their periods exercised as much as the athletes who retained their periods, their levels of ghrelin were significantly higher, leading Misra and colleagues to wonder whether high ghrelin levels could disrupt the menstrual cycle (Lohr, 2008).

It's easy to see the connection. After all, animals and humans that can't produce leptin are infertile. The brain and body don't believe there are enough food sources to sustain pregnancy or offspring, and so reproduction ceases. Since leptin is the opposite of ghrelin, perhaps high levels of ghrelin also affect reproduction. Except that abnormally high ghrelin levels might just be a marker of inadequate energy intake, and it's the lack of nutrition that affects menstruation. Nor did the researchers say they assessed eating-disordered thoughts and behaviors or body fat levels, both of which would have given a better idea about the link between ghrelin and amenorrhea.

"In women with anorexia, because of the chronic starvation and stress on the body, the reproductive system sort of goes into hibernation," Lawson said. "There's a reverse to pre-pubertal patterns of signaling in the brain, so the ovaries don't get the correct signals to produce hormones that result in a normal menstrual cycle and reproduction."

The eating disorder community is especially worried about the causes of amenorrhea in anorexia because the loss of menstruation, even for a short period of time, dramatically decreases bone density. Since anorexia not uncommonly strikes during adolescence, this decrease in bone density is especially detrimental since this time should be devoted to bone strengthening, rather than deterioration (Teng, 2011).

"Bone loss is a major problem in anorexia," Lawson said. "Bone remodeling is a constant process. Bone is formed, and bone is being resorbed. But until you reach the mid-twenties, bone formation is greater than bone resorbtion, so you're building bone. People tend to reach their peak bone mass when they're in their twenties, so if women develop anorexia nervosa during their adolescence, then they fall off that normal curve [of bone development], they don't reach their normal peak bone density, and they have much more severe bone loss."

Approximately 75 percent of adolescents with anorexia nervosa show a significant decrease in bone density compared to other girls their age. An illness duration of just one year can lead to significant decrease in bone density (Wong *et al.*, 2001). As length and severity of illness increases, so does the likelihood of osteopenia and osteoporosis, a clinical thinning of the bones. Among women who have had anorexia for approximately ten years, three-quarters of them had femurs that could be easily fractured (Baker *et al.*, 2000).

Bone thinning is common in anyone who is starving, Lawson told me, due to insufficient nutrient consumption that can cause the body to leach calcium from bones and teeth to meet its immediate needs. But it's especially prevalent in anorexia nervosa due to the complex series of hormonal and endocrine changes that occur as a result of the disease.

The appetite hormone PYY, which is produced in the gut, generally increases after eating and decreases during food deprivation (Murphy and Bloom, 2006). Anorexia patients generally have abnormally high levels of PYY, which is evidence for yet another hormone that decreases appetite and increases fullness in anorexia (Misra *et al.*, 2006). "When these women recover, this signal is still high, so one of the questions is if this hormone could contribute to the symptoms of anorexia nervosa," Lawson said. "You would think it would certainly perpetuate symptoms."

Researchers have found that elevated PYY appears to contribute to many of the physical side effects of the illness. A study by Lawson and her colleagues compared PYY levels in anorexia patients to their levels of bone loss. Those patients with the highest PYY levels also had the greatest bone loss, especially in the spine (Utz *et al.*, 2008). Although researchers aren't exactly sure how PYY levels contribute to bone loss, it may be that chronic undernutrition relative to energy needs simultaneously elevates PYY and decreases estrogen levels (Scheid *et al.*, 2011). So PYY itself may be just a marker of malnutrition, with other hormones, like decreased estrogen or an increase in the stress hormone cortisol, leading to bone loss directly.

"In anorexia, there's increased cortisol production, and we think that this is probably an adaptive response to the chronic stress of starvation. But it has consequences. It can potentially contribute to bone loss and changes in mood," Lawson said. As in the PYY studies, when Lawson and colleagues compared cortisol levels in women with anorexia to bone density, they found that higher levels of cortisol led to greater bone loss (Lawson *et al.*, 2009).

When scientists have used CT scans to study microscopic changes to the architecture of bone in women with anorexia, they have found significant abnormalities. These changes, which are impossible to see on traditional bone scans, greatly contribute to bone weakness and an increase in risk of fractures and bone breaks in anorexia (Lawson *et al.*, 2010).

While Lawson was talking, I could barely suppress an inward cringe, remembering all too well my own brittle bones and subsequent breaks and fractures. The first (and most memorable) incident occurred one frigid February evening—ironically just a few months after I first hefted Keys' starvation study that day in the graduate student library. That morning, my apartment complex had plowed the sidewalks and driveway after overnight snow, which had begun to melt slightly after spending all day in the sun. But as the sun slipped below the horizon, the meager heat disappeared, and the ground re-froze into a sheet of nearly invisible black ice. Exhausted after spending nearly ten hours in class that day, I barely noticed the sheen on the pavement.

Which is how I found myself suddenly sitting in the middle of the driveway of my apartment. I got a passerby to help me to my feet to see if I could stand enough to at least stop sitting on the ice. I couldn't. An evening in the ER revealed the worst: my ankle had simply disintegrated as I fell. My three ankle bones weren't just broken, they were totally shattered. A week later, surgeons tried to put my ankle back together again, as if I was a living Humpty-Dumpty. My bones were in such bad shape that they could barely attach the rods, pins, and screws to my leg and foot.

The incident, and the excruciating pain, terrified me. I had only been without my period for around a year. Yet the bone scan I had in the months following my surgery showed me to have very significant osteoporosis. My bones were in worse shape than my sixty-something mother. I began different regimens of birth control pills (to supplement any estrogen deficiencies) and osteoporosis medication, none of which had much effect.

Researchers now know they generally don't. A 2011 study showed that physiological estrogen replacement, rather than with oral contraceptive mimics, does help to improve bone density in adolescents with anorexia (Misra *et al.*, 2011). These estrogen replacements wouldn't be used in place of refeeding and other existing anorexia therapies, but in addition to these techniques. What researchers are sure helps to improve bone density, after all, is weight gain.

"The best thing women can do is recover weight and restore their menstrual cycle. We think that, independently, each can improve bone density," Lawson said. "But this doesn't fully restore bone density. It doesn't get them back to normal." It's something I've found as well. Even after several years at a healthy weight (with an occasional downward blip), I still have significant bone loss. It has definitely improved, but it will likely never fully return to normal. As difficult as the process was, returning to a healthy weight for me (which was ultimately about 10–15 pounds above my pre-anorexia weight) was the first part of the healing process.

"A lot of the hormonal changes we see in anorexia nervosa are thought to be adaptations to starvation," Lawson said. "The abnormalities seem to normalize with recovery."

Still, the question remains as to why anorexia has remained in the gene pool for as long as it has. The disease is deadly and often leaves sufferers with lifelong medical issues that can require ongoing attention. One evolutionary psychologist believes that, as harmful as anorexia may be, it may have originated as a beneficial adaptation to help humans survive regular bouts of famine. Anorexics, then, may be history's super-starvers.

7 Adapted to Flee Famine

Several years ago, the theme of National Eating Disorders Awareness Week was "Listen to Your Body." The posters printed for the event had a picture of a girl slurping a milk shake with a straw. Another version had a cafeteria tray with different foods—I distinctly remember carrots on the tray. If we ate when we were hungry and stopped when we were full, and if we ate a variety of foods that we loved, then eating disorders would cease to exist. Listening to our bodies was seen not only as a universal prevention tool, it was also touted as the ticket to recovery.

My psychiatrist refused to hang up the posters. He hated the message. I found this baffling, coming from a man who was so helpful in my own recovery. What could possibly be wrong with listening to your body?

"If I told you to just listen to your body," he said, "you would probably be dead. Your body is telling you to keep starving, to keep exercising, and that you don't need to eat. Recovery means tuning that out. It means not listening to your body, at least for now."

It took me several years to fully grasp what he was saying. After all, during most of the anorexia, I did feel hunger. Maybe not as frequently as others might have, and maybe not as strongly, but I did feel it. The problem is that every instinct I had, from the top of my head down to my toenails, told me not to eat. Eating meant sloth and gluttony. It meant tolerating nearly unbearable guilt for needing and wanting and *consuming*. Eating required me to actually have food in my stomach, something I found rather repulsive. Although my desiccated, thinning hair and bruised limbs may have lodged a protest, my body and brain were telling me not to eat.

It was, perhaps, the most frustrating and difficult pieces for friends and family to understand. In their eyes, I was willfully not eating. Considering I hadn't had a proper meal for months, how could I not feel the drive to open the refrigerator and pull out a yogurt or an ice cream? How could I sit at home, night after night, with a pizza delivery service only a phone call away? No wonder anorexia was usually explained using supernatural forces—how else could someone starve themselves to death while surrounded with bounties of food?

Less-than-helpful physicians told me to "eat a cheeseburger" and "get over myself." I found that suggestion odd. First of all, I wasn't stupid. I knew that the treatment for starvation was food. Although I might admit if waterboarded that I occasionally felt the sensation of hunger, I wouldn't have classified myself as starving. Eat a cheeseburger? Why would I ever want to do that? I felt no real internal drive to increase my food intake.

The previous chapters have explored a lot about the psychology of anorexia. Maybe self-starvation decreases someone's anxiety, or their dopamine system malfunctions and they find the starved state to be rewarding. Maybe someone with anorexia is extremely rule-bound and too focused on the minutiae of calories and fat grams to look up and see that they should probably get something to eat. Maybe they value thinness very highly, or they're using the anorexia to solve a family problem.

More recently, discussions of what might cause or maintain anorexia nervosa have begun to incorporate physiology. Perhaps what separates those with anorexia from the general population is a physiological difference in the way they (don't) experience hunger signals. An initial energy imbalance from increased exercise, efforts towards more healthful eating, a growth spurt, or even an illness sets off a cascade of changes that prolongs the semi-starved state into what can be diagnosed as anorexia nervosa. What's more, this ability to withstand starvation could be passed from parent to child.

Every organism needs food. It's one of the strongest bodily drives there is—without food, an animal will die. This means that the forces of evolution and natural selection have helped make hunger an unpleasant state, such that an animal will feel the need to go out into the elements and risk death in order to find food. Still, most animals will face periods of famine or extreme food shortages. Those who can survive these shortages will go on to eat and reproduce another day, thus passing their genes onto the next generation. Hundreds of thousands of years ago, the disorder we know as anorexia may have originated in a small group of humans as a novel way to survive famines.

Anorexia typically harms fertility in both women and men during the active disease process, which may make the heritability of these genes questionable. After all, if someone with anorexia has trouble reproducing, they're not going to be passing these genes onto anyone. Which is true during the acute starvation phase, but studies following women with anorexia have found that they do, in fact, have children.

If the aberrant response to starvation was initially self-limited to the period of food shortage—if the proto-anorexic was able to start eating freely when food became more abundant—the damages to future fertility would also be more limited. What's more, siblings and children of those who were able to thrive when everyone else struggled also benefitted. They could have been more likely to get food if their close relative was able to do without. And since close relatives can share up to one-half of their genes, these relatives could also pass along the ability to withstand starvation.

"I'm Not in the Pleistocene; I'm in High School"

It's an idea that psychologist Shan Guisinger calls the "Adapted to Flee Famine" hypothesis (Guisinger, 2003, 2008). Initially trained as a behavioral ecologist (someone who studies foraging and mating strategies in animals), Guisinger ultimately found her calling in both evolutionary and clinical psychology. When she opened her practice in rural Montana in the mid-1980s, her very first client was a young woman who had developed anorexia.

"This girl was not ambivalent at all about getting better. She desperately wanted to get well, and that was part of the reason that I began to think there was something fishy with current theories about anorexia," Guisinger said.

This woman, Guisinger told me, worked as a hairdresser and tried to squeeze in extra hours to afford Guisinger's fee. Guisinger said she really liked the woman, who Guisinger described as "conscientious and hard-working," traits typically associated with anorexia, and so kept lowering and lowering her fee to fit within the woman's limited budget. "I tried to help her with what I had learned in graduate school at [the University of California at] Berkeley. I said this is really about your relationship with your mother. As it happened, she loved her parents and thought they were great," Guisinger said. "It wasn't that she had a controlling mom or a critical dad or any of those things."

So Guisinger turned next to the young woman's perfectionism. Not surprisingly, the woman espoused views of perfectionism and, also not surprisingly, her perfectionism worsened as her weight decreased. But working on her perfectionism issues didn't loosen the grasp of anorexia. "She told me, 'Shan, I would eat if I could, but I can't,'" Guisinger said.

A stomach virus during the time the pair was working together caused the woman's weight to drop even lower. "Eventually she told me that she felt she shouldn't even drink water," Guisinger said. It was a confession that got Guisinger thinking. Water didn't have calories, and, if anything, thirst would kill someone faster than starvation. Something was driving this woman to deny herself food and water—but what?

It was something Guisinger couldn't figure out in her small Montana practice. Current theories about eating disorders didn't give Guisinger a way to help this woman, and so she eventually stopped coming to therapy. But the young woman's effects on Guisinger lasted long after their therapy sessions eventually ceased. Guisinger found anorexia interesting, and spent several years at Yale University in the late 1980s as a post-doctoral researcher in their eating and weight disorders program. There, she saw many more patients with anorexia.

"I noticed that they all seemed to report the same kinds of feelings," Guisinger said. No matter what might have caused their illness, and no matter how much insight they had into this cause, she said, they almost all said "I'd eat if I could, but I can't."

Another piece of the puzzle fell into place when she did a study comparing the parenting styles of the mothers and fathers of anorexia and bulimia patients.

Current theory held that parents of those with bulimia were overly emotional, while those of anorexia patients were under-emotional and over-controlled (Johnson and Flach, 1985). Except that's not what Guisinger found. Parenting styles seemed to have no relation to eating disorder diagnosis. Because the study didn't find an association, it was placed in a drawer and never published, a sadly common habit in the scientific world. Still, the research profoundly changed Guisinger. "Maybe the parents aren't what are causing these things," she said. So she began to look elsewhere for what might be causing such severe illness.

After Guisinger completed her postdoc at Yale and returned to Montana, she became known as the eating disorders therapist in her area. As she saw more and more patients, one question nagged at her more than any other. "Why would a starving body ever turn off hunger, or give you the idea that it was wrong to eat," Guisinger wondered. "It really made no sense."

And then there was the compulsive, driven exercise. "A starving person normally conserves their energy," she said. Her anorexia patients didn't, instead burning thousands of precious calories in their frenetic activities.

Then, after finishing a session with one of her clients, Guisinger's brain returned to her behavioral ecology training. Humans are animals, after all, and the forces of evolution and natural selection act upon us as surely as they do the birds and the bees. Maybe, Guisinger realized, anorexia was an evolutionary relic from the days when famine was common. Maybe the traits that have become what we know as the illness of anorexia nervosa began as a beneficial response to a food shortage.

"From college, I've been an evolutionist. I see everything through that lens," Guisinger said, inadvertently paraphrasing the eminent evolutionary biologist Theodosius Dobzhansky, who wrote a famous essay titled "Nothing in biology makes sense except in the light of evolution" (1973). "In the Pleistocene, if you were starving, it meant everyone was starving, because hunter-gatherers share food. It's really striking to our individualistic culture, where everyone is on their own, just how much [hunter-gatherers] share food. That's how it was for millions of years," she said.

So if someone in the Pleistocene lost 15 percent of their body weight (as specified in the DSM-IV diagnostic criteria for anorexia nervosa), it meant that everyone was starving. Essentially, Guisinger said, people could choose from one of two options. "The typical one is that you can hunker down and wait for spring to come and the bison to return. You basically conserve your energy, and that's what most starving people do," she said.

But Pleistocene humans had a second option. As bands of humans spread out from Africa, into the Middle East, and from there to Europe and Asia, food shortages were often very local. New groups of hunter-gatherers would arrive in an area, eat most of the big game and edible plants, and then find themselves short of food (Diamond, 2000). If this group could keep moving—if even just a few members of the band could mobilize their last reserves and venture to the next mountain top—total disaster could be averted. Those humans that could ignore the deleterious effects of starvation could go out and find food, saving their friends and family from death-by-famine.

With this scenario, moving to a new location was a great short-term strategy. Desperate, yes, but it was also often successful. The problem, Guisinger said, is that "hunger is very distracting. If you're hungry, if you're starving, and you don't have anorexia, you're not thinking about much else. If what you needed to do was cross a mountain range or get on a boat and row to Australia, and you stopped because you saw a few good berries, you're not going to make it. It's really important to turn off hunger."

Physiological evidence seems to indicate that people with anorexia can often dial down their hunger, even if they can't shut it off entirely. It wasn't that I didn't feel hungry while ill, it was that I didn't deem the hunger that important, certainly not important or uncomfortable enough to stop pursuing my obsessive exercise and minimal food intake. Nor did my illness stop me from finishing college and pursuing graduate degrees. Like the proto-anorexics in the Pleistocene, I could keep going.

Switching off hunger isn't purely a volitional thing. Plenty of animals do it. In the 2005 documentary *March of the Penguins*, I watched the heroic efforts of Emperor penguins (*Aptenodytes for steri*) lay their eggs and raise their chicks in the middle of the Antarctic winter. Mothers often lose one-third of their body weight as they try to feed their chicks, and fathers lose even more—up to half their weight. Clearly, these birds were starving, and yet they didn't abandon their young to go seek food (Groscolas and Leloup, 1989).

Of course, no one knows if these penguins don't actually feel hunger, or if their drive to feed is superseded by another drive: to reproduce. "That's the way it is with anorexia. It's not that you don't feel hunger, but you have these cortical responses, these higher brain phobias, that develop the feeling that it's virtuous not to eat. And I suspect that this is what happens with the penguins, that they feel almost virtuous for not eating," Guisinger said. "We don't know whether they're hungry or not, we can just observe that they act like they're not hungry because they don't eat."

Guisinger gave me another example, this one from her own backyard. She raises hens, and knew that chickens generally stop eating while incubating their eggs. One of her hens was "getting broody," sitting on her clutch of eggs and ignoring the chicken feed Guisinger had set out. Even after Guisinger had collected the unfertilized eggs (zoning laws in Guisinger's town meant no roosters), the hen still wouldn't leave her nest. So Guisinger set some feed right next to the hen, so she wouldn't have to leave her nest. "She took a few pecks, and then she lost interest. She stopped eating," Guisinger said.

These animal behaviors might help explain why someone with anorexia can deny his or her hunger, but they still don't explain the ceaseless exercise seen in some anorexia patients. Which is when Guisinger remembered another avian behavior, known as migratory restlessness. At around the time birds traditionally migrate, they become hyperactive and jittery (Helm and Gwinner, 2006). If you place migratory birds in a cage around the time they usually migrate,

Guisinger said, they will often hop endlessly at the north or south side of the cage, depending on what season it is and where the bird usually flies.

"So I suggested these ideas to one of my patients. 'I wonder if this is what is going on,' I told her. And it really seemed to help," Guisinger said.

As Guisinger began to search for more information on her ideas that became known as the "Adapted to Flee Famine" hypothesis, she came across studies highlighting the many neuroendocrine changes that happen to those with anorexia. Levels of leptin, a hormone that signals satiety, decrease, but not as much as would be expected given the degree of weight loss seen in anorexia (Adan and Vink, 2001). Some young women with anorexia have unusually high levels of vasopressin and abnormally low levels of oxytocin (Kaye, 1996). Other studies have indicated that vasopressin and oxytocin have profound effects on memory, oxytocin by helping women forget the pain and discomfort of childbirth (Lee *et al.*, 2009), and vasopressin by improving memory of aversive circumstances (Engelmann *et al.*, 1996). This has led some scientists to hypothesize that "high vasopressin and low oxytocin levels in AN might enhance retention of the aversive consequences of eating" (Guisinger, 2003; Demitrack *et al.*, 1990), while simultaneously blunting memories of how uncomfortable starvation really is.

Both serotonin and dopamine are also thought to play a role in the two primary, paradoxical symptoms of anorexia: self-starvation and hyperactivity. Researchers have linked high levels of serotonin in the starved state to hyperactivity and excessive exercise (Favaro *et al.*, 2000). Some of the otherwise healthy young men in the Keys starvation study admitted to extra physical activity outside of the 22 miles they had to walk each week. The researchers wrote this off as the men's attempt to finagle extra food rations (Keys *et al.*, 1950), but Guisinger suspects starvation-induced hyperactivity may have been the real culprit (2003). High serotonin levels also exist after weight recovery from anorexia and are thought to be present before the onset of illness, given the neurotransmitter's links to perfectionism and obsessionality (Kaye *et al.*, 1998).

Given dopamine's link to rewarding behavior, the high levels of dopamine seen in those with anorexia nervosa seem to indicate that the stress of starvation and hyperactivity has become rewarding and self-perpetuating (Bergh and Sodersten, 1996; Weinberger and Zink, 2010), which Guisinger says is consistent with the Adapted to Flee Famine hypothesis. "The more I researched, the more I became convinced that this was going on. I used it in my therapy practice more, and again, people found it really helpful," Guisinger said. "Thinking that 'my body is trying to migrate' allows you to say 'But I'm not in the Pleistocene; I'm in high school.'"

Anorexia is seductive. The vast majority of modern-day anorexia sufferers live amongst adequate, if not abundant, amounts of food. But the body is confused. It interprets the weight loss diet, the stomach virus, or the healthful eating attempts as famine throughout the land, and responds accordingly. It drives sufferers to think of eating as greedy and distasteful, and to endure punishing exercise routines. What makes anorexia different from a Pleistocene famine is the fact that food is abundant and those with anorexia are still unable to eat.

Food is always over the next mountain. Starvation is a solo endeavor in anorexia, not a communal trauma as in the Pleistocene. Evolution simply hasn't
caught up yet.

"We believe what we feel, and with anorexia treatment it's so hard because
you're asking yourself to go against what your body feels. It feels like it's
wrong to eat. It feels like it's right to move," Guisinger said. Treatment means
learning how to override those tremendously powerful, biologically driven
feelings.

It wasn't until I spoke with Guisinger that I truly understood why my former
psychiatrist had hated that "Listen to your body" poster. Although he never
mentioned the Adapted to Flee Famine hypothesis to me by name, so I have
no way of knowing for sure whether he knew of Guisinger's work, he intui-
tively grasped the same concept. More than 30 years of treating eating disorder
patients had taught him the same thing: it's not a refusal to eat; it's an inability
to eat. And recovery means fighting powerful biological drives that keep the
illness going.

If the Pleistocene Had Photoshop

Guisinger's work also accounts for the body image distortions and anosognosia
that characterize many cases of anorexia. Just as it was almost impossible for my
friends and family to understand how I could turn down a cheeseburger while
starving, they also had a tough time grasping how I could see myself as anything
but skeletal. But I didn't; I just saw a rather average-looking person staring back
at me in the mirror. I clearly wasn't too thin, so how could I have a problem?

To Guisinger, the Adapted to Flee Famine hypothesis is predicated on the fact
that the starving person needs to be unable to recognize their own emaciation.
If they did that, she said, they might be shocked out of their food denial and
hyperactivity. This could put countless Pleistocene people in danger if hunter-
gatherer groups didn't have at least one person able to ignore the starvation
and search for food. Thus, far from being rather bizarre and crazy-making,
the profound body image distortion and an inability to recognize that there's
anything wrong are actually helpful, if you view anorexia from the point of view
of the Pleistocene.

One of the most striking studies, Guisinger told me, is a brain imaging study
in which underweight anorexia patients looked at both pictures of themselves
and pictures of other people (Sachdev *et al.*, 2008). When these women (all the
study participants were female) looked at pictures of other people, the activity in their brains looked almost identical to the activity in control women.
A patchwork of activity appeared across the brain, from the frontal lobes to
the fusiform gyrus, specialized in facial recognition. But when the women with
anorexia looked at pictures of themselves, their visual cortex went completely
blank. It was as if they literally did not see themselves.

"The visual change is always in one direction: it's always adding fat to the
body. It's never reducing fat. Someone with anorexia never looks in the mirror

and sees themselves as thinner than they are. And they seem to feel fatter the thinner they get," Guisinger said.

As well, this visual distortion is only self-directed. If a Pleistocene proto-anorexic couldn't recognize that everyone in their group was starving, they would have no reason to summon their last reserves of energy and make the journey to new hunting and foraging grounds. So they need to be able to perceive everyone else accurately but be able to ignore (or at least discount) the effects of famine in themselves. It's almost as if someone with anorexia needs to be out of touch with reality to pursue self-starvation in spite of the physical and psychological side effects, whether in the Pleistocene or in modern-day America.

There's a reason for this. "If you look at your body when you're starving, the primal response is terror. You think, 'Oh my God, I'm not going to make it.' But if you think you're not going to make it, then you're not going to take that risk and head over that next mountain," Guisinger said. "Presumably, the people that went over the mountain sometimes made it and those that stayed often did not."

The Adapted to Flee Famine hypothesis offers an alternative lens through which to view these seemingly maddening symptoms. "For me," I told Guisinger, "the typical theories of parental conflict and a desire to be thin didn't really jive with my own experience. My eating disorder started in college when I got really depressed and thought that eating better and exercising more would make me feel better. Lo and behold, it did, but it also got me in trouble. The five pounds I'd hoped to lose turned into 50. Yet I never read fashion magazines, and I got along just fine with my parents."

Although the reception of her hypothesis by the eating disorder community at large was less than cordial (attending eating disorder conferences "was a lot like middle school," she confessed), patients and their families, in contrast, have welcomed Guisinger's ideas. "I don't think I've had anyone who didn't immediately think it made sense of their experiences," she said. "And the parents, of course, weep. 'You mean it's not my fault?' They're in tears."

"When I look at biology, it makes it so much clearer why recovery was so hard and why I got stuck," I told Guisinger. "It didn't necessarily get me unstuck, but it stopped me from the pointless search for what caused it."

"And this questioning can do so much damage to the people who love you the most," Guisinger replied.

"Yes," I nodded. "Exactly."

"To know that recovery is hard not because you're unconsciously sabotaging yourself, but because your body is fighting you, is so helpful to my patients. I tell them that your body has its own idea about what's required here," Guisinger said.

The eating disorder world shouldn't embrace Guisinger's theory just because parents and sufferers and ex-sufferers-turned-authors find it helpful. They should embrace it because it has a large range of evidence supporting it, and because it explains so many different aspects of anorexia. Guisinger has amassed hundreds of studies that support this idea, and it can be used to help explain why such deleterious genetic variations came to exist in the gene pool in the first place: they were once beneficial. The Adapted to Flee Famine hypothesis also explains many of the personality traits that place people at risk for anorexia, why females are disproportionately affected, and why relapse rates are so high upon discharge from treatment.

The perfectionism and people-pleasing so frequently seen in those who develop anorexia provide the mindset necessary to not only endure starvation, but to seem to thrive while not eating. Writes Guisinger in her 2003 paper in the journal *Psychological Review*:

> Clinicians have long known that a risk factor for developing AN is being compliant and driven. … Perfectionism is the personality trait most consistently associated with AN. … Hunger is generally extremely aversive; most American women say they would like to lose what would be unhealthy amounts of weight …, but thankfully, only a few actually achieve this. Presumably the same qualities that help perfectionistic individuals succeed in school and work—the ability to work hard, delay gratification, and ignore suffering in pursuit of a goal—help these dieters drive their weight dangerously low.
>
> (p. 755)

Yet these perfectionistic traits exist across the lifespan. So why does anorexia disproportionately affect adolescent females? Psychodynamic theories have hypothesized that adolescence is a time of individuation and sexual maturation. Anorexia is a way to physically remain pre-pubescent, and it also stops the young person's flight from the family home, maintaining the enmeshment.

On the other hand, researchers have noted that body mass index changes across the lifespan. Although body weight continues to rise until the early twenties, body weight relative to height is typically at its lowest point for females in early puberty. This means that an adolescent girl has the least amount of weight to lose before her body starts to go into starvation mode. At other times in her life, she has more weight to serve as a buffer. Hebebrand *et al.* (1995) speculate that "The hormonal changes associated with puberty might lead to intermittent weight loss with or without the psychopathological features of AN in genetically predisposed females during their puberty or adolescence" (p. 1624).

What's more, females who go on to develop anorexia generally weigh less than their similarly aged counterparts, even before illness onset (Strober, 1995). If inadequate amounts of body fat trigger the Adapted to Flee Famine response, then this leanness loads the gun with even more ammunition. Combine this with a perfectionistic temperament, and you end up with someone with the psychological endurance to withstand deprivation and very little buffer between their normal weight and the havoc of starvation.

Once this weight loss starts, the body essentially panics. In normal dieters, this is registered as extreme hunger and the diet generally ends. In someone with a predisposition to anorexia, you get the Adapted to Flee Famine response. But this response doesn't shut off once refeeding starts, once an anorexia patient is discharged from the hospital or treatment center, or even once the individual returns to a biologically appropriate weight. It can take weeks or even months for the body to escape from "panic mode."

Thus even after an individual regains physical health, the biological drive to restrict food and over-exercise remains. No wonder relapse rates from inpatient treatment are so high, Guisinger says. Someone with anorexia will continue to fight their biological drives to eat less and exercise more for quite some time, and often needs lots of extra support during this time. As well, any future weight loss can trigger a re-emergence of anorexic thoughts and behaviors even after a lengthy period of remission.

"You have to have food every few hours for a long time to convince your hypothalamus that you're not going to go through famine again. If you skip one meal, it's so tuned to danger that it can flip you back into anorexic thinking," Guisinger said.

On a summer vacation to Germany and Austria (ironically, following a trip to Salzburg, Austria, for an international eating disorders conference), I picked up a nasty stomach bug on my travels. For over 24 hours, I only sipped on apple juice. For several days after that, my food intake was very limited because of ongoing nausea. Not surprisingly, my weight dropped. Before I got sick, my eating-disordered thoughts were minimal. I was eating freely, enjoying hiking and other moderate physical activity, and in good spirits. But after I was ill for several days, I was catapulted back into full-blown anorexic thinking.

As much as my brief sickness interrupted an otherwise lovely European vacation, it also taught me something important. My body responds very differently when deprived of food or even when I lose just a few pounds. I find myself once again yearning to cut back on my eating and to increase my exercising. My body wants to migrate.

After talking with Guisinger, though, I can now tell myself that I'm not in the Pleistocene. Starving and migrating aren't adaptive here and now. What is adaptive is picking up the fork and taking off the running shoes and resetting my hypothalamus, one meal and one snack at a time.

Ancient History

Other studies have raised the intriguing possibility that the genetic variations that make anorexia possible are far older than even the Pleistocene. After all, 100,000 years is an evolutionary blink of an eye. Nor were bands of nomadic *Homo sapiens* the first organisms to struggle against hunger and famine. Finding enough food has been a battle since the very first organisms emerged several billion years ago.

In that time, life on Earth has learned to guard against starvation. Microbes can shut down unneeded enzyme production to preserve precious energy (Vazquez *et al.*, 2008). Animals can hibernate for the winter (Davis *et al.*, 1990) or lay down extra body fat (Lockwood, 2006) to survive lean times. Failure to do this can be deadly. Scientists believe that a fungal infection known as White Nose Syndrome is driving brown bats to near extinction in the eastern United States because it interferes with the bats' normal hibernation process. This causes the bats to burn through their fat stores long before spring, and eventually the animals starve to death (Cryan *et al.*, 2010).

But the origins of anorexia may predate even brown bats and polar bears. If you look at the right genes, says Donard Dwyer, a professor in the Department of Pharmacology, Toxicology, and Neuroscience at Louisiana State University, you can trace anorexia back to yeast (*Saccharomyces cereviciae*). Dwyer, who studies how antipsychotic medication affects metabolism, hypothesized in a *Molecular Psychiatry* paper that anorexia results from an altered starvation response due to variations in a gene called FOXO (Dwyer *et al.*, 2011).

FOXO (pronounced "fox-oh") is a type of gene known as a transcription factor. Think of many of the genes in your DNA as light bulbs. Like the chandelier over my dining room table, many of your genes have a dimmer switch. Rather than being either off or on, like a normal light switch, genes can be expressed at a variety of levels, similar to how I can adjust the lighting in my dining room from very dim to bright with the twist of a knob. A specific type of gene known as a transcription factor acts as this dimmer switch. Some transcription factors act on many genes, whereas others act on just a single gene. A transcription factor works by binding directly to the DNA and making a gene or genes more readily available to the enzymes that transcribe and translate a gene into RNA and protein, respectively.

The FOX (short for forkhead box) family of transcription factors controls a wide range of genes, everything from liver cells (FOXA; Bingle and Gowan, 1996), to embryo development (FOXC; Tuteja and Kaestner, 2007), to cellular metabolism (FOXO; van der Horst and Burgering, 2007). Because organisms depend so heavily on the FOX transcription factors for so many different functions, these genes have been highly conserved throughout evolution. That is, the FOX genes in organisms from yeast, to the fruit fly, to humans have a very similar DNA sequence, which means they likely have a similar function in all of these different species.

An organism experiences profound physiological changes as it starves. Insulin levels drop, as do blood glucose levels. Hunger and food-seeking behavior increases. Growth stops as the organism tries to conserve as much energy as possible. Central to all of these changes is a protein known as insulin-like growth factor 1 (IGF-1). IGF-1 is a growth hormone that has a similar structure to insulin (as you might expect from the name), and helps promote growth in younger organisms as well as creating large molecules out of smaller building blocks in animals of all ages (Scarth, 2006). Without adequate energy intake, however, IGF-1 levels drop, leading to many of the physical and psychological changes associated with starvation and anorexia nervosa (Brick *et al.*, 2010).

The FOXO transcription factors control levels of IGF-1. Although the three FOXO genes seem to have nothing to do with starvation (they code for butter-fly-shaped proteins that bind to DNA), they actually play a crucial role in how the body responds to low food intake. If the FOXO regulation of IGF-1 and the associated starvation-related changes is somehow defective, it could result in anorexia nervosa, says Dwyer.

When people with normal FOXO pathways starve, their bodies command them to seek out food. Some of the men in the Keys starvation study ate food out of dumpsters (Keys *et al.*, 1950). Shipwrecked sailors on the nineteenth-century whaleship *Essex* resorted to cannibalism (Philbrick, 2001). Yet people with anorexia either resist these drives or don't appear to feel them. If the FOXO pathway is malfunctioning, then appetite regulation can go awry. When researchers disturbed FOXO in organisms like yeast, roundworms, fruit flies, and mice, feeding and body weight were affected.

Too much FOXO in yeast meant they didn't make the required physical changes to absorb extra nutrients in a food-scarce environment (Zhu *et al.*, 2000). When researchers eliminated the ability of the worm *Caenorhabditis elegans* to sense IGF-1, the worms essentially stopped feeding and searching for food (You *et al.*, 2008). Fruit flies (*Drosophila melanogaster*) that made too much FOXO showed characteristics similar to anorexia: they didn't approach food as frequently, they ate less, and they had a smaller body size than flies with normal FOXO (Kramer *et al.*, 2003). And researchers found a close relationship between FOXO and serotonin in starving mice (Liang *et al.*, 2006).

"These FOXO-related proteins are controlling a very primitive foraging response in organisms all the way back to yeast. This said that there's something fundamental going on here," Dwyer said.

Yet yeast and worms and flies are far different from humans. It seems odd to think that organisms with very primitive brains can teach us anything about a complex mental illness. But if you strip anorexia down to its barest essentials—if you remove the illness's cultural baggage—what you are left with is a self-starvation syndrome. Someone with anorexia has access to food, but they don't seek it out. Learning how and why other organisms are able to achieve this same feat can teach scientists a lot about what goes wrong in anorexia.

"Essentially anyone who undergoes starvation starts to show some of the signs that we attribute as causative in anorexia. Which causes us to ask what is the normal response to starvation and what is adaptive about it," Dwyer said. Figuring out if and how this differs in people with anorexia should yield new clues to what might cause or maintain the illness.

One of these clues comes from the fruit fly study mentioned above. When scientists cranked up the amount of FOXO in fruit fly larvae in a previous study, they found that the flies spontaneously wandered away from food. They ate less, had smaller bodies, and reached reproductive maturity later than flies with normal FOXO levels—all characteristics of people suffering from anorexia nervosa (Kramer *et al.*, 2003).

"This sounds pretty close to what you see in anorexia nervosa," Dwyer said. "If you can see that with the simple manipulation of a single gene, it made me wonder about the accepted idea that this disorder is a psychosomatic illness.

Maybe things like perfectionism are secondary to anorexia, or maybe they're a smokescreen, but it seems there are bigger things going on metabolically."

If a young girl has inherited this FOXO mutation, Dwyer said, she might very well become anorexic or have a tendency towards anorexia based on this simple genotype. "It doesn't mean that she's trying to lose weight or look like a supermodel. All of that might be an element of it, but it could be much more fundamental than that," he noted.

A second clue comes from studies of social feeding behaviors in the nematode *C. elegans*. These worms can feed both individually and in groups, depending on how they respond to different chemicals in the environment. Individual feeders find signs of other worms aversive, whereas these same chemicals attract social feeders (de Bono *et al.*, 2002; Coates and de Bono, 2002). "Although this isn't exactly what is going on in anorexia, I'm imagining that this is part of the same genetic vulnerability," Dwyer said.

Considering that so many people with anorexia say they prefer to eat alone, I told him, it's not surprising. "Part of this preference may be so that the person can eat less without anyone noticing, but some of it might be that eating with others is very stressful. It's not a pleasant experience," I said.

A third clue to anorexia comes from mouse studies. Not only does FOXO affect appetite and eating behaviors, it also helps control some of the enzymes that make serotonin and dopamine, both of which are also affected in anorexia. High levels of FOXO can mean extra enzymes that synthesize serotonin and dopamine, which can lead to an increase in levels of both of these neurotransmitters (Liang *et al.*, 2006; Zhou and Palmiter, 1995). Write Dwyer and colleagues (2011):

> Thus, a bias toward denial of food leads to a reduction in calorie consumption, and weight loss. As weight loss proceeds, production of ancillary signals to initiate feeding, such as IGF-1 and dopamine (controlled by FOXO), is diminished and the starvation response is further activated. However, because this response is defective in AN, counter regulatory (or exigenic) mechanisms are ineffectual, and a persistent catabolic state develops, much like anorexia associated with cancer or infectious diseases. The fact that some anorexic patients literally starve themselves to death attests to the failure of evolutionarily conserved survival strategies in AN.
>
> (p. 599)

The main dysfunction in anorexia, Dwyer speculates, could be the fact that the body doesn't respond appropriately to even moderate food restriction. Instead of receiving signals to eat more, the body of someone with anorexia receives the message to eat less via high levels of serotonin and dopamine. It's an effect I know all too well. When I would skimp on a meal or snack, even inadvertently, my urges to restrict increased. This response might be normal for someone with anorexia, but it's profoundly different and dysfunctional compared to what my body actually needs me to do.

Starvation Adaptation

What complicates matters, Dwyer said, is that the body can adapt to consistent over- or under-consumption of food. When someone continues to overeat, even when full, the body becomes resistant to the effects of leptin and insulin, two hormones that signal satiety. Helping a chronic overeater or binge eater to resume more normalized eating patterns can't be done with a simple command to put down the damn fork. "It's hard for them to do because they have to overcome this poor signaling" that's not telling them to stop eating, Dwyer said.

Something similar might be going on in patients with anorexia, especially in patients who have been ill for many years. They might become resistant to the effects of appetite-promoting hormones like ghrelin, neuropeptide Y, and BDNF (brain-derived neurotrophic factor). Messages like "listen to your body" and "eat when you're hungry and stop when you're full" can be counterproductive to someone with chronic anorexia.

"The body adapts to too much or too little food over time in ways that become their own pathology," Dwyer said. "It happens in someone who starves, whether they're a hunger striker or someone with anorexia. They have undergone some adaptations that are counter-productive. They may actually have some evolutionary protective role in surviving times of starvation, but they've become counter-productive from the standpoint of reinitiating normal eating patterns."

"We might very well find that these regulators that he's pointing to are implicated in anorexia. It's not a mistake," Guisinger responded. "But the characteristics of anorexia are really hard to do. You're asking the body to do something very remarkable, very exceptional. It doesn't look like dysfunction. It looks like an adaptation. I believe it's way too extraordinary to be a dysfunction."

Look at anorexic mice and rats, Guisinger said. Studies have shown that, under starvation conditions, the cells of these animals remodel themselves to become supermice and superrats (Komatsu *et al.*, 2007; Scott *et al.*, 2004). Under starvation conditions, the fact that mice and rats "run 12 miles a day on their wheels when normally they would run just one is a result of metabolic changes," Guisinger noted. "And that's not what you get from a dysfunction. It's what you get from an adaptation. If it was a dysfunction, you would expect it to be all over the place and not result in super-abilities."

As much as Guisinger might have a bone to pick with Dwyer and other researchers, like Bryan Lask, who regard the profound changes undergone by the anorexic brain and body as a dysfunction rather than an adaptation, she nonetheless greatly admires their work. "I think that Lask and others have found one of the ways that evolution works in anorexia. The hypoperfusion of the insula helps people with anorexia not to process what they feel. Their body is feeling hungry but their mind doesn't really get it. This hypoperfusion is part of the adaptation, too," Guisinger said.

Not surprisingly, this is one of the biggest hurdles in anorexia treatment. Persuading someone who might not be especially hungry, and who is simultaneously terrified of food and weight gain, to resume eating isn't the world's easiest task. Psychological therapies for anorexia have thus far remained inadequate, Dwyer said.

Dwyer compares talk therapy for anorexia to talk therapy for diabetes. Someone who regularly and consistently overeats will gain weight and may become obese. As a result of their overeating and excess weight, they may develop diabetes. Although psychotherapy may help someone address the emotional reasons behind their overeating, it won't treat their diabetes. To do that, someone needs dietary changes and/or medication, not just talk therapy. Anorexia, Dwyer says, is like diabetes. The profound metabolic changes that accompany anorexia make the disorder more physiological than mental.

It's one of the many reasons that Dwyer remains hopeful that a medication may one day help treat anorexia by facilitating eating and weight gain. The medications that show the most promise to Dwyer are the atypical antipsychotics: second- and third-generation antipsychotic medications, like olanzapine (Zyprexa), risperidone (Risperdal), and quetiapine (Seroquel). All of these medications work by blocking the effects of dopamine in the brain. In patients with psychosis, atypical antipsychotics help block their abnormal motor movements, delusions, and hallucinations (Ananth *et al.*, 2001). Given their ability to soothe physical agitation and delusions, these drugs have become attractive to clinicians treating eating disorders. Besides the general sedating effects, the atypical antipsychotics have a side effect that has made them seem especially useful in the treatment of anorexia: weight gain (Lock and Fitzpatrick, 2009).

However, simple weight gain isn't why Dwyer sees these medications as useful in the treatment of anorexia nervosa. Some of Dwyer's own previous research showed that olanzapine increased appetite and feeding behaviors in the worm *C. elegans* by acting on the proteins in the FOXO pathway (Donohoe *et al.*, 2008). Since Dwyer believes a dysfunction in this pathway is crucial to the development and perpetuation of anorexia, olanzapine and similar drugs may help target the broken metabolism that he sees as the core of anorexia.

"Even though olanzapine and other drugs do cause weight gain, we're more interested in what they do in the short term to re-stimulate and normalize the appetitive drives that have been blunted by this long-term starvation," Dwyer said. "Perhaps these drugs have a place in treatment to re-normalize this physiology that has been disturbed, while also recognizing that these medications are far from ideal."

In recent years, scientists have begun to formally study the usefulness and efficacy of atypical antipsychotic medications in eating disorders. Numerous case studies have shown that olanzapine (the most studied of all of the atypical antipsychotics in eating disorders) helped anorexia sufferers gain body weight and maintain these gains (Mehler-Wex *et al.*, 2008; Powers *et al.*, 2002), as well as decrease obsessive thinking about food and weight (Mondraty *et al.*, 2005; Bissada *et al.*, 2008). Despite the relatively positive evidence supporting the use of atypical antipsychotics in anorexia treatment, many clinicians continue to urge caution in their use, seeing as all of the trials have been small and safety information isn't well-studied (McKnight and Park, 2010).

Dwyer says the use of medication isn't meant to negate psychological factors that can precipitate the illness, nor the learned behaviors like calorie counting and compulsive exercise that frequently accompany anorexia. "Regardless of how these issues got there, you have two main issues that need to be dealt with. You have the learned behaviors and psychological issues to manage, and you also have to reset the metabolic system because of starvation or chronic food restriction," Dwyer said. "And unless you deal with both of those, someone isn't going to see a lot of improvement."

Still, the physiology of starvation in general and anorexia nervosa in particular takes an important hypothesis about the development of eating disorders and reverses it. Instead of causing anorexia, the obsession with calories and thinness, as well as the significant body dysmorphia, are a result of starvation. They're a side effect of food restriction. So to target these symptoms, psychotherapy shouldn't focus on why these symptoms developed or their meaning. Instead, treating the malnutrition and starvation that accompany anorexia will help reverse the food obsessions and body image issues.

This reversal is important, says child and adult psychiatrist James Greenblatt, author of *Answers to Anorexia*, because it dramatically changes how we treat this disorder. Nutritional rehabilitation needs to be a priority, Greenblatt says, because it does so much to treat the debilitating psychological symptoms.

"I have just as many patients without anorexia that have those same issues with their mother or father. Only one percent of girls are getting anorexia, but we're all looking at the same magazines and movie stars, and only a tiny fraction develop a delusional disorder about their body," Greenblatt said.

These cultural influences are very relevant, Greenblatt said, because they often trigger a young person's desire to diet, exercise more, or otherwise attempt to change their weight and shape. "But it's not what keeps them in a pathological illness that kills," he said.

What kills in anorexia is the extreme, long-lasting malnutrition, whether through its physiological effects on the body or by creating a brain that becomes so ill and depressed that suicide seems like the only way out. Focusing on the nutritional aspects of treatment not only prevents deaths but also begins to bring the patient to a state of recovery. Although most anorexia patients are severely malnourished in all areas, Greenblatt says that achieving adequate zinc levels should be the cornerstone of treatment.

The symptoms of zinc deficiency are eerily similar to anorexia nervosa: weight loss, appetite loss, changes in taste abilities, lethargy, and depression (National Institutes of Health, n.d.). What's more, low zinc levels affect the functioning of several neurotransmitters implicated in anorexia, including gamma-aminobutyric acid (GABA), which has led some clinicians, including Greenblatt, to suggest that zinc supplements should be one of the standard treatments for anorexia (Birmingham and Gritzner, 2006). Other randomized control trials, however, have shown no real benefits of zinc supplementation on weight gain and remission of psychological symptoms (Lask *et al.*, 1993).

Even if the link between zinc supplementation and anorexia treatment remains somewhat controversial, numerous other studies have shown a direct link between nutritional deficiencies and mental health. Some of the newest—and perhaps most intriguing—have found that your gut bacteria have a tremendous effect on your brain. Not surprisingly, a person's diet can alter the microbes that live in their intestinal tract. A 2006 study showed that the microbes living in the guts of obese individuals were different than those in normal weight people. What's more, when the obese people were put on a weight loss diet, their gut microbes began to more closely resemble the microbes in the intestines of normal weight people (Ley *et al.*, 2006). A follow-up study showed that the bacterial species found in the gut can rapidly adjust to diet (Jumpertz *et al.*, 2011).

Although no one has yet studied the intestinal microbes in people suffering from anorexia, the existing scientific literature would indicate profound microbial changes. And changes in intestinal microbes in mice had dramatic effects on their mental health. Disrupting the usual intestinal balance with antibiotics in mice increased signs of anxiety and depression (Denou *et al.*, 2011). A preliminary study in humans found that probiotic supplements (superconcentrated forms of healthy gut bacteria) decreased symptoms in patients with anxiety disorders (Messaoudi *et al.*, 2011).

Regardless of whether these physiological changes are cause or effect, and whether or not the psychological symptoms of anorexia are a by-product of starvation, the ongoing food restriction traps sufferers in their illness. It sets off a cascade of physiological changes that prevent those with anorexia from eating when they're hungry, recognizing their fullness cues, and breaking free from the disorder. Recovery, at least at first, means ignoring the strong biological drive to starve, purge, and over-exercise. Treating anorexia means helping sufferers to stop listening to their bodies, return to a normal weight, and then tackle the psychological issues that contributed to the anorexia.

8   Gym Rats

Some people exorcise their demons. I exercise mine. The steady whir of the elliptical trainer, the slow blink of the red display as it tallies how long I've been running, how far I've gone, and how many calories I've burned—it's almost hypnotic. The gentle sway of my body in motion lulls my brain into thinking that everything is going to be okay. *Just a little farther, just a little longer,* I think. My destination isn't so much a completed workout as it is a state of mind.

If you would have told me before my eating disorder began that I would find myself in the grips of a powerful exercise compulsion, I probably would have laughed. Athletic pursuits were never my thing. I was neither physically coordinated nor particularly sporty. I was always picked last for teams in gym class. In college, however, working out was *de rigueur* in some of my friends, and so I found myself traipsing to the fitness center along with everyone else lest they think of me as lazy and uncaring about my health.

Mostly, I stuck to the exercise bikes because I could study at the same time. By my sophomore year, the stress of my workload increased alongside my devotion to exercise. Although my workouts were still well within the standard recommendations to promote health, I had started to grow dependent on fitness for a release of anxiety. Since so many health professionals touted exercise as a great way to handle stress, I thought all of my workouts were beneficial.

When I was seized by a particularly bad bout of depression and anxiety during my junior year, I responded by further increasing my workouts. While working out, and for a short period after, the fog would lift. I would feel okay. Without exercise, I couldn't cope. And the more I exercised, the more I found my food intake dwindled. I was trapped.

As my eating disorder evolved, so did my affinity for exercise. Besides being a powerful tool with which I could modulate anxiety and mood, exercise was how I justified eating. If I didn't exercise, I would slash my calories or stop eating all together. If I ate too much, I added extra exercise. As time passed, however, I began using food to justify exercise. If I couldn't exercise, there was no point in eating. Many days, I forced myself to at least eat minimally so that I would have the energy to complete my workout. The endorphin rush of extreme exercise only added to the high of starvation.

No one questioned my fitness devotion. Instead, I received almost endless praise. I was "dedicated." I was "good" for my thrice-daily treks to the gym, not to mention the endless pacing and secret stash of workout DVDs. I had "willpower." This praise only played into the anosognosia of anorexia. Far from being problematic, my exercise was a good thing. People admired it. People didn't praise heroin junkies or the wino on the corner. They had problems. I didn't.

I even shrugged off the injuries and physical problems that accompanied my exercise. That tendonitis in my foot? Totally from the high-heeled sandals I wore the other week. My ankle is swollen because of a change in the weather and overly salty Chinese takeout, not because my intense workouts might have caused a stress fracture. It wasn't until a searing pain developed in my left foot that no amount of pills would conquer that I reluctantly visited a doctor. By the time I walked in the door to his office, I only had one pair of shoes that I could bear to have on for more than a few minutes.

He quickly diagnosed a stress fracture and I had to wear a walking cast for the next six weeks. Had I been rational about exercise, I would have taken my diagnosis as a sign that I needed to lay off my daily workouts. Except I wasn't. So the day I got permission to remove the cast, I was back in the gym and as gung-ho as ever about continuing my workouts. Exercise became the center of my universe. I altered my work schedule to accommodate my exercise. I stopped going to social events because it might disrupt my workout schedule. I was working, exercising, or sleeping.

Eventually, both my body and mind gave out. I was shaking with anxiety, suicidal, and a physical wreck. I couldn't keep working, and my therapist again gave me an ultimatum: move home or go into the hospital. Either way, my time as a gym rat was over. I was torn between relief and utter despair. If I wasn't Carrie the Fitness Freak, then who was I? How could I cope without working out? And what in the hell would I do with all of my spare time?

Answering those questions took years. In some ways, I'm still answering them. Part of how I began to fill my spare time was researching the ideas that ultimately became this book. I couldn't understand how someone with an almost virulent hatred of sports and gym class could find herself with a life-threatening exercise addiction. Learning exactly what it was about working out that was so addicting, and what factors in my life made me so vulnerable, helped me connect the dots and create a more nuanced understanding of what made me tick.

Whether you call it exercise dependence, compulsive exercise, excessive exercise, or exercise addiction (the terms seem to be used relatively interchangeably in the literature), it's exceedingly common in eating disorders. Italian researchers assessed 165 people receiving inpatient eating disorders treatment and found that that 45 percent of them—and 80 percent of people with the restricting type of anorexia—had a clinically unhealthy relationship with exercise. One of the primary motivators of this intense activity was to burn calories, and this motivation was most prominent in individuals with the highest levels of control over their food intake (Dalle Grave *et al.*, 2008).

A trip to any commercial gym will tell you that exercising to control weight and shape is hardly unique to eating disorders. Almost any time I have a meal or snack with a group of otherwise well-adjusted women, someone will order dessert and lament the next day's treadmill penance. Although these women don't (to the best of my knowledge) have a clinical eating disorder, they do share our culture's messed-up attitude towards eating and exercise. But if many people in our society equate exercise with weight loss, then researchers need to identify other criteria that separate people with problematic exercise from the rest of the general exercising population.

Part of the problem in delineating exercise dependence is that small amounts of exercise are healthy and have a variety of health benefits. Think of it like alcohol, Brian Cook, a sports psychologist and expert on exercise dependence at the University of Kentucky, told me. "If you drink one glass of red wine each day, we know that's associated with health benefits. If you drink a bottle of red wine each day, however, we might call you an alcoholic," he said. It's easy enough to say that someone who chugs several bottles of red wine each day has a drinking problem. Most people who have alcohol dependence or addiction, however, often live in an area much more nebulous. So, too, do most people with exercise issues. It leaves researchers and clinicians without a way to draw even a tentative line between healthy and problematic exercisers.

Perhaps, they thought, the amount of time spent exercising would separate these two groups. One of the hallmarks of anorexia that has existed even in the earliest case reports is excessive physical activity (Beumont *et al.*, 1994), which could mean that exercise duration is significantly greater in the eating-disordered population. Immediately the researchers began running into problems. Elite athletes exercise and train for long periods of time, many of whom don't have a clinical eating disorder or an unhealthy attitude towards fitness (Greenleaf *et al.*, 2009). This doesn't mean that the amount of time exercised per week isn't unrelated to problematic exercise habits, just that it's not the only factor.

So in the mid-1990s, sports psychologists in the UK set out to develop a set of criteria that would easily and accurately identify exercise dependence in people with and without eating disorders. Taking a cue from the addiction literature, David Veale had previously defined someone as being dependent on exercise when they found that they needed an increasing amount of exercise to get their fix, they experienced withdrawal symptoms when they couldn't work out, and their exercise interfered with different areas of their life (Veale, 1987). Veale set out with two of his colleagues to further refine these criteria. Together, they came up with a set of seven different criteria that they believed would accurately identify exercise dependence:

- **Tolerance.** Someone finds they have to increase the amount of exercise they do in order to receive the same physical and psychological benefits.
- **Withdrawal.** If someone doesn't exercise or tries to delay exercising, they might report getting shaky, irritable, distracted, or depressed—the same signs of withdrawal seen in the abuse of illegal drugs.

- **Intensity.** Not only is someone working out longer, they're working out harder. They will increase the speed on the treadmill or increase the resistance on the exercise bike or elliptical trainer.
- **Lack of control.** Someone can't seem to stop or decrease their exercise for a significant amount of time. Their need to exercise dominates their life.
- **Duration.** Someone spends more time exercising than they would really like to. In other words, exercise becomes a giant time suck.
- **Interference with other activities.** Not only is someone spending more time working out than they want to, their physical activity is also beginning to interfere with other areas of their life, such as school, work, or social activities.
- **Continuance.** Someone might know, deep down, that their exercise is excessive and that it's causing physical and psychological harm, but they keep exercising regardless.

Veale and his colleagues developed these criteria into a 76-question Exercise Dependence Questionnaire to assess the presence and severity of the above symptoms (Ogden *et al.*, 1997). Other scientists have developed similar questionnaires, such as the Exercise Addiction Inventory (Terry *et al.*, 2004) and the Exercise Dependence Scale (Hausenblas and Downs, 2002). When these tests were administered to a general population of university students, researchers found three percent of the students met the criteria for exercise dependence or addiction (Terry *et al.*, 2004). Interestingly, measures of exercise dependence didn't seem to be related to body image concerns among university students (Hausenblas and Fallon, 2002). This seems to support the idea that the most important factors in exercise dependence are when it interferes with other areas of functioning and when someone can't decrease the amount of time they exercise (Bamber *et al.*, 2003).

"If you exercise in appropriate amounts, you can have certain benefits. But, obviously, the more you exercise, the more demand you're placing on your body," Cook said. "If that becomes something where you can't stop even though you want to and recognize that it's a problem, then that's where you start to develop exercise dependence."

The serious physical and mental harm done by exercise dependence and eating disorders is precisely why scientists and therapists need a better understanding of exactly what exercise dependence is, says eating disorders and exercise therapist Ron Thompson, co-author of the book *The Exercise Balance*. "Exercise is viewed as a positive behavior, even by people who don't exercise. Often, people assume that 'you can't get too much of a good thing.' Many think this about exercise. That is, if a little exercise is good then a lot of exercise would be better; they believe that more is better. It is not unlike how some people think about eating. That is, if fewer calories are good, then a lot fewer would be even better. Or, if low fat is good, then no fat must be better. People think these things without regard for their health," he told me. "Many assume that eating and exercise are simple processes rather than complex ones that are affected by many factors. Thus, they believe that they know all they need to know to lose weight by dietary restriction and exercise, when in fact they do not really know how their body works. Regarding eating and exercise, we need to listen to our bodies. Our bodies will communicate with us if we will listen, and the body doesn't lie. The head lies. Because many people don't listen to their bodies to tell them when they are exercising too often, too much, or too strenuously, we need criteria by which those determinations can be made."

Running Rats

Scientists' understanding of exercise dependence in humans is partially based on studies done in exercising rodents. Rats might not run on treadmills, but they do run on wheels. In the 1960s, researchers discovered that if you limited a rat's access to food and simultaneously allowed it to run on its wheel as much as it wanted, the rat would rapidly run itself to death, a phenomenon that looked eerily similar to what psychologists diagnosed as anorexia nervosa. The researchers called this behavior activity-based anorexia (Spear and Hill, 1962).

These animal models have been crucial in helping researchers understand eating disorders and excessive exercise. As their name suggests, however, animal models are only representations of what is likely to be happening in humans. A rat on a running wheel is probably not wondering whether her tail makes her butt look big or whether she should have eaten that last piece of kibble. "These models tell us a lot about the neurobiology that underpins a lot of these behaviors," says Charlotte Keating, a researcher in the Department of Medicine at Monash University in Melbourne, Australia, "but it really can't get into the complex emotional and cognitive factors that motivate people with anorexia. It's one of those areas where there's been almost an exhaustive amount of work in animal models, but the part that makes us human—the psychological side—is really underdeveloped."

These models might not tell us much in the way of what motivates a person in the midst of anorexia nervosa, but they do indicate that their brains are being held in the thrall of a powerful neurobiological drive that compels them to starve, binge, purge, and over-exercise. Especially for exercise, researchers are still trying to parse out whether that biological drive stems from an unceasing search for reward.

Discussions of exercise are generally done with a tone of dread. Exercise is something people feel they "have to" do in order to maintain their physique, burn calories, and stay healthy. Before I started exercising regularly while in college, I, too, thought exercise and gym class were appalling inventions. If working out so commonly fills people with dread, it made me wonder how exercising could become addicting in the first place. Generally, people don't find themselves addicted to something they find seriously unpleasant.

Although many people regard exercise as a "have to" rather than a "get to," researchers have known for decades that moderate exercise provides some well-known physical and mental health benefits. The physiological benefits of exercise aren't nearly as important as the psychological ones in understanding how a sports-phobe like me can get hooked. For many psychologists treating depression and anxiety, exercise remains at the top of the list for simple ways people can start to feel better.

A 2009 study presented at the annual meeting of the Society for Neuroscience found that rats who exercised regularly were better able to cope with stress. In their experiments, neuroscientists at Princeton University divided rats into two groups, one of which exercised regularly, whereas the other did not. The researchers placed each rat into a deep pool of cold water that required them to swim to safety. The rats find this task stressful and unpleasant. When the researchers looked at each rat's brain, they found that the stress of swimming had activated genes in neurons throughout the brain. But when they looked closer at the brains of the exercising rats, they found that the new neurons created by running didn't show these same signs of stress. Exercise had protected the brain from stress (Reynolds, 2009). "The rats had created, through running, a brain that seemed biochemically, molecularly, calm," wrote Gretchen Reynolds in the *New York Times* (n.p.).

Considering that people with anorexia have high anxiety (Kaye *et al.*, 2004) and high levels of serotonin (Kaye and Weltzin, 1991), a molecularly calm brain would be rather spectacular. It turns out that exercise's ability to reduce stress might be partially explained by its modulation of serotonin levels. When researchers at the University of Colorado, Boulder continually stressed rats, they found that serotonin levels in their brains zoomed upwards. In rats that ran on a running wheel for several weeks before being stressed, however, serotonin and anxiety levels remained low. This means, the researchers concluded, that exercise has both anti-depressant and anti-anxiety effects (Greenwood and Fleshner, 2008).

All of these results may help explain why psychologists have long noted links between anorexia, obligatory exercise, and obsessive-compulsive disorder. In anorexia, exercise is often linked to specific numbers, whether it's calories burned, distance covered, or time spent exercising. Whether laps, minutes, miles, or fat grams, exercise is carefully measured. Anything less than the desired number means the entire workout session doesn't count. In this sense, it sounds a lot like the rituals seen in OCD.

Canadian researchers compared obsessive-compulsive traits in a group of 53 women with anorexia nervosa, of whom 22 had signs of excessive exercise and 31 did not. The women with anorexia who exercised excessively had more signs of obsessive-compulsive beliefs, behaviors, and personality characteristics, as well as higher levels of self-oriented perfectionism, than anorexic women who didn't over-exercise (Davis *et al.*, 1998). In a separate study, these researchers found that, in general, the higher a person's symptoms of OCD, the more they exercised (Davis *et al.*, 1995).

Some of the obsessive beliefs about exercise in anorexia seem to be linked to exercise's ability to modulate mood and anxiety (Naylor *et al.*, 2011). *If I can't exercise*, I remember thinking, *I will go crazy*. Exercise became a compulsion I used to relieve any uncomfortable feeling, from sadness to frustration to fear. The use of exercise as a compulsion to control negative mood was especially prominent in patients with long-standing eating disorders (Bratland-Sanda *et al.*, 2011).

Excessive exercise seems to be linked not only to OCD but also to obsessive-compulsive personality traits (Davis and Kaptein, 2006; Shroff *et al.*, 2006), like a need to follow the rules, perfectionism, and the desire for objects to be organized and symmetrical (Anderluh *et al.*, 2003). Just as these personality traits seem to be heritable in anorexia patients, so, too, does excessive exercise. The parents of children with anorexia appear to be more active, on average, than parents of healthy controls (Davis *et al.*, 2005). In anorexia nervosa, Davis and Kaptein (2006) hypothesize that obligatory exercise may be "a culture-bound variant of OCD" (p. 209). The researchers concluded that OCD and excessive exercise create a feedback loop that sufferers find hard to break (Davis *et al.*, 1995).

Climbing the StairMaster to Nowhere

Exercise's powerful mood-altering and anxiety-lifting properties provide a doorway through which people can become addicted. My friend Ruth has been struggling for years with a serious exercise addiction, and she told me that this aspect of exercise has been the hardest thing for her to shake. I first met Ruth online more than five years ago, and our shared love of biology, books, and All Things Nerdy cemented our friendship. When I finally met her in person last year, I felt as if I had known her most of my life. Even the role of exercise in both of our eating disorders had an eerie parallel. Although Ruth was an active kid—her favorite sports were softball and rock climbing—she began to exercise for the purpose of burning calories when her eating disorder developed at the age of 12.

"When my eating disorder first started, I was exercising, and it was really obsessive and rigid, but compared to what it became later, it wasn't all that much," Ruth said. "But I was so rigid with my running, and never taking a day off even when I was extremely nutritionally stressed, that I basically destroyed my knees by the time I was 21."

Ironically, Ruth's compulsion to exercise, combined with self-starvation, left her with neither the time nor the energy to pursue the team sports she loved. As she told me this, I nodded in agreement. I stopped playing flag football and intramural basketball and volleyball in college as I felt I could get in a better workout on the stair stepper. In high school, Ruth became such a fixture on the treadmill at her local YMCA that when she didn't show up one day, the staff there called the police and asked them to go check on her. Ruth was fine, but she had bought herself a treadmill and so saw no need to keep going to the Y.

As Ruth went off to college, exercise began to eclipse the food restriction in importance. "Every time I've had a crash and a recovery, food has become less of an issue and exercise more of an issue with each iteration, mostly as a means for compensating for the extra food, and then it just sort of took on a life of its own," Ruth said. "When I couldn't run any more, the exercise got really out of control volume-wise. I needed that endorphin hit, and no matter what I did or for how long, I couldn't get the same hit as I did with running."

While at college, Ruth realized that, in order to do all of the things she dreamed of doing, she needed to tackle her eating disorder. Like I learned the hard way, conquering the exercise demon can be a very difficult task. "It became more of an OCD or anxiety thing than anything else. Not that there isn't a fear of gaining weight or of having a fat day if I feel I haven't moved enough, but it's mostly OCD. Stopping two minutes ahead of when I normally do on the machine is really stressful, even though I know that I will burn a completely insignificantly fewer amount of calories," she told me. "If I was anxious, exercising made me feel like I had done something about it."

The years dragged on, and although her desire to get her exercising under control remained as she left college to begin graduate studies at a different university, her ability to actually do so remained much more nebulous. "It's just how my day is. It's what I do, what I'm used to. It gets really hard to change that because all of a sudden you don't know how to structure your day because your routine has all of these big holes," Ruth said.

Just a few months ago, Ruth had a discussion with her boyfriend (who is, ironically enough, pursuing his own Ph.D. in clinical psychology) about her desire to be a university professor and all the work that would entail. As the pair chatted, it became clear to Ruth that, to live the life she desired, the exercise addiction would have to go. With the help of a supportive therapist and dietitian, Ruth has taken small but serious steps to decrease her workouts. "I'm at a point in my career where I just can't let it consume and structure my day," she said. "I want to be more involved with my community and my co-workers. I just reached an exhaustion point with how much exercise was controlling my life."

Talking to Ruth made me realize just how addictive exercise could really be. Neither of us realized at first that exercise really could be addicting until we were already trapped. Even now, when my exercise addiction is under good control, my first impulse when stressed is to hit the gym. I crave it, like an alcoholic craves booze or a junkie craves heroin. The biggest difference between us is that society gives Ruth and me a gigantic pat on the back when we go in search of our next hit.

One of the most common phrases when discussing exercise addiction is "endorphin high," and these powerful chemicals produced during intense exercise can induce a euphoric feeling. An endorphin is an opiate chemical synthesized by the body, and it gives the same pain-relieving and exhilarating feelings provided by morphine and heroin. The body makes endorphins to help blunt the pain of childbirth and dull the muscle and joint aches that build up while running or exercising for long periods of time (Goldfarb and Jamurtas, 1997).

Endorphins work by, among other things, stimulating the release of the neurotransmitter dopamine. The flood of dopamine in the brain not only causes the euphoric feeling (similar to the high experienced by users of illicit drugs) but it also leads to changes in how neurons connect to one another. Repeated floods of dopamine essentially rewire the brain and a person can find they are dependent on exercise. At this point, exercise is as much about avoiding withdrawal as it is about seeking the endorphin high.

The physical signs of exercise dependence look remarkably similar to the abuse of heroin and other opiates. Robin Kanarek, a psychologist at Tufts University in Boston, initially began studying the relationship between dopamine and exercise as a potential treatment for addiction. To replace the dopamine surge from their illicit drugs, Kanarek thought, perhaps moderate exercise would be a feel-good substitute. So Kanarek divided rats into two groups, one of which was allowed continuous access to a running wheel, whereas the others weren't. To simulate activity-based anorexia, she then placed half of each group on a food-restricted diet, only allowing them access to kibble one hour each day.

Not surprisingly, the rats with restricted food intake and continuous wheel access lost the most weight. The researchers then gave the rats a drug called naloxone, which blocks the body's ability to respond to opiates and is used to stimulate withdrawal in heroin addicts. The exercising rats began trembling, chattering their teeth, and drooping their eyelids—all signs of opiate withdrawal. The food-restricted exercising rats showed the most signs of withdrawal. "Excessive running shares similarities with drug-taking behavior," the authors concluded (Kanarek *et al.*, 2009, p. 911).

The Punishment Paradox

Unlike drug-taking behavior, however, exercise has an element of punishment to it. This punishing aspect can be seen in descriptions of exercise even from people without eating disorders. People describe an upcoming exercise session as penance for eating too much. I meted out the most unpleasant and grueling workouts after I over-indulged or bombed a test at school. Even as I actively sought to marinate my brain in endorphins, I was attempting to punish myself.

Keating calls this curious blend of pain and pleasure "reward contamination." The brain processes both reward and punishment in an area of the brain called the anterior cingulate cortex (ACC). The ACC is filled with dopamine receptors, which is what makes it so sensitive to both reward and punishment. People find something rewarding when they experience an unexpected burst of dopamine. Dopamine and the ACC are also involved in punishment, only it involves a drop in dopamine instead of a surge (Schultz, 2007). The neurons responsive to reward and punishment in the brain are very close together—so close, Keating says, that their messages can sometimes be confused. This neurological confusion, Keating believes, may help explain why so many sufferers cling to their illness even as it destroys their lives.

"Despite being very sick and in a very dire situation, individuals [with anorexia] engaged in really damaging behaviors. It seemed like there should be a point at which the brain said you have to stop, that it's not as healthy and rewarding behavior as it should be. The behaviors should have a natural limit of escalation," Keating said. In anorexia, however, there wasn't. As a person's health deteriorates, in fact, eating-disordered behaviors only seem to escalate.

Keating (and many others who work with eating disorders) couldn't quite explain this. If starvation and excessive exercise were so rewarding, then why did people continue even when the rewarding aspect had stopped? And how did such punishing behaviors become rewarding in the first place? Keating found part of her answer when she read a 2007 study by Angela Wagner, Walter Kaye, and colleagues. Because of this conflict between reward and punishment, and the predilection towards asceticism and the denial of pleasure, researchers wanted to know how the brains of women recovered from anorexia processed rewards. With this answer, they could better understand how they could endure starvation and why they might seek it out to begin with.

Wagner, Kaye, and their colleagues asked 13 women who had recovered from the restricting type of anorexia (the restricting type has the strongest association with asceticism) and 13 healthy control women to participate in a gambling game while inside an fMRI machine. The game was simple: guess whether a hidden card was greater or less than five. Study participants could choose any number between one and nine, except for five. A person won $2 if she was right, lost $1 if she was wrong, and lost $0.50 if she didn't make a guess within the allotted time.

Right after they learned whether they had guessed correctly, the fMRI analyzed how their brains processed that information. In the control women, the brain's response to winning and losing looked very different. Someone could tell whether a control woman had guessed correctly just by looking at a graph of activity levels in the anterior ventral striatum, another area of the brain involved in reward processing. With the recovered anorexic women, however, winning or losing looked the same. Just like a color-blind person can't distinguish between red and green, people with anorexia can't tell the difference between reward and punishment. It all feels the same (Wagner *et al.*, 2007).

"This seems like a validation to the idea that there may be some sort of neural mechanism that fails to appropriately process the rewarding or punishing behaviors or external stimuli," Keating said. To someone with anorexia, food and eating don't carry the normal rewards, nor do starvation and compulsive exercise elicit the standard punishing feelings. They all get blurred together in the brain, similar to how someone with color blindness may grab a red crayon to color the grass. They can't tell the difference between the two.

"There's lots of evidence to suggest that patients process reward and punishment using the same neural mechanisms, whereas healthy controls don't," Keating said. An anorexia patient who looks at images of underweight people will show activation in the areas of the brain associated with reward, and will be far more satisfied with these images than healthy women.

"It seems that the same reward-linked stimuli for a healthy control are not necessarily the same for an anorexia patient. It does seem to be linked to very key symptoms of the illness, like body image disturbances, excessive exercise, and self-starvation," Keating said. People with anorexia seem to find satisfaction with starved bodies and demanding exercise that other people find punitive or even repulsive. This satisfaction, then, helps explain why starvation can persist even in the face of grave bodily harm: the punishing nature of these behaviors is exactly what makes them rewarding.

"Is the opposite also true?" I asked Keating. We had spent the last chunk of time discussing how someone with anorexia could find a normally punishing activity like excessive exercise rewarding, but I wanted to know whether researchers had studied whether other anorexia sufferers also found seemingly rewarding activities to be rather torturous.

I told Keating about a birthday party my parents had for me two years after my initial diagnosis and hospitalization. I met them at a local deli for dinner, and then we went back to my apartment for cake. A simple enough shindig, but I couldn't wait for it to be over. The idea of eating at a restaurant was enough to fill me with dread, not to mention cake and a celebration. I picked at my dinner, miserable, and the cake was an encore presentation of dinner. Then, I had to unwrap presents that I was convinced I didn't deserve or even want. "These normal things that should have been rewarding felt, ultimately, very punishing," I said.

"It's such a good example because it's one of those things where, if you look at it objectively, you think that it's a party, so it must be good, you should enjoy it, it's about you, it's a celebration of you," Keating said. "But, as you said, it's actually torturous."

"I remember thinking that I wished no one would have come so that I could have had my apple for dinner and then gone for a run for several hours. I just wanted everyone to go away," I said.

"It's something that's not really talked about in terms of the scientific literature," Keating said. In so many of my interviews with sufferers and loved ones, however, I heard tales of difficulties at Christmas, birthdays, and other holidays. Patients were convinced they didn't deserve their gifts, refused to accept them, and stormed out of the house in a whirlwind of frustration and despair. Looking at these situations through the lens of Keating's reward contamination theory, I understood my own behavior better. This hatred of celebrations didn't confirm my awfulness as a human being, as I thought, it only meant that my brain was seriously confused.

Here, too, I could see aspects of asceticism coming into play, I told Keating. "The punishing nature of denying yourself gets blurred and starts to feel rewarding because you feel good that you're able to do without," I said.

"It's a conflict," Keating responded. "In one aspect there's the part where you know that what you're doing isn't good for you, but it also feels good, in a way."

In my search for understanding my exercise issues, I was coming to understand so many other quirks of my psyche. Why, for example, I felt tremendously guilty about owning nice things. I refused to fix the air conditioning on my car, even in the sweltering Southern summer, because it made me feel less guilty. Or why I had trouble spending money when going out shopping with my friends. Except for books, the thought of buying something filled me with dread. Reward contamination seemed to explain all of these seemingly unrelated behaviors.

Whether anorexia is a cause of or results from this neurological confusion remains to be seen. Researchers also haven't yet studied whether reward contamination results from an inability to distinguish pleasure from punishment or that people with anorexia find punishing activities rewarding.

"There's not a lot of work that's been done on the rewarding nature of excessive exercise in humans," Keating said. One of the reasons for this is the difficulty in getting an exercising person to remain still while inside a brain scanner. If the person inside the scanner moves their head even just a fraction of a millimeter, they can distort the image of their brain's activity (Van Dijk *et al.*, 2012). Getting an accurate image of brain activity in someone running on a treadmill or even sitting on a stationary bicycle has thus far remained out of reach.

Keating is far from the only scientist researching the hypothesis that the excessive exercise often seen in anorexia is linked to altered reward processing. An article from the Dana Foundation (a US-based non-profit organization that provides research grants and public information about brain science) called anorexia nervosa "a mortal clash between reward and hunger" (Dietrich and Horvath, 2009). In their article, they write:

> One clue to the intensity of this clash is the elevated level of physical activity in patients with anorexia nervosa, a symptom that people have reported for more than 100 years. Several studies have established a relationship between obsessive-compulsive characteristics and exercise frequency in women with strenuous daily exercise routines and in hospitalized female patients with anorexia nervosa. In the patient group, preoccupation with weight was associated with both the frequency of exercise and pathological attitudes toward it. Addictive and obsessive-compulsive personalities contributed to excessive exercise because of their obligatory, pathological thoughts promoting it. Among anorexia nervosa patients, those who exercise excessively have more bulimic symptoms, higher levels of general psychopathology about eating and a greater degree of body dissatisfaction, anxiety, somatization (physical symptoms with a psychological origin), depression and irritability. Scientists view the tendencies toward mental alertness and continued normal-to-high activity levels (despite insufficient nutrition and weight loss) as being relatively unique to anorexia nervosa patients, versus individuals who experience semi-starvation due to causes such as illness, chemotherapy or famine.
>
> (n.p.)

"It's definite that things like endorphins, dopamine, serotonin, and any other reward-linked chemicals, are involved in exercise when it's normal, and exercise when it becomes pathological. I think that's consistently an aspect of runner's high. When patients engage in the behavior that leads to a release of neurochemicals that enables them to push through a barrier, their brain is bathed in a protective mechanism that doesn't allow them to realize the pathological nature of their behaviors. The brain fails to let the body know that enough is enough," Keating said.

This happens, Keating noted, not only in patients with eating disorders but also in elite athletes, like marathon runners. "When you look at the relationship between exercise and eating disorders, distance runners were one of the first groups to be studied," Cook said.

A 1983 paper in the *New England Journal of Medicine* raised the intriguing idea that many male distance runners appeared to share many similar behaviors with female anorexia patients. In interviews with more than 60 marathon and trail runners, Alayne Yates, a psychiatrist at the University of Arizona, and colleagues found that these men shared many personality traits with women with anorexia. They were driven, and had high standards for themselves, a tolerance of physical pain, and a tendency towards depression (Yates *et al.*, 1983). A more rigorous study published a year later found that these male runners didn't share the same degree of psychopathology that the women with anorexia did (Blumenthal *et al.*, 1984). However, when researchers looked more closely at female distance runners, they found that 14 percent had symptoms of anorexia, and that the most highly ranked athletes were the most likely to have these symptoms (Weight and Noakes, 1987).

A desire to become better at cycling was what triggered Scott's downward spiral into anorexia at the age of 14. "I'd ridden bikes with my dad since I was eight years old, and I wanted to get more into racing," he said. This desire to improve at his sport was combined with Scott's new awareness of food and calories. The first time he thought about calories or restricting, he said, happened when he was visiting his older sister at college. Eating with her in the cafeteria, Scott became painfully aware of the values society attached to different foods.

"I didn't want the pasta, and I thought I should have more vegetables," Scott said. Always a picky eater, his initial interest in healthful eating seemed like a good thing—the teenager was expanding his palate. Except that Scott wasn't expanding his palate as much as he was substituting higher calorie foods for fruits and vegetables at the same time he was increasing the amount of time he spent cycling. As his exercising increased, so did his restrictive behaviors, and his weight began to drop.

The combination of Scott's gender (many doctors still believe that eating disorders and Y chromosomes are mutually exclusive) and his inability to see his behavior as problematic (common in anorexia in males and females) meant that it took nearly two years for Scott and his parents to receive a diagnosis of anorexia. "I was really baffled when the doctors told me I had anorexia nervosa," Scott said. "I didn't know too much before that about eating disorders, and really didn't have an idea of what they involved. I never thought of it as a disease as I do now."

With the help of his parents and a supportive treatment team, Scott began putting on weight, although tackling the exercise piece remained more difficult. "Riding was my way to get out of the house and away from my need to eat," he said. "If I went riding, I had to have more to eat to make up for it, but this was easier than not riding."

Ironically, what helped Scott reduce his compulsive exercising was actually his love for cycling itself. While he was ill, Scott tried to do a bike ride across Indiana with his dad, but wound up injuring his knee and couldn't complete the ride. Getting healthy enough to do this helped prod him through many difficult moments. "I wanted to do the things I wanted to do, and not be held back by anything," Scott said.

Scott, a recent high school graduate now in his twenties and doing well, like many men, fell into anorexia through exercising. Although the studies are limited, researchers have found that compulsive exercise is even more common in males with eating disorders than it is in females. A 2002 survey published in the *Journal of American College Health* found that eight percent of college-aged men met criteria for a clinical exercise disorder (O'Dea and Abraham, 2002). One study done by the Eating Disorders Program at Rogers Memorial Hospital (one of the only programs in the United States to have a separate program for men with eating disorders) reported that men were more likely than women to use exercise to compensate for calories eaten (Weltzin *et al.*, 2005). As well, men had more trouble managing their eating disorder symptoms during treatment (Bean *et al.*, 2005).

Besides a mentality that can handle the dogged persistence necessary to run 26.2 miles or exercise on a machine for hours at a time, the excessive exercise in elite athletes and eating disorder patients of both genders, to me, shares another peculiar similarity. The repetitive motion of such activities becomes hypnotic, whether it's the rhythmic pounding of feet on pavement or the endless whir of an elliptical trainer. The body slips into a mindless rhythm and seems almost to propel itself forward on its own accord, no mental input necessary. Behavioral addiction and gambling researcher Natasha Schull at the Massachusetts Institute of Technology calls this "the zone."

It's not the reward of the big win that keeps gamblers coming back for more. Instead, it's the lure of the zone, which Schull describes as:

> a dissociative state or trance in which players lose a sense of time, space and physical embodiment, consumed totally by the spinning numbers, symbols or electronic card hands before their eyes. Because gambling machines don't require social interaction (as is the case in table games such as poker), they let people get into and stay in a state that is not dissimilar to, but far more intense than, watching TV; players describe the zone as a compelling, mesmerizing condition of intense concentration—an almost out-of-body experience. Heavy machine gamblers come to crave this state, says Schull. "It's about wanting to keep playing," she says. "People will actually get disappointed or irritated if they win a jackpot because it may

freeze up the machine and interrupt their flow. Then they have to sit there until they lose it. Walking away with the jackpot is not an option" in their state of mind.

(Schorow, 2009, n.p.)

I first read this description of the zone, and I immediately started yelling "Yes!" in my apartment in what must have sounded like a re-enactment of Meg Ryan's famous scene in *When Harry Met Sally*. Exercise didn't give me an out-of-body experience as much as it gave me an out-of-my-life experience. When I was in the gym, plugged into my iPod, smartphone blissfully out of reach and switched off, all of the stressors in my life seemed to melt away. Upcoming tests and papers didn't matter, nor did that looming due date on a work project. I'll confess that the knowledge of burning calories did hold some sway over me, but what I loved most was the zone. However exhausted I might have been at the end of a workout, and however alluring a nice, long shower sounded, I felt a knot of dread in my stomach as I climbed off the machine. I had to return to real life—talk about a downer.

Physical symptoms of exercise dependence are significant, Cook noted, but the psychological aspects of an exercise compulsion are under-studied. Cigarette smokers usually know that smoking is bad for them, and that they should quit, but their inability to do so is frequently linked to nicotine addiction. Which is true, Cook pointed out, but there are also significant behavioral and psychological reasons that people find themselves unable to put out that cigarette. They might smoke to relieve stress, or look cool, or maybe even just out of habit. It's the same with those addicted to exercise. Besides the endorphin rush and calorie burn, the people I interviewed for this book frequently cited the mood-regulating effects of exercise, the relief of stress and anxiety, and their identity as a so-called gym rat as reasons that kept them going to the gym.

"Too much exercise has negative effects on the body. It may stop menstruation. It may cause stress fractures or overuse injuries. The immune system in the body is usually facilitated by exercise, but it works on a volume threshold basis. That is, up to a point, immunity increases, but it begins to decrease when too much exercise creates a stress response," Thompson said. "Basically, the people who exercise too much are out of balance and are exercising for the wrong reasons. They often believe that their motivation is to improve health but actually compromise their health. Those who exercise healthfully are probably more balanced in terms of their exercise, their eating, and the balance between their exercise and eating, rather than exercising solely for the purpose of burning calories. Many of these unhealthy exercisers cannot change this without professional help, but they don't even know they need assistance."

Getting that assistance isn't always that easy, however. Not all therapists understand the danger of compulsive exercise, nor is it easy to stop exercising on your own. It took many years and even more false starts before I was able to integrate a healthy level of physical activity into my life. Thoughts of burning calories still occur to me, of course, but I try to focus on the other aspects of movement that I find enjoyable: the wind in my hair, the satisfaction of a job well done. I still feel the occasional twinge pulling me back to the gym, but I try to focus on the tremendous time suck that exercise addiction really is.

9 Stepping Up to the (Dinner) Plate

I stared at my plate of fish sticks, tater tots, and cold green peas. After a two hour-long staring contest, I knew every ridge of minced fried fish and every contour of pea almost by heart. Despite my protestations that I could not, would not, eat this fish (not in a house, not with a mouse, I will not eat it, Sam I am!), the tray remained in front of me. In order to leave the table, I had to eat.

It was the second day of my third hospitalization for anorexia, and I had only picked at the food on my trays until then. No stupid doctors or padded rooms or threats of nasogastric tubes were going to get me to eat. No siree.

My psychiatrist had been treating eating disorders for more than 20 years by the time he met me, and I'm fairly certain he had encountered my type before: stubborn, angry, and utterly terrified of eating. He didn't shame me and tell me how much I was hurting my parents or how much the hospital stay was costing. He didn't mention my weakening vital signs or ask why someone with so much potential would throw away her life. He simply instituted a strategy known as tray sitting.

Tray sitting meant the following: at meal times, you sit in front of your tray until every bite of food is gone. That means no visitors, no bathroom breaks, nothing. Just you, your chair, and your tray. When my doctor told me that he had put me on a tray sitting protocol , I almost laughed. Surely they were joking. They weren't.

When I was called down to the dining room for dinner, I brought a book to read. If I was going to have to sit here all night, I figured, then I may as well not be bored. A tech pulled up a chair and sat down beside me. I pulled out my book and started to read. I hadn't made it past the first paragraph when the tech neatly plucked the book out of my hands. I gaped. The tech looked almost amused. I hurled invective at him—how *dare* he take away my reading material? Would *he* want to eat this crap? Hadn't he heard of something called *obesity*?!? I was not eating, and that was that.

He raised an eyebrow and calmly drawled, "Honey, I got all night. I don't mind sitting here. I don't get to sit down much on the job, and this is a nice break. So take as long as you want. I have plenty of crossword puzzles to catch up on."

"You can't stay here all night," I told him. "Eventually, you'll have to go home and I can have my book back."

"There's a night shift that is probably as eager to sit here as I am," he replied. "You'll get your book back as soon as you finish your dinner."

Which is when the staring contest started. As I stared down my long-cold dinner, I snuck furtive looks at the tech sitting beside me. He seemed totally unbothered by his task. He finished one crossword puzzle, then another. Visiting hours were soon, and if I wanted to see my parents, I had to finish my dinner. I truly didn't have an out. If I didn't eat everything on my tray, I knew my doctor would order a nasogastric tube. If I refused that, he would get a court order to have one placed. So ever reluctantly, I picked up my fork and started eating.

My recovery didn't stay on some sort of magical trajectory after the Curious Incident of the Fish Sticks in the Nighttime. I relapsed hard, again and again. I entered other treatment facilities that made eating and weight gain much more optional. Choosing to eat would be empowering, I was told. I needed to work on the issues first. Then I would eat. I needed prayers and magic ponies to help work through the resistance. The fact that many of these theories had no evidence to support their use didn't stop some of the best-known eating disorder treatment facilities in the United States from using them.

Eventually, I burned through all of my money and a large chunk of my parents' in a desperate attempt to figure out how to choose to overcome my eating disorder. A new therapist I started seeing after the longest and most expensive of treatment stays used the same tactic as my psychiatrist did so many years ago. Eating wasn't optional. If I wanted to live at home (broke and jobless, as much as I hated being nearly 30 and still living with my parents, I realized it was still better than living in a box on the street corner), and if I wanted to continue seeing my therapist (who I adored), then I needed to eat. I wasn't given a choice. My back against the wall, and having officially run out of options, I gave in and started eating.

For a disorder that is supposedly "about control," it seems almost counterintuitive that having no say in one's food intake, exercise habits, and about a bazillion other little daily things would be so successful. Orders to recover didn't work. Cajoling didn't work. Bribery didn't work. Eliminating every option but recovery, however, did work. Reading a recent study in the journal *Psychological Science* made me realize why.

Two groups of students read a mock news article about how lowering speed limits in their town would make everyone safer. One group read that the new laws were definitely going into effect, whereas the other group read that it was likely the laws would go into effect, but there was a small chance the government would overturn the suggestion. Neither group especially liked the new restrictions, but the first group had significantly more support for the new law than the second group. Our brains have very contradictory responses to rules, the researchers concluded. We do our best to get around rules we don't like, devising elaborate plans and equally elaborate excuses to get away with it. Once we realize there's no way out, however, we do our best to try and live with it (Laurin *et al.*, 2012).

It's why the ability not to eat was always enough for me to evade recovery. In a press release from the Association for Psychological Science (publishers of *Psychological Science*), lead author Kristin Laurin compared the findings to why playing hard to get can be so effective in romantic relationships. She says:

> If this person is telling me no, but I perceive that as not totally absolute, if I still think I have a shot, that's just going to strengthen my desire and my feeling, that's going to make me think I need to fight to win the person over. If instead I believe no, I definitely don't have a shot with this person, then I might rationalize it and decide that I don't like them that much anyway.
>
> (Menon, 2011, n.p.)

A person with an eating disorder might rationalize eating and weight gain, then, as it being forced upon them by parents and doctors. It makes the anxiety bearable because there really is no way out. My therapist calls this "choice amongst lack of alternatives." Eat at home, eat in the hospital, or eat at a treatment center. Not eating is not a choice.

Holly felt backed into a corner for different reasons. Holly, a 37-year-old lifelong Midwesterner, has struggled with anorexia since her early teens. "I always did weird things with food," she said. "Like every Halloween I would come home with these big bags of candy, and I would sort them real meticulously, put them in a special drawer in my room, and then I wouldn't allow myself to eat any of it. I would open the drawer and look at the candy, but I would never eat any of it."

She also liked to play what she called The Starving Game, where she wouldn't go home for lunch from her elementary school. Holly simply pretended that she was a kid with no food. "For whatever reason, that sort of game was pleasurable for me," she said. Her odd food behaviors took on a more sinister turn in middle and high school, when she began more systematically restricting her food intake. But Holly, a self-described odd ball, deflected any concerns about her dwindling food intake and weight with an aura of black eyeliner and hostility. If anyone expressed care or concern, Holly responded with venom, almost like a mama bear protecting her cub. No one could touch her eating disorder.

Her eating disorder continued to escalate when she was in college until she met Mark, the man who eventually became her husband. For the first time, Holly found someone or something that could break through anorexia's iron grip. She began to force herself to eat one meal a day in the college cafeteria—previously uncharted territory—and gagged on every bite. Slowly her weight rose, and Holly began to think she had put anorexia behind her.

She hadn't, of course, and her eating disorder became a quiet but steady presence in her life, accompanying her through her wedding day and the birth of her two little boys. The stress of caring for two boys began to take its toll, and Holly once again found herself cutting back on eating. One day at lunchtime, Holly found herself unable to get up off the couch. She had gone far too long without eating and was too weak to stand. Knowing that her children needed lunch, Holly phoned her sister to come over and get them some food. Her sister called Holly's husband, and both of them dragged Holly to the doctor.

Which is how, over 20 years after her disorder started, Holly found herself addressing anorexia with a therapist for the first time. Tired of fielding incessant questions from concerned family members, but still wanting their support, Holly created an email support group that consisted of her husband, mother, four older sisters, and six friends. When she needs extra support, something changes in her treatment plan, or when she got together with her family for her first Christmas in recovery, Holly sends a message with updates and helpful advice about how to be of support. Replies aren't mandatory, Holly said, but she still receives at least two to three replies per message.

"You can't do it alone. You need your family's support," Holly said.

Shortly before I spoke with Holly, she began backsliding. Faced with an ultimatum from her therapist that it was turn things around or go into the hospital, Holly's mom came to live with her and her family to give her more support. Within a few weeks, Holly had regained the weight she lost, although her mom continues to stick around full-time. "If she wasn't here and I was making my own lunch, I can tell you it would be a heck of a lot smaller," Holly said.

Holly's family has closed ranks to protect her from the eating disorder. It's something I know she's grateful for, even if she can't always appreciate it every day (I never did). But their unflagging support has given Holly the motivation to push forward, even when times get tough. "When I weighed in at the dietitian's office and she told me all the weight had come back on, it was so distressing, and yet everyone else around me had these big smiles on their faces," she said. "And I thought, you know what? That's worth something."

Whereas parents have traditionally been blamed for causing an eating disorder in their children, a growing amount of research is pointing to the opposite fact: not only do parents not cause eating disorders, they can also be crucial to helping their sick child get better (le Grange *et al.*, 2010). Much of this shift in thinking has come from the promising results of a treatment for adolescents with anorexia and bulimia known as family-based treatment (FBT), popularly referred to as the Maudsley Method.

Named for the eponymous London hospital where it was developed, the Maudsley Method was developed in the early 1980s when researchers wanted to do something to stem the tide of relapse and hospital readmissions. The families they worked with were far from perfect, but the researchers figured they were good enough to be trained to help their children through the rocky phase immediately after hospital discharge. The parents could emulate the firm but supportive stance of the nursing staff and ensure that their children ate and digested all their food. Much to the eating disorder community's surprise, this approach worked. Teens who received this type of family therapy had better outcomes and fewer readmissions than teens who received individual therapy (Russell *et al.*, 1987).

Over the next few years, psychologists at the Maudsley Hospital further refined and manualized their treatment into what is now known as FBT. Its developers divided FBT into three phases. Phase One requires parents to take over control of what the adolescent eats and when. The primary focus of treatment at this point is weight gain and returning the teen to more normal eating habits. Phase Two usually begins after the teen is at or near a normal weight, and the parents begin to hand control of food and eating back over to their child. And Phase Three deals with any co-occurring diagnoses, family issues that haven't been resolved, and the normal tasks of adolescent growth and development.

The success of these early trials meant that clinicians needed to rethink the role of the family in the development of an eating disorder (Dare *et al.*, 1990). If parents were so toxic that they caused an eating disorder, then they shouldn't be expected to help their children get well. Except that psychologists at the Maudsley were finding that was exactly what was happening (le Grange *et al.*, 1992).

It's all well and good that FBT appears to help adolescents with a relatively short course of anorexia (less than three years) recover faster, but scientists needed to know whether these changes held up over the long term. A five-year follow-up study found that they did (Eisler *et al.*, 1997). Patients who had presented to treatment within three years of illness onset had better FBT outcomes than more chronic patients, although no treatments work as well on chronic anorexia as they do on a shorter course of illness.

More recently, a larger, controlled trial of FBT showed the same results. For the trial, 120 teens with anorexia were randomly assigned to either FBT or individual psychotherapy. Teens receiving FBT gained weight and returned to normal teenage life more quickly than those receiving individual psychotherapy (Lock *et al.*, 2010). This trial was important both because of the larger number of participants, which allowed researchers to identify more subtle differences between the two treatments, and because the patients and families were randomly assigned the different treatments. This showed that it wasn't just "special" families that could make FBT work. With the right coaching and support, many families could find FBT a successful treatment for their sick child, even for young adults (Chen *et al.*, 2010) and those with bulimia (le Grange *et al.*, 2007).

Despite being colloquially referred to as "highly effective" and the "gold standard in anorexia treatment" (Mitchum, 2010), most teens and their parents aren't offered FBT, says clinical psychologist Sarah Ravin. Typically, they discover it on their own and have to demand better treatment. "It's pretty much the rule, rather than the exception, that a previous clinician who was an eating disorders specialist, quote-unquote, has said that won't work for your family," she said.

"I've worked with many families very successfully in FBT who have been told by another clinician that it won't work for them," Ravin said. She told me of a family she's currently working with where the 15-year-old daughter was in traditional individual psychotherapy for anorexia. The parents found out about FBT through online research, and told the therapist that they would like to try this with their daughter, especially since she wasn't making much progress in her current therapy. Both the therapist and dietitian told the parents that using FBT would be "absolutely detrimental" to their daughter. The parents persevered, however, and ultimately began FBT with Ravin. Three months later, the daughter has dramatically improved, although she still has a way to go.

The reasons many psychotherapists seem to advise against FBT seems to have more to do with the therapist's own beliefs about the role of parents in eating disorders than it does with the actual family. Ravin said that most clinicians treating eating disorders believe that parental support hobbles the young person's recovery. "This really stems from myths about etiology, that people with anorexia have over-controlling and over-bearing parents, and they need to find their voice and assert their needs, and empower themselves and all that stuff," Ravin said.

My mother wasn't remotely over-controlling, I pointed out, until I got sick. "Most therapists don't seem to realize that the over-controlling parents might be a result of the eating disorder, rather than the cause," I said. While it's true that temporarily turning over control of my food to my parents did rein in my independence, it was a necessary, short-term step. When I busted up my ankle, I had to wear a cast and use crutches for several months while the injury healed. No one was afraid that I would never walk again if I used crutches or that I would never be independent. It was seen as a necessary step to promote healing. The same thing happened with my eating disorder.

Parents generally don't instinctively know how to support their children through anorexia, but with the right coaching, many parents can heroically step up to the plate and be their child's greatest allies in recovery. Rebeckah Peebles, an adolescent medicine specialist at the Children's Hospital of Philadelphia, puts it like this:

> I continue to be impressed by how, for lack of a better word, demonic some kids are when in the early stages of refeeding. They hit, scream, throw things, cut, and wield threatening objects or language to try and avoid eating. They are not at all themselves—sweet and compliant good kids. Consequently, their parents are often truly surprised and fearful of their kids in this phase, and need lots of support to stay firm. ED [eating disorder] puts families under siege and disempowers parents profoundly, and many parents don't behave their absolute best when they see their kids wasting away and don't know what to do. If they tend to be on the overprotective or anxious side, their reactions may appear to be very controlling or lacking in boundaries. However, this truly does improve when they enter into family-based therapy with an experienced clinician.
>
> (Liu, 2011, p. 33–34)

What Ravin and I, and other research-oriented folks in the eating disorders field, find astounding is that finding FBT is so difficult, especially when it's the only treatment for anorexia with any amount of empirical support. "What it comes down to is that using evidence-based treatment dramatically increases the likelihood that the person is going to recover," Ravin said. "It doesn't guarantee recovery, but it dramatically increases the likelihood. To me, it's sort of a no-brainer. Start with evidence-based treatment unless there is a very specific reason why it would be contraindicated."

Even in the UK, where FBT is supposed to be the first-line treatment for anorexia, it's rare to see a family offered this treatment. Charlotte, a farmer living in Suffolk in the UK, stumbled across FBT while she was researching anorexia online. Her daughter, Georgie, had developed anorexia shortly before her twelfth birthday, and was hospitalized for a month after becoming afraid of water. After she was discharged with an 1,800 calorie per day meal plan (less than the recommended amount for a girl Georgie's age, let alone one who needed to restore weight), Georgie started a course of cognitive behavioral therapy that failed to break through her illness. Frustrated and at the end of her rope, Charlotte stumbled across an online forum known as Around the Dinner Table, where parents provide support to each other, with a special focus on FBT.

There, Charlotte learned that the dietitian's meal plan was woefully inadequate, and that Georgie wasn't choosing not to eat, she was literally unable to eat enough. So Charlotte rolled up her sleeves and began plating up more food for her daughter, which was when the crap hit the fan and the yogurts hit the ceiling. Literally. Georgie pleaded and raged at the increase in calories, hurling food and expletives with equal venom. But the parents on ATDT told Charlotte that this was normal, and to stand firm.

"The most important thing I learned," Charlotte said, "was how to separate the anorexia from my daughter." Georgie's illness was making her call her mother names or negotiate for fewer calories. Georgie herself was hidden somewhere inside, alone, scared, and desperate for food. Charlotte stopped letting her daughter provide input on her meals and made all food-related decisions for her. Charlotte's job was to prepare and serve the food, and Georgie's only job was to eat. It might sound cruel, Charlotte pointed out, but not giving Georgie any choice actually relieved her of anxiety.

The weight slowly began to return, and with it came a growth spurt, which left Charlotte playing catch-up to keep Georgie's weight proportionate to her height. After about 18 months of re-feeding, the fog slowly began to lift. "I don't know how much of it was the food or how much of it was the routine," Charlotte said. "It was a combination of several things. It was learning to be calm, it was food, food, and more food, and it was just the constant routine—whatever happened, whatever we planned, whatever was going on, nothing got in the way of eating. I think that made a really big difference."

The other thing that made a difference for Charlotte was the presence of other parents going through the same thing. She could go online at 3:00 am and find support. She could learn how other parents dealt with the rages, the resistance, or the hiding of weights in clothes to artificially increase weight. She could complain (or, as she puts it, "have a whinge") and vent and feel less alone in her family's struggle. "If it weren't for the forum, Georgie would have been back in hospital," Charlotte said.

Not all anorexia sufferers live at home with their parents. Recent media coverage of eating disorders indicates that a growing number of anorexia sufferers are in their mid-thirties and beyond (Epstein, 2009). Although a small portion of these women's disorders actually start in middle age, most women either have never before sought treatment or are suffering a relapse (Gura, 2007). Noting that FBT was so successful with adolescents, psychologists Cindy Bulik, Jennifer Kirby, and Donald Baucom at the University of North Carolina, Chapel Hill decided to try and harness a similar support for older women. They called their intervention UCAN—Uniting Couples against Anorexia Nervosa.

When researchers asked women who had recovered from anorexia about what contributed to their recovery, many of them said that having a supportive partner was key (Tozzi *et al.*, 2003), as was helpful friends and family (Nilsson and Hagloff, 2006). These findings, combined with studies showing that 80 percent of couples where one member has anorexia report significant marital difficulties (Woodside and Shteker-Wilson, 1990; Timini and Robinson, 1996), led Kirby and colleagues to try and harness the positive couples relationship to help people recover from anorexia.

To participate in the initial treatment trial, the woman with anorexia had to be medically stable and living full-time with her partner (although the couples that have participated in the UCAN trial so far are all heterosexual, researchers believe UCAN will also be successful for same-sex couples). Like FBT, UCAN consists of three phases. The first phase lays the foundation for the therapeutic work to come. The therapist allows the couple to discuss how anorexia has affected the relationship, provides psychoeducation about anorexia and the recovery process, and also teaches the couple effective communication skills. The second phase has the couple address the eating disorder together, including the aspects of the disorder perceived to be the most challenging (e.g., restricting, purging, binge eating, exercise, etc.). The couple works together as a team to figure out how to best support the patient and work on recovery. Phase two also addresses the body image and sexual issues that typically arise when a partner has anorexia, not so much to eliminate the body image issues but to bring a greater understanding of the subject and help the couple function better within the limitations of the current recovery stage. The third and final phase helps the couple enact a plan for relapse prevention and shows them how they can keep working together as a couple against anorexia in the future (Bulik *et al.*, 2011).

Thus, write Bulik and colleagues:

> UCAN addresses multiple aspects of AN from a couple's perspective, leveraging the patient's key relationship in a variety of ways to address the eating disorder. By integrating UCAN into a broader intervention for AN, we acknowledge the critical role that a committed partner can play in recovery from AN and anticipate that it will lead to more favorable and lasting treatment gains.

(p. 25)

Although the results of the first UCAN treatment trial haven't yet been formally published, Bulik presented preliminary results at the 2011 International Conference on Eating Disorders. The most interesting—and heartening—finding is the low dropout rate associated with UCAN. Treatment dropout rates in individual therapies for adults with anorexia routinely approach 50 percent (Halmi *et al.*, 2005). The dropout rate for UCAN was only five percent, Bulik said, and the reason for that dropout was the husband's job was transferred across the country.

I dug up my notes from that conference section, and I have the number "5" underlined several times and circled vigorously. In a treatment trial of adults with anorexia, this low dropout rate was almost revolutionary. What seemed to make the difference in UCAN, Bulik noted, is keeping everyone on the same page. Whereas a person can quietly discontinue individual therapy when the going gets tough, having a partner involved creates an expectation that treatment will continue. This expectation is a powerful thing. Simply showing up at a therapist's office every week is no guarantee of recovery, but UCAN and FBT helps loved ones create an aura of recovery and eliminates the secret hiding places where anorexia can fester.

Although Hannah and Jonathan didn't participate in UCAN, the couple used similar tactics in Hannah's recovery from anorexia and bulimia. Like so many other people I interviewed for this book, Hannah described herself as very anxious, and the onset of puberty sent that anxiety skyrocketing. At age 13, depression began in earnest. Hannah's mental despair didn't always seem evident to the people around her, especially since she was a talented gymnast. But an injury, combined with the depression, effectively ended her career. "When I quit the gym, it dawned on me that, oh shit, I'm not going to be working out for all these hours, and I better change the way I eat," Hannah said.

Hannah didn't initially lose weight, but she didn't gain weight as she grew taller, which had the same effect. She would restrict her food during the day, but eat more normally at home. This, combined with the lack of weight loss, meant that no one had a clue about Hannah's eating issues. She completed high school without ever receiving diagnosis or treatment, and went off to college, when everything came crashing down. Unable to complete school, Hannah dropped out and got a job at a local bookstore. She met Jonathan when she was 21, although she tried to hide her eating disorder. Eventually, Hannah became so ill that hiding her disorder became impossible. After Hannah was kicked out of several treatment programs, the pair ended up tackling her disorder together.

"He had no idea what he was dealing with," Hannah said. "I don't know how it came about—we didn't sit down and decide to do something about it—but I was pissed off at treatment for kicking me out and so was he. Jonathan seemed to know, though, that I needed to eat. He wasn't buying the idea that I would talk about my feelings in therapy and eventually I would want to eat."

Instead, Jonathan started eating lunch and dinner with Hannah, as the bookstore was near his office. Hannah refused to let Jonathan cook, so the pair ate dinner at the same two restaurants for months. "I essentially lived at his apartment, even though I had my own place," she said. "I don't know what made him decide that this was a situation he should get involved in. I don't think it's something that most people would jump at the chance to do."

Slowly, over several years, Hannah's eating disorder improved. Regular meals helped decrease her urges to binge eat and purge. And the couple has stayed together, even though their relationship isn't perfect. "For a long time, even though his support really helped me, the eating disorder just dominated our relationship. He was constantly worried about me. He felt incredibly responsible and incredibly resentful," Hannah said. "Now, we can go days without talking about it. The eating disorder isn't the third person in our relationship any more."

Melting the Iceberg

Yet all of the treatments in the world seem useless when someone with anorexia insists they are fine and don't need treatment. Whereas the parents of adolescents have the legal authority to insist their sick children receive care, they generally lose this power at age 16 or 18 (depending on country or local laws). Plenty of legal and medical minds have debated this issue (Goldner *et al.*, 1997), and, in general, legal coercion of treatment for anorexia is considered a last resort and reserved for the most dire of situations.

The reality is this: most anorexia patients are resistant to treatment and will not uncommonly refuse care if given the choice. Besides the anosognosia of anorexia that prevents the person from seeing that they have a serious problem, they must also contend with an overwhelming fear of eating and weight gain—not a combination that causes people to dance happily into a therapist's office. A concerned parent can obtain guardianship or conservancy of their sick adult child if a court deems them unable to make their own medical decisions (Griffiths *et al.*, 1997). In other cases, a person can be deemed an immediate danger to themselves and legally detained in a locked psychiatric unit.

Involuntary treatment of psychiatric disorders remains contentious and the debate centers on a patient's right to refuse medical or psychiatric care. Coerced treatment infringes upon a patient's free will and right to control the fate of their body, say some legal scholars. Which is, to some extent, true. Yet the question remains whether a person with a severe eating disorder is mentally competent to make these decisions. Is the patient doing the choosing, or is their illness? Although studies are limited, researchers know that starvation shrinks the brain, especially the areas involved in reasoning and logical thinking (McCormick *et al.*, 2008), which likely impairs a person's ability to make rational decisions about their care.

Although these descriptions of coerced treatment seem fairly bleak (and, to some extent, they are), compulsory treatment doesn't necessarily signal that the person's life is forever ruined. Many patients say that being forced into treatment was ultimately a positive thing (Watson *et al.*, 2000), and another study reported that, after the second week of hospitalization, many anorexia sufferers who felt coerced into treatment were able to admit that inpatient treatment was necessary (Guarda *et al.*, 2007).

"The illness is complex, and the process of recovery is equally complex," said psychiatrist Blake Woodside, director of the eating disorders program at Toronto General Hospital. "When people are sick with anorexia, they're sick behaviorally. They have abnormal eating habits, they have low weight, and they can have purging behaviors."

But these behaviors only tell part of the story. "They're not well cognitively. People have a particular way they have to look at the world to be anorexic. You have to think in a specific way to do the behaviors that lead to the clinical manifestations of the illness," Woodside said.

Anorexia made my world very black and white. Food was good or bad, safe or not. Exercise had to be done for a very specific time period or it wasn't any good. If I didn't get a perfect score on a test, I was a failure. I felt worthless, that I didn't deserve to eat or take up space or even exist. The perfectionism that existed before anorexia was only amplified under the illness, and it was this way of thinking that enabled the illness to take root and persist for so long.

These feelings of perfectionism and worthlessness made it almost impossible for me to engage in treatment. I wasn't thin enough to have anorexia. If I did seek treatment, I would be the fattest one there. If someone was thinner than me, I wasn't sick enough. I didn't deserve treatment anyway. The world would be better off if I just starved. It's not a mentality that lends itself well to accepting help.

Coupled with these cognitive difficulties are problems in overall general mental health. "There's something that got people sick in the first place, something that was eating at them that was never resolved while they were ill. And they'll pick up other problems along the way that have to be dealt with," Woodside said.

To Woodside, anorexia is like an iceberg. "The behaviors are the tip of the iceberg. They're the ten percent of the iceberg that's out of the water, and that's what everyone sees. But that's only a tiny fragment of the condition," he said.

Most of what anorexia is sits below the surface of the water. It's the cognitions, the perfectionism, the anxiety. It's the depression, the alterations in hunger cues and appetite, and the interoceptive difficulties. It's also why weight gain alone isn't enough to treat anorexia. "To recover, you have to melt the whole iceberg," Woodside said.

Weight gain and behavioral recovery is like melting the top ten percent of the iceberg. You can't recover from anorexia without returning to a weight that is appropriate for your height and build, but that alone isn't recovery from anorexia. If it was, relapse rates from anorexia wouldn't be so high. To recover fully, you also have to work through the other cognitive and psychological issues that accompany anorexia, which means melting the 90 percent of the iceberg that's below the surface.

This melting occurs underwater and unseen, long after the sufferer looks and appears, for all intents and purposes, almost normal. The tip of the iceberg is gone, but the illness remains underneath the surface, ready to reemerge at any time. This was the hardest phase of recovery for me, and for many anorexia sufferers. The weight loss that accompanied the illness made it obvious to everyone that I was ill and that I needed help. One of the things that terrified me about recovery is that I would be just as ill but I would look completely normal. I found a normal appearance to be tremendously invalidating of my inner turmoil. I felt like the world around me was expecting me to suddenly pop out of bed and be totally relaxed around food. Instead, I was in the kitchen, as paralyzed as ever, and trying to figure out how to function without the shield of anorexia.

"In the same way it is for substance use disorders, there's a behavioral piece that has to happen first. There's no scientific evidence that you can psychotherapize your way out of anorexia," Woodside said.

Yet this remains the treatment of choice for many people treating anorexia, I told Woodside. I told him of the years I spent trying to "dig deep" and "get to the root of my issues." "I confused understanding my eating disorder with beating it," I said. I understood anorexia all too well, and yet I remained in thrall to its ever-increasing demands. Part of this inability to break free of anorexia might have to do with the thinking styles that made me so vulnerable to the disorder in the first place. A new therapy called cognitive remediation therapy (CRT) is targeting this way of thinking to help make behavior change possible.

Targeting Thinking

"'Thinking style' is the way you process information, and the strategies you use," commented[1] Lock. Researchers have identified two major thinking styles that are common in anorexia and appear to complicate treatment. "For a long time, clinicians have noticed that people with anorexia have problems with being flexible. They're pretty rigid in their thinking style, pretty rule-bound," he noted.

In formal research-speak, this is known as difficulties with set-shifting. "Set-shifting is your ability to move from one set of information to another quickly and easily and fluidly. Some people do it really easily and other people struggle. They get stuck and they can't move. There are some advantages to being less flexible, because you can be highly focused and get in there on a topic. There are disadvantages, too, obviously, when you need to bring in new information," Lock noted.

The other major thinking style that psychologists have identified in individuals with anorexia is being overly detail-oriented or, in other words, having difficulties with central coherence. Central coherence is how you process

---

1 Information in this section that is designated as Lock "commented" or "noted" means that the information was transcribed from a video interview with Lock on cognitive styles in anorexia for the group Maudsley Parents. Any quotes with "Lock said" means that I got this information from an interview I did with Dr Lock.

general information, how you identify a forest when you're looking at lots of trees. "People with anorexia tend to have an overly detailed focus. So they're highly skilled at puzzles where you look at all the details and sort them out, but they have trouble with puzzles where they have to see the big picture," Lock commented.

Lock's description of this detail focus reminded me of the time when my college roommate was watching me highlight my biochemistry textbook. I dutifully dragged my fluorescent green marker across lines of text, thinking I was marking up the most important sections of the chapter. My roommate looked over and asked why I bothered highlighting if I was just going to turn the whole page green. "I skipped some words," I pointed out indignantly.

"True," she said. "I think you missed a 'the' up top."

In my biochemistry text, as in so many other areas of my life, I was so overwhelmed by the details of the information that I lost track of the entire point of highlighting. I only needed to highlight the key points, except I couldn't figure out what those key points actually were. I literally couldn't see the forest for the trees.

Interestingly, the thinking styles seen in anorexia are rather similar to those with schizophrenia: both groups cling tightly to ideas that aren't based in reality and fixate on tiny details that are irrelevant to the big picture. This similarity led Kate Tchanturia and other researchers at the Maudsley Hospital in London to adapt CRT, initially developed as a treatment for schizophrenia, to anorexia. The idea was to target the specific neurocognitive processes that helped maintain the rigid food restriction, weight obsession, and compulsive exercise characteristic of anorexia.

Instead of targeting food and weight directly, which are often so fraught with anxiety and contention in anorexia, CRT uses a series of brain games that focus on more neutral subjects. "People with anorexia often don't agree that there's a problem around their weight and their dieting, but they can agree sometimes that there is a problem with them being not very flexible in their thinking or they get lost in the details," Lock told me. "They can see that this affects my school and this affects my work. Therefore, working on something that's not directly taking on the eating problem can make the beginning of therapy sometimes better."

During a session of CRT, someone may be asked to look at a map and describe a route from Point A to Point B. Then, they are asked to find another route, and another. The idea isn't to teach a bunch of starving youngsters how to read maps, but to help them learn the idea that there are many different ways to achieve the same outcome. Another game asks the person to read a short story and provide a one-sentence summary to help them get better at seeing the big picture (Arnold, 2011). Despite being a writer, this is something I struggle with immensely, as my experience with highlighting my biochemistry textbook indicates.

In 2007, Tchanturia and colleagues published the first case series of CRT in four patients with anorexia nervosa. Each patient received ten 45-minute sessions of CRT. All patients said they found the therapy to be beneficial, and all the patients had improved cognitive flexibility by the end of the study. And even though food and weight weren't targeted, all the patients gained weight, either during the study itself or during the 18-month follow-up period (Tchanturia *et al.*, 2007). A separate study indicated that patients liked CRT specifically because it didn't focus on food and eating (Whitney *et al.*, 2008).

Initial success with these small trials of CRT has led Tchanturia and colleagues to begin testing new ways of delivering this therapy. Offering CRT in a small group setting appears to yield the same positive outcomes as individual CRT (Genders and Tchanturia, 2010), and another study demonstrated that these outcomes can also be seen in adolescents with anorexia (Wood *et al.*, 2011). Researchers in Wales also found that CRT helped to improve perfectionism in outpatients with anorexia (Pitt *et al.*, 2010).

"The idea of cognitive remediation therapy is to make someone more flexible in their thinking and better able to see the big picture so that when they start a therapy, they'll be more able to use it," Lock noted. "Another way to think about it is if you have this in addition to other kinds of therapy, it would prevent your getting lost in that kind of thinking again because your cognitive processes would have been improved."

Still, Lock and other researchers caution that CRT isn't a substitute for nutritional restoration and other behavioral changes that need to occur in anorexia. CRT is an add-on, an adjunct to traditional therapies, Lock told me.

"You can't enact psychological change and then the behaviors will fall away. It doesn't work like that. The first thing you have to do if you get help for alcoholism is to put down the bottle. With anorexia, the first thing you have to do is correct the behaviors. By correcting the behaviors, you will start to get other help. But treatments for anorexia that don't involve behavioral change are not known to have good outcomes in the scientific literature," Woodside said. "And that's a hard one, because lots of people have this idea that, if they can figure out something psychologically, then the behaviors will disappear. And unfortunately, that doesn't occur."

Some of the latest evidence-based treatments for anorexia, like family-based treatment and cognitive remediation therapy, prioritize behavioral change. According to the tenets of FBT, normalized eating and weight restoration are the primary goals of treatment. Addressing other adolescent or developmental issues occurs after the adolescent is well on the road to health. Cognitive remediation therapy seeks to unlock the ways of thinking that are so destructive in anorexia. Although it doesn't prioritize weight gain per se, preliminary trials have found that CRT makes behavioral change easier and helps sufferers begin the weight gain process.

Regardless of which evidence-based therapy is most appropriate at the time, seeking out treatments that have been shown to be effective in research studies is crucial, Woodside said. "Some people will benefit from almost anything. If you came to me and told me that tai chi was what did it for you, I would say that I'm very happy for you and congratulations," he noted. "For most people, you want to have expert treatment. You want to have treatment delivered by someone who is properly trained, thoroughly evidence-based, and is providing what would be described as standard of care."

Everyone's road to recovery will be different, and everyone's recovery will look different. "We've got a definition of recovery, which is a full behavioral, psychological, and cognitive recovery, which involves normal functioning, good relationships, doing something in your life that you feel good about doing—Freud's definition of recovery, which is to work and to love," Woodside said.

"My personal belief is that people who talk about living with your anorexia as the best outcome are practicing a cruel deception on individuals who are ill," he continued. "I don't think that's the best that can be accomplished. It matches neither with our research, nor my 25 years of clinical experience. That's a hopeless position that is not true and should not be promulgated. People should never give up. In my view, there is a chance of recovery regardless of the duration or severity of illness. The chance does alter with time, but it never goes down to zero as long as the person is alive. There is *always* hope for a full recovery, no matter how long a person has been sick."

Getting there, however, is often a bumpy and difficult ride, filled with wrong turns and relapses. Learning from these relapses can be the key to creating a lasting recovery.

10 Oops, I Did It Again …

From the outside, I looked totally healthy. My weight was low but normal (according to the BMI charts). I had just finished a second grueling graduate course at one of the top universities in the United States and was working at a coveted position in public relations at a well-respected scientific institution. The new job and accompanying move meant that I was going without weekly psychotherapy for the first time in nearly a decade. But I was ready, I thought. I wasn't "recovered," but I thought I was on the upswing.

Just like Newton's Laws of Motion, however, what goes up must come down. The first sign of trouble came almost immediately as I learned my office had an in-house gym, as did my apartment complex. My activity level increased almost automatically. The next indication of a problem didn't come until I had been at my new job for about six months. Shortly after Christmas, I was walloped by another bout of serious depression, and turned to exercise to help regulate my mood. And it worked—the increased activity made me feel better, but only temporarily.

A small mistake at work blew up in my face on the same day that I was diagnosed with a stress fracture in my left foot from all of my exercising. I had been grimly holding onto recovery until then, but the stress at work, combined with my newfound inability to exercise, left me flailing. I grew so anxious and depressed that I started to find food physically revolting, and I immediately cut back on my intake. The depression, anxiety, and anorexia continued to spiral. Several times, I showed up at my office and stared at the blinking cursor on the screen. I would look up at the clock only to find that hours had passed. I was paralyzed by feelings of inadequacy and despair.

The day the walking cast came off my foot, I returned to my rigorous exercise regime and slashed my intake even further. I felt the anorexia was the only thing holding me together. Even with the eating disorder in full control, I was consumed by feelings of hopelessness. Every morning, I walked into the elevator at work and pressed the button for my office. In reality, I wanted to head up to the rooftop terrace and throw myself off. I hated myself for thinking this, but I hated myself even more for being too chicken to actually follow through.

Eventually, I called my old therapist and told her everything. I was miserable. I wanted to stop but I couldn't. "My brain is scaring me," I whispered into the phone. I wasn't in control of my behaviors and that terrified me. Within the week, I had quit my job and was moving back home, having barely escaped hospitalization for medical and psychiatric instability. My heart was a wreck and my brain was even worse. For the next four months, I barely moved off my parents' couch except to eat and go upstairs to sleep. With food, lots of food, time, and a new love for crappy television, I slowly began to heal.

This tale is far from my only relapse, but it was the last major one. I am far from alone in my story of relapse—in fact, I don't really know anyone who has recovered from anorexia without relapsing in some way. Months and years of behaviors become seared in your brain, becoming habits and safe havens from which escape is treacherously hard work. Despite the near-universality of relapse in eating disorder recovery, it's surprisingly not very well studied in the research literature.

"The literature on this is pretty limited, and we've written about half of it," Blake Woodside, director of the eating disorders program at Toronto General Hospital, said.

Woodside divides these outcome studies into two different groups: treatment response and long-term outcome. He defines treatment response as completing the treatment program, which includes total weight restoration, and a total cessation of binge eating and purging behaviors. The likelihood of completing treatment in the Canadian system (who don't have to worry about insurance companies declaring treatment "not medically necessary" or simply refusing to pay, even when a person is very ill and severely underweight, in the American system) depends on the subtype of anorexia the person has and whether they've received treatment before. "The binge/purge type is almost like a different illness. It's a much more severe, malignant, and treatment-resistant form of anorexia," Woodside said.

The best prognosis for treatment completion, Woodside said, is for people with the restricting subtype of anorexia who have never been in treatment before. About three-quarters of these people complete treatment. People with the binge/purge subtype of anorexia who have previously sought intensive, inpatient treatment have a much harder time reaching weight restoration and behavioral abstinence: only 25 to 30 percent complete treatment. People with the restricting subtype who have sought previous treatment and people with the binge/purge subtype who haven't sought treatment lay somewhere in the middle. Interestingly, duration of illness and BMI at the start of treatment seem to play less of an important role, Woodside noted.

Weight gain during hospitalization or intensive treatment is crucial, researchers have found, and a faster rate of gain makes it significantly more likely that the other physical and psychological gains from treatment will be maintained at one year (Lund *et al.*, 2009). Although rate of weight gain is important, so is the weight at which someone leaves the hospital. Prior to the mid-1980s, hospitalizations for anorexia were relatively rare and relatively lengthy. With the advent of managed care in the United States, hospitalizations for anorexia have become much shorter (often solely for medical or psychiatric stabilization) and patients are frequently discharged at very low weights. This has primarily served to increase rehospitalization after discharge (Wiseman *et al.*, 2001; Willer *et al.*, 2005) and decrease the likelihood of a positive outcome. Low discharge weights are significantly associated with higher relapse and lower overall functioning two years after admission (Baran *et al.*, 1995). In one US study, length of hospital stay was determined not by clinical status but by whether private insurance would pay for further care or the family could afford to pay out of pocket (Robergeau *et al.*, 2006). The short-sightedness of this policy, especially in light of the research literature, is obvious to everyone but insurance companies themselves.

Staying in the hospital or a treatment facility isn't foolproof; people can and do relapse back into anorexia even after they've reached a seemingly healthy weight. Younger patients, those with more abnormal eating-disordered thoughts and behaviors, and a slower rate of weight gain all predicted rehospitalization in teens who had reached a healthy weight before discharge (Castro *et al.*, 2004). Anorexia patients with immediate family members who also had anorexia, those who were overactive, and those with alcoholic fathers were also more likely to need additional hospitalizations (Steinhausen *et al.*, 2008). Adolescents who maintained their weight post-hospitalization had a higher readiness to change and had higher body weights at admission (Castro-Fornieles *et al.*, 2007).

There's No Place Like Home

Today's cost-conscious environment, combined with a growing desire to keep patients in the least restrictive environment conducive to recovery and a growing awareness of the downsides to hospitalization (Gowers *et al.*, 2000), has made long-term anorexia hospitalizations less desirable or even feasible. Increasingly, the metaphorical heavy lifting needed to make recovery possible in many anorexia patients has fallen on the shoulders of outpatient teams, the patients themselves, and, when available, their parents and loved ones. It's not necessarily all bad—after all, recovering from an eating disorder means functioning well in the world at large, not functioning well in a treatment facility, and engaging in the hard recovery work while supported by loved ones can be beneficial and therapeutic.

Through her daughter, Margaret found out the hard way that anorexia recovery is a protracted process and that parents are needed to provide ongoing support and relapse prevention long after a patient flies the nest. Margaret's daughter, Leslie, descended into anorexia rapidly at the age of 17 after participating in a 30-hour famine at church, where Leslie fasted for 30 hours to raise money for starving children around the world. Within three months, Leslie's weight plummeted and she became one of the starving children she was trying to save. After a brief hospital stay, Margaret returned her daughter to a healthy weight almost as rapidly. Leslie's mental recovery, however, lagged long behind her physical recovery. Although her attitudes towards food were reasonably healthy, Leslie's anger, anxiety, and hostility towards food had transferred to Margaret.

"All the psychosis around food was redirected," Margaret told me. "There was such a change in her when I came into the room. Her face would change, her body language would change … everything. It was like an electrical storm happening in her head." Just as Leslie had been starving for food, she was now starving for love.

So Margaret used the same techniques to extinguish Leslie's hostility towards her mother that she had once displayed towards food. Margaret began to require that Leslie interact with her like a normal teenage daughter. Instead of recoiling when their hands would brush, Margaret kept her hand on Leslie's, just for a minute, just to let her daughter know she was loved and that her mom wasn't going anywhere. Over the course of a year, Leslie's mind began to heal. Their relationship was literally knitted back together over a long weekend the pair spent at a remote cottage on the Oregon coast.

"We were both really dreading it, but it turned out to be a good thing. It was a long time of exposure," Margaret said. The turning point for the pair came when Leslie found some yarn in a shop and Margaret offered to teach her daughter how to knit socks. Leslie agreed, and the pair literally began to knit their relationship back together.

That fall, Leslie went off to college with a contract in place: regular weigh-ins wearing a hospital gown and after emptying her bladder, daily brief check-ins via phone, and no judgment if Leslie did need to come back home temporarily. The college health clinic was less than thrilled with Margaret's plan. The university didn't want Leslie to sign the releases and told her she didn't have to sign. "Oh yes, she does," Margaret said, and the requisite forms were ultimately signed. Having those safeguards in place was crucial, as Leslie later admitted that she intended to return to college and start restricting again. "Leslie said the impulse was there, but it was weaker, and she thought, nah, I'm just going to get caught, so why bother," Margaret recalled.

Yet Leslie maintained her weight and even gained a few pounds up until the end of her junior year. Then, over the summer, her weight dropped by just a pound or two. Since Leslie's mental state was so good, Margaret initially wrote it off as Leslie's body settling in to her setpoint weight. Early in the fall semester, Leslie's weight again dropped by two pounds. Again, since everything else about Leslie looked healthy, Margaret simply encouraged her daughter to put on a few pounds and sent her on her way. By Thanksgiving, however, Margaret was noticing signs that seemed almost reminiscent of her daughter's initial descent into anorexia.

Margaret asked Leslie to hop on the scale, just to check, since her weight was no longer monitored at the student health clinic. Leslie had lost an additional 12 pounds, and was in the midst of a full-blown relapse. "She was shocked," Margaret said. "She said she had been eating three meals every day, and snacks, and was eating the same as she had been the last year. Leslie said she wasn't having any eating-disordered thoughts." Which could be true, Margaret said, but was really beside the point as normal people don't accidentally lose 12 pounds. The weight had to come back on.

The good news is that Leslie has regained almost all of her lost weight and is making progress towards the last few pounds. Margaret also helped her daughter find a therapist to help Leslie unload some of her stress and to teach her skills to help prevent another relapse. "This might be the best thing that could have happened, because now Leslie has a better understanding of anorexia and is able to start talking about it," Margaret said. "Leslie had our support all through this, even if she didn't realize it. I just hope this relapse is a good, teachable moment."

Leslie's story illustrates not only the power of a mother's love—something no doctor or treatment facility, no matter how devoted, could duplicate—but also the importance of maintaining a healthy weight to promote ongoing recovery. Even as I was finishing this book, I was struck by two viral infections, one right after the other. Both of them meant I was unable to eat properly as I was violently ill. Those two weeks saw my weight drop by nearly ten pounds, and suddenly I found myself questioning whether I really needed to eat, and that I could probably stand to get in better shape. I had experienced this before, of course, and expecting the return of the anorexic thoughts gave me the power and foresight to keep the weight loss from getting worse. Still, the experience was humbling. I live with the knowledge that I am only one skipped meal or a few pounds away from a devastating relapse.

Woodside's years of clinical experience have also shown him the importance of maintaining a healthy weight. "In our research, getting all the way to a normal weight is a requirement for a good outcome at a year. People who fall short of that definition of treatment completion, even by a small margin, are extremely unlikely to maintain their gains," Woodside said. He wasn't exaggerating when he said "small margin," either. Falling short of their target weight by even one kilogram (2.2 pounds) dramatically decreased a person's likelihood of recovery.

Imagine recovery like trying to bike up a steep hill, Woodside said. Stopping even just a little short of the hill's crest means that you will start rolling backwards because you're still on the incline. "There's a profound difference from having your bicycle at the top of the hill and having your bicycle 20 feet from the top of the hill," he said. That one kilogram difference, he said, is what pushes a person to the top of the hill.

That last kilogram is often the hardest bit of weight to put back on. I had long since started to look healthy and normal, and my behavior was evening out, too. Since I was already at what the BMI charts told me was a "healthy" weight, I saw no need to add those last few pounds. After all, plenty of people weighed less than me and no one was telling them to consume high-calorie nutritional supplements every day. Plus, I was tired of treatment and weight gain and consuming vast quantities of food every single day. I had little energy left and just wanted to stop pedaling. And so the slow slide back to the bottom of the hill would begin, again and again and again.

The top of the hill was scary for me as well. It meant having to live without an eating disorder, something I hadn't done for over a decade. It meant giving up the only way I knew to manage my anxiety and depression. It meant relinquishing the constant praise about my small size, seemingly impeccable eating habits, and draconian exercise regime. And I couldn't yet see the benefits that lay just on the other side of the hill.

"What being at the top of the hill means in anorexia recovery is complicated. It's the physiological and biological meaning of being at a normal weight. Your body functions differently when it's at a normal weight. It's also the psychological meaning of being and staying at a normal weight. That's what being at the top of the hill means. Twenty feet down means that you're holding something back. There's something you're not giving up, something you're protecting," Woodside said.

As Mary learned, even holding on to something small can start to set a relapse in motion. Several months before I sat down with her, Mary entered residential treatment in Denver for a relapse of her eating disorder. Her eating disorder first surfaced at the end of elementary school when she first started skipping lunch. "I didn't think it was that weird of a thing to do. It was just a self-soothing behavior," Mary said. "I didn't even know what anorexia was until seventh grade, and then I did my best to hide what I was doing."

Her food and exercise obsessions stayed mostly under the radar throughout middle and high school, largely because they weren't accompanied by a visible weight loss. However, when Mary went away to college in 2009, her weight rapidly plunged. "When I came home for Thanksgiving, there was no hiding it any longer," Mary said ruefully. She dropped out of school and started outpatient therapy, and her eating and exercise habits slowly began to improve, along with her weight.

Two years later, however, Mary's family moved and she found herself in a new location with no friends and not much to do while she waited for her school semester to start. "I was alone all day with so much time on my hands, so I ran and ran and ran, probably over a thousand miles that summer," Mary said. Simultaneously, she cut back on her food intake, which caused her weight to drop again. She made it partway through the school term before having to drop out and enter residential treatment. The structure of an intensive treatment program helped Mary gain some weight and get some insight into what made her disorder wax and wane over time, but she still has a way to go to achieve full recovery.

"My parents are very watchful, and they know what they're looking for at this point," Mary said. "But I'm still struggling with the exact same things I was before I went to treatment." She still has trouble managing urges to over-exercise, and hasn't yet broken her categorization of foods into "safe" or "unsafe."

What Mary is currently working on—eating a wide range of nutritious foods and maintaining a healthy weight—have been shown in the scientific literature to be important factors in preventing relapse. Even in recovery, people with anorexia tend to avoid foods that are higher in fat and calories, said Tim Walsh, eating disorders expert and director of the eating disorders research program at the New York State Psychiatric Institute.

"It's a tale we're still trying to put together," Walsh said, "but we're quite convinced—and it's consistent with lots and lots of descriptions from the data—that folks with anorexia nervosa very characteristically avoid high-fat food, or energy-dense food, and also tend to eat the same foods over and over again. They have a more limited diet variety than folks without anorexia." These techniques, ironically enough, are exactly what are used by many commercial diet programs to help people lose weight, Walsh pointed out.

The problem with anorexia is that weight loss is the one thing that needs to be avoided above all else. "We couldn't figure out why all these people were relapsing," he said, even after they had been weight-restored in a rigorous, state-of-the-art hospital program. To find out why, Walsh and his colleagues tracked 47 patients as they left the hospital and reintegrated with normal life. They tracked not only what the patients weighed and their eating disorder cognitions, but also what they ate. Those patients who ate a wider variety of energy-dense foods were much more likely to maintain their weight after hospitalization than patients whose diets were more limited and tended towards foods with fewer calories (Schebendach *et al.*, 2008). Researchers repeated this study in another group of patients several years later and found the same outcome: preventing relapse means expanding food variety and encouraging fat intake (Schebendach *et al.*, 2012).

"I wouldn't be surprised that the degree to which people tend to eat a diet that's low in fat and low in variety increases the chances that they're going to lose weight and relapse," Walsh said. What he doesn't yet know is whether these dietary factors alone increase the chance for relapse, or whether they are markers for increased anxiety and other anorexic thoughts and behaviors. Still, Walsh noted, they give psychologists a target upon which to focus behavioral change.

Woodside sees some of these factors—limiting the range of foods you eat and maintaining inadequate body fat—as a lit match. Recovery, especially at the beginning, is like dry kindling. One tiny spark from a lit match is all that's needed to get a fire going. "People can take tiny actions that aren't intended to lead to relapse that can light a fire in the dry tinder of recovery, and get a relapse started," he said. "It might take a number of months to be completed, but it started from some tiny action that they then don't take steps to deal with."

Some new treatment trials are trying to pour some water on the dry kindling by specifically targeting these dietary behaviors linked to relapse. If psychologists can expose patients to their feared foods enough times, hypothesize Walsh and his colleagues at the New York State Psychiatric Institute, then perhaps anorexia patients can overcome their fears. It's known as exposure and response prevention. "It might be a useful treatment target in the short-term, rather than waiting until someone is crashing and burning and on the wrong path," Walsh said. "That's why I think it's worthy of further study."

Extinguishing these fears isn't that simple. People with anorexia become afraid of high-fat foods through a process known as fear-based learning.

Natural selection has primed our brains to pay close attention to our environment when we're afraid, which makes humans really good at learning when we're scared out of our minds. Those things stick in our minds for a really long time because of the particular brain circuits activated during fear (McGaugh *et al.*, 1996). For someone with anorexia, it's much easier for their brains to learn that cake is scary than to be reassured that nothing bad will happen if they eat that slice of cake. The strength of this fear-based learning may help explain why relapse rates are so high in anorexia, researchers believe (Steinglass and Walsh, 2006).

If you practice any behavior, no matter whether it was learned in a time of fear or relative peace, it can become a habit. Researchers say that a behavior has become a habit when the person keeps doing it long after it has ceased to become rewarding. They do it without thinking, whether it's placing their keys on a hook by the front door or gnawing their nails while on hold. Some of the behaviors seen in anorexia, Walsh said to me, fit this neuroscientific definition of habit.

"It makes all kinds of sense that dieting and weight loss are somehow rewarding," Walsh said. "But then, as a clinician, I often see that it takes on a life of its own, often to the degree that patients will say 'Man, this isn't working for me.'" Yet the behaviors persist, despite the fact that the initial reward isn't there any longer, essentially making them a habit. Walsh described some studies done by cognitive neuroscientists in rats that may help explain this phenomenon.

You can train a rat to press a bar to receive a food pellet when the light switches on. The light goes on, the rat presses a bar a bunch of times, the rat receives a tasty reward. What's interesting isn't that you can get a rat to do this, but that they will continue to press the bar when the light goes on even after food is no longer given. It's the default response in the rat brain: lightbulb means bar pressing time, food be damned. Something similar may be going on in the brains of people with eating disorders. "The process of dieting and avoiding high-fat food may become habitual and disconnected from the rewards that were there," Walsh said.

Treating these behaviors has taken a page right out of the OCD literature, using the technique of exposure and response prevention. For OCD, exposure and response prevention may require a person to touch an object they perceive as dirty and then not wash their hands after. For anorexia, however, this may require eating cake or another feared food and then not exercising or purging afterwards. The idea is to teach the person that these feared items really aren't all that scary. A study that used exposure and response prevention in nine people hospitalized for anorexia found that this treatment helped increase caloric intake (Steinglass *et al.*, 2011). A study of adolescents being treated with family-based treatment (FBT) showed that FBT also uses a form of exposure and response prevention by requiring the teens to eat a wide variety of foods, day after day (Hildebrandt *et al.*, 2012).

"I'm not trying to over-simplify these things," Walsh emphasized. "Anorexia isn't just about eating or not eating high-fat foods. These things are connected to psychological processes, but they are a final common pathway leading to a target that we can aim at."

Helping people with anorexia change their behaviors remains a daunting task. "Why is it that once this pattern gets established, it's so hard to break?" Walsh asked. Perhaps it's a combination of different things—the fear-based learning, the OCD-like rituals, the stickiness of thoughts and ideas while someone is underweight. In this sense, it really is like Woodside's analogy of a fire: with the right amount of fuel, a single lit match can start a blaze that burns out of control.

Playing Smokey the Bear with someone with anorexia—"Only YOU can prevent forest fires!"—isn't always the most effective. I am notoriously bad at noticing the first signs of relapse. I often didn't find thinking about skipping meals and losing weight to be repugnant or even worrisome. Just as a stray blaze might be welcomed by a homeless person on a cold night, the initial descent of a relapse can seem almost friendly and inviting.

Woodside and other researchers have tried various tactics in their metaphorical stance as Smokey the Bear, and very little has borne fruit. Cognitive behavioral therapy after inpatient treatment of anorexia did seem to decrease the likelihood of relapse. Approximately three-quarters of the women receiving treatment as usual (in this case, it was nutritional counseling) either relapsed or dropped out of the study before finishing treatment. Only about one in five of those receiving CBT relapsed or dropped out. The proportion of patients with a good outcome was also higher in the CBT group: 44 percent versus 7 percent of the treatment-as-usual group. The cognitive therapy also seemed to decrease the speed at which patients relapsed (Pike *et al.*, 2003). A second study in 2009 by Woodside and colleagues replicated these findings, indicating that CBT after weight restoration did seem to be useful (Carter *et al.*, 2009).

Although scientists continue their quest for medications that can improve treatment and decrease relapse, thus far no drugs have been shown conclusively to prevent relapse in anorexia. The most recent study appeared in the *Journal of the American Medical Association* in 2006. Tim Walsh and colleagues at the New York State Psychiatric Institute randomly assigned 93 women with anorexia who had been weight restored to a minimum BMI of 19.0 to receive either fluoxetine (brand name: Prozac) or placebo. The women also received weekly CBT and were followed for a year. The women relapsed at the same rate in both groups; overall, just under 30 percent of the women relapsed. Selective serotonin reuptake inhibitors, then, do not appear to be effective at preventing relapse in anorexia (Walsh *et al.*, 2006).

And those several studies are pretty much it when it comes to figuring out the best ways to keep women from relapsing after weight recovery. Getting people with anorexia to participate in treatment trials is notoriously difficult (Halmi *et al.*, 2005), which means that researchers are left with a very small pool of individuals with whom to conduct relapse prevention studies. The other problem researchers face is time. Tracking people over a year or more is both time-consuming and expensive, which can make it hard to find the funds to complete these studies.

From my admittedly non-scientific interviews, conversations, and personal experiences, however, time seems to be one of the most crucial things in relapse prevention. Not that you can just wait for anorexia to go away, but it also takes time for new behaviors to take root and the brain to rewire itself. This rewiring is what scientists call neuroplasticity: the brain is continually shaped and molded not only by what we do, but also by how we act. Neuroplasticity is what allows stroke patients to re-learn the use of a limb that was thought to be paralyzed. It's how thinking and behaving differently can help relieve the symptoms of depression and anxiety. And it's how even long-term anorexia sufferers can re-learn how to eat and how to maintain a healthy weight (Doidge, 2007).

Recovery in eating disorders is often talked about as a lightbulb moment, or as some sort of mythical destination. I wrote of "working towards recovery," and tended to emphasis the "recovery" bit while neglecting the "working" bit. The fact is that recovery is a lot of hard work. It takes skills and practice, which is something many researchers and clinicians fail to account for. I never had an "aha!" moment when I suddenly understood that the anorexia was bad and asked for a slice of cheesecake. It didn't work like that. For me, recovery came with the dogged repetition of recovery behaviors over a long period of time.

According to Norman Doidge, author of the book *The Brain that Changes Itself*, neuroplasticity requires both adequate practice and adequate time. Yet I've never been able to find a single study that assesses neuroplasticity in anorexia, nor any measurements of how much time and how much practice of recovery behaviors is required for a good outcome. In popular psychology books, the magic number required to become an expert at something is 10,000 hours (Syed, 2010). Mozart was a musical genius, yes, but part of his brilliance was that he practiced the piano very intensely. Picasso would have had artistic talent even if he became a plumber, but it was the fact that he painted that made him an art master.

Nor did Mozart just learn where middle C was on the piano and then bang away for the next 10,000 hours. He had teaching and coaching from his father and others. The feedback was constant. Little Wolfgang didn't have just a year or two of piano lessons, he studied for years. He didn't become a brilliant composer on his own—he had support, and lots of it.

It helped me to re-frame recovery not as some sort of nebulous process, like watching a pot of water boil, but as a skill set I had to master. I had to become an expert at recovery behaviors. I had to become the Mozart of Recovery. It definitely made the task sound more glamorous than "Thirty-something woman learns to eat!" I had to give up on lightbulb moments and start acting like a person in recovery. I had to practice, make mistakes, and seek feedback even when I didn't want it. I had to try new things. Mostly, I had to push myself harder than ever before. This process took years and is still ongoing, long after I've been out of inpatient treatment.

Expecting a brief hospitalization for anorexia to re-wire the brain is like trying to create another Mozart with just one piano lesson. Despite Einstein's brilliance, he probably couldn't do calculus as a five-year-old. Discharging a malnourished anorexia patient after a week in the hospital and expecting them to feed themselves properly is as absurd as expecting a five-year-old to do calculus. It doesn't mean the five-year-old will never learn calculus, just that they can't do it yet. They need to learn long division and multiplication tables and infinite sums before they can get to differential equations. All the potential in the world doesn't matter if you don't acquire the skills to use it. Everyone has the potential for recovery, but reaching this potential takes lots of practice and lots of hard work. It's the type of thing that often happens in the home environment, and it's one of the reasons why I've found on-the-ground support, whether from parents, partners, friends, and other loved ones, to be so crucial.

The work required to re-wire the brain is invisible, but grueling nonetheless. Therapy helped me; so did nutrition counseling and medication for my underlying depression and anxiety. What ultimately got me better, however, was the constant prodding to eat three meals and two snacks every day, no matter what. I was lucky—I had the support of my parents, who were willing to let their adult daughter move back home and to require me to work on recovery while living under their roof.

Perhaps this is part of the reason why FBT has such a good long-term response rate. The importance of this kind of live-in recovery coaching can't be underestimated. With every meal, every snack, every pat of butter, new brain connections are being formed. Every time someone distracts you from purging or stalls off a binge, your brain is healing. When you pick up your knitting after a stressful day (or hug your dog or catch up on your favorite television program) instead of hitting the gym, you are learning. Your brain is changing. And it takes 10,000 hours of this type of practice to make someone an expert at recovery.

A few back-of-the-envelope calculations told me that 10,000 hours of recovery was a little over a year—59.2 weeks, to be exact. It's interesting to note that the first year after hospital discharge is the highest risk period for future relapse. A potential explanation could be that, after a year of recovery, the brain has re-wired itself, which dramatically decreases a person's risk of backsliding. It means recovery is the new habit, the go-to mechanism even when things get tough.

The research on what leads to relapse in eating disorders, both in that crucial period and beyond, is relatively sparse. Scientists know that relapse is exceedingly common, and that people don't always relapse into the same behaviors with which they were initially diagnosed. It's known formally as "diagnostic migration" or "diagnostic crossover," and it happens when someone with the restricting type of anorexia develops binge eating and purging behaviors. Or when someone with bulimia starts losing weight but still binge eats and purges regularly, changing their diagnosis from bulimia to binge/purge anorexia. And so on.

To measure the frequency of diagnostic migration, researchers at Harvard University followed a group of 136 women presenting at an outpatient clinic with clinical anorexia nervosa for eight to twelve years. The researchers found that 62 percent of the women diagnosed with the restricting type of anorexia had crossed into the binge/purge type, and only 12 percent of the people diagnosed with the restricting subtype hadn't regularly binged or purged in the eight-year follow-up (Eddy *et al.*, 2002).

Despite several studies, trying to predict which people with restricting anorexia will go on to develop significant binge eating and purging behaviors remains a bit of a guessing game. A personality trait known as low self-directedness—that is, difficulties with adapting behavior in different situations to be consistent with personal values and goals (Cloninger, 1993)—seems to be the main factor predicting who will switch diagnoses, whether from anorexia to bulimia or from bulimia to anorexia (Tozzi *et al.*, 2005).

What sometimes happens, Woodside said, is that the switch from primarily restricting behaviors to binge eating and purging behaviors happens during a relapse when a person's weight is slamming downwards. Every person, he told me, has a genetic threshold for starvation and for binge eating, as well as a genetic tendency towards behaviors like vomiting, other forms of purging, and excessive exercise (Devlin *et al.*, 2002). Someone with normal-weight bulimia has a low threshold for binge eating and a high tendency towards purging. Someone with binge/purge anorexia has a higher tolerance for starvation but a lower resistance to binge eating. The restricting type of anorexia has a high tolerance for starvation and a high resistance to binge eating. But if you starve someone enough, almost everyone's threshold for binge eating will be crossed. The downward spiral of a relapse can often be when that threshold is crossed, which activates the switch from restricting anorexia to binge/purge anorexia or bulimia.

What Woodside found in his own experience that also distinguishes patients with the binge/purge type of anorexia from the restricting type is a history of trauma. "Dealing with the sequelae of post-traumatic stress disorder (PTSD) is related to the eating disorder—the two sort of feed off of each other. It's a very, very difficult job for people in that circumstance to make a full recovery, because as they start to eat more, the PTSD gets activated, and the eating problems are a great way to suppress the effects of post-traumatic stress disorder. It takes ages and ages for people to sort that out," Woodside said.

Using information gathered from 824 women with anorexia who participated in a genetics study with the National Institutes of Health, researchers found that 103 of these women (13.4 percent) met the DSM criteria for PTSD. Further analysis confirmed Woodside's clinical experiences: women with the binge/purge subtype of anorexia were twice as likely to have PTSD as women with restricting anorexia. As well, the traumatic event generally occurred before the onset of the eating disorder, which has raised questions about the role of PTSD in the etiology of eating disorders (Reyes-Rodríguez *et al.*, 2011).

Melanie, a 41-year-old woman with a 30-year history of anorexia, experiences this link on a daily basis. "I know that I am not 'fat,' but the underlying trauma that is the causation of my anorexia still is causing me enormous anxiety even after multiple treatments," she told me. "I wish I could find something, anything that would prevent me from hitting that panic trigger as soon as I get to that point when my body gets to the point when there is just enough flesh on it that my bone structure is covered. I no longer wish to be emaciated, but I cannot seem to get to the point where I can be comfortable maintaining anything above very low-normal, no matter what type of therapy I try, after three decades of this disease. At least I have made progress to the point where I no longer wish for the death-like numbers that I wanted before, ever again, and I have a strong desire for recovery. I just came out of inpatient just two months ago again, and I still have very high distortions, even though my restored weight is not high by any means. I suppose it will always be a day-to-day process."

Despite her long history of illness and numerous relapses, Melanie is keeping up the good fight. "I am 41 years old, damn tired of this crap, 30 years of this, and I intend to win," she said.

Backseat Drivers

Other untreated co-occurring disorders also make anorexia more difficult to treat. Untreated OCD increases the chances of relapse by 75 percent, Woodside said. Also increasing the chances of relapse in the first year after weight restoration is physical activity (as little as 30 minutes per day, Woodside said) and even just urges to exercise compulsively (Davis and Kaptein, 2006; Carter *et al.*, 2004).

"For a restricting anorexic with a good prognosis who starts walking, even for just 30 minutes a day, their chance for being well at a year drops from about 70 percent to about 30 percent," Woodside said.

Although I was in treatment a couple years after this study was published, no one ever mentioned these results to me. It's entirely possible that the danger wouldn't have registered or I wouldn't have cared, but I find it astounding how little of these research results had been relayed to me by treatment providers. Exercise has been a relapse trigger for me on several occasions, and I had to learn the hard way just how difficult it is to juggle physical activity and anorexia recovery. I had to stop all activity for quite some time before I was able to exercise without immediately overdoing it.

"We tell people that we don't know whether it will be safe for them to exercise again. We just don't know," Woodside said. "If people want advice that is conservative, that maximizes their chances of being well, we tell people to just lay off it for a couple of years."

I keep my exercise compulsions in check, I told Woodside, by very strictly limiting the amount of activity I do and my access to exercise equipment. As much as that home elliptical machine might be awfully convenient, I know my exercise would spiral out of control very rapidly if I had 24/7 access to it. It's also why I avoid gyms and try to be active outside as much as possible. Besides the mood-lifting effects of being outdoors (Barton and Pretty, 2010), I love the feeling of the wind in my hair as I pedal my bike or hike local trails. Of course, I can become compulsive about these activities, just as I can become compulsive about the red blinking numbers on indoor exercise equipment, but focusing on the joy of movement and nature steers me away from compulsion and back towards recovery.

My biological predisposition to anorexia will never go away. It's like living with a permanent backseat driver. They rarely start out by suddenly grabbing the wheel away from you. Rather, they creep up in importance and influence. We do, ultimately, remain the driver of our lives, but, as anyone who has followed GPS directions only to end up at the wrong place knows all too well, bad directions can lead to a very different road traveled. Our predispositions towards eating disorders or anxiety or bad boyfriends tend to nudge us. They change what environments we're likely to seek out, and our environments can provide new backseat drivers (or new directions for the existing ones). They can be annoying passengers in our lives, but there's also not a lot we can do about them. We're often stuck with them for the ride.

The goal is to diminish their influence. Most backseat drivers I know don't change, no matter how many times you tell them to shut their traps. It's much easier to deal with them effectively once you know that a) they're a backseat driver and b) their sense of direction really sucks. Treatment means figuring out how to wrest control back from this backseat driver. You might not always be able to toss the SOB out of the car and watch him go *kathump kathump splat* on the highway, but you can turn up the radio to drown out his directions. Or you can work to push him back to the backseat, and ultimately to the trunk. I also have to remember that the wannabe driver is going to be trying to give directions for a good long time, and that he might figure out how to get out of the trunk and back into the car at some point. I have to be ready for that. I have to get my own directions and be confident in that. I also need a killer playlist for my iPod so I can drown out his racket.

Living with a predisposition to anorexia isn't the same as living with the illness, just as having a backseat driver in the car doesn't mean you let him give you directions. I have begun, slowly and tentatively, to refer to my eating disorder in the past tense. I *used to* over-exercise and restrict my food. I *used to* freak out about calories and weight. *Used to.* My recovery, however, remains present tense. I *still eat* three meals and two snacks every day. I *still exercise* in moderation and for the joy of moving my body. *Still.*

It is like this that I and many others like me are re-building our lives after our eating disorders and figuring out everything that life has to offer.

11 Standing at the Buffet of Life

Usually in the last chapter of an eating disorder book, the heroine leaps off the page, recovered, and yammers on endlessly about how great her life is. She loves her body! and how she looks! and food is just this wonderful, delicious thing! and so on. This is not that book.

Anorexia isn't really a factor in my day-to-day living any more. I mostly don't stress about food or weight. I don't look in the mirror and think how great I look. Honestly, I still don't particularly like my body—but then, I never really did, even before the eating disorder. The difference is that now, I don't think about it all that much. My size doesn't particularly bother me. Yes, I would like to have thinner thighs, but I don't, and that's that. Sometimes I still think that eating is a pain, but it now stems from the fact that I am involved in so many things that can more easily hold my attention than food porn and nutrition information.

As the haze of anorexia began to lift, my life didn't instantly become wonderful. I found myself a thirty-something young woman who had never dated, and never held down a steady job for longer than a year without having to leave and return to treatment. On paper, my life looked great. I had several graduate degrees and an impressive pedigree. But when people talked about parties or college life or going out with friends, I was totally lost. I couldn't talk about that crazy night when I turned 21 and could legally drink alcohol because I was in the hospital and couldn't even have a Diet Coke, let alone a shot of vodka. These things were not a part of my experience.

At 30, as I truly began to leave the eating disorder behind, I was lonely, sad, and angry. Despite my knowledge of anorexia, I blamed myself for years of failed treatments, for the financial and emotional pain I caused my family, and for being dumb enough to start down this road in the first place. I also had boatloads of wisdom—a Ph.D. from the School of Life—that many of my peers didn't have. It gave me a self-awareness that was hard to put into words. I find myself simultaneously wiser and immature compared to people my own age. I had to literally rebuild my life from the ruins, and it's an ongoing process.

Part of this process means maintaining the cornerstone of my recovery: regular eating and a healthy weight. Without that, all of my other hard work goes down the drain. It's why I still use a meal plan to guide my eating. No, I don't painstakingly measure all of my food as I did before, but because my hunger and fullness cues don't always register, I need a plan to help me eat properly. I have worked with my therapist and dietitian to integrate plenty of flexibility into my plan so that I can eat in restaurants and with friends easily and worry-free.

It's also why I am still weighed regularly. As much as I hate climbing on the scale, I know that staying at a healthy weight is important. These regular weight checks also help alleviate the anxiety that I'm constantly gaining weight. Regular weigh-ins are part of my health routine, just like refilling my prescriptions or having my blood pressure and electrolytes checked. I might not always like it—in fact, I frequently don't—but I've come to accept it as necessary.

It took more time and more work than I ever thought possible, but I have taken my life back from my eating disorder. No more is my life ruled by an evil whisper that only I can hear. My relationship with my parents no longer consists of frightened phone calls or shouting matches. We are closer than ever. As other families have found, this closeness is a direct result of my recovery. Family healing didn't make recovery possible; rather, it was my recovery that made this healing possible. Not all relatives are on board. To some, I will remain permanently sick and crazy, and that's a reality I have to get used to.

It took years of work, but it was only as I was writing this book that I reached a stage where I actually felt any confidence in my own recovery. Previously, I had strung together a week or two behavior-free, but these always collapsed under the weight of my anorexic perseverations and compulsions. Anything that might be called "recovery" always seemed like a fluke. I knew, deep down, that it wouldn't stick. I might very well have created a self-fulfilling prophecy in the process.

Slowly, however, with a lot of hard work, I found that the slips grew fewer and further apart. When I did slip, I wasn't finding myself in a catastrophic spiral. Rather, it was an extra exercise session or a skipped snack. These things definitely needed immediate attention, but I wasn't finding myself narrowly avoiding hospitalization. At some point, I realized that I had been doing this recovery thing for several months straight, with no substantial slips. The momentum began to build on itself, and I started to feel that I could keep it up.

Only after I had a substantial amount of time at a healthy weight and with a very low level of eating disorder behaviors did I find myself actually wanting recovery. I had wanted to be rid of the eating disorder for a very long time, but I was simultaneously fearful of recovery. Essentially, I tried my damnedest to figure out a way to stay underweight and not be miserable. Not surprisingly, I wasn't successful.

Defining Recovery

I asked my blog readers who thought themselves in recovery from their eating disorder to chime in and share what they felt being in recovery actually means. The comments I received in response to this question provided a breadth and depth to my understanding of recovery that I hadn't anticipated. Some pearls of wisdom:

- Recovery to me is first about getting physically healthy and ED [eating disorder] behavior free. To sit with the anxiety and fears that come with it and not engage in the ED. Even if you don't feel 100 percent about recovery, you go through the healthy steps until you feel it 100 percent. I agree that physical health is number one, then you can work on the why behind the ED, coping skills, and building a life outside the ED. There is not that mental battle. The anxiety, fears, and depression lesson. The rigid behaviors around food, weight, activity, and so on are very little. You feel recovery in your heart and that you deserve it.

- A life outside the eating disorder, including going out and eating with friends and be able to eat off a food plan. Much of a social life revolves around food—from Thanksgiving to a cup of coffee in town when shopping. Not having to plan this or think about it but just doing what your peers do—having a muffin because it's cold! The return of hunger cues and the ability to eat when hungry. Food as pleasure as well as fuel. You recognize ED thoughts for what they are—thoughts, not orders. You cope with anxiety/depression, etc. in ways other than restricting food. You accept perfectionist tendencies and realize that perfection is not attainable. Settling HAPPILY for second place! You can recognize and react to other people's feelings and emotions.

- Recovery for me means no emotional attachment to food or using it as a mask for my feelings. Food is fuel for giving my body and mind the strength to face my emotions and feelings head on and doing something about them, should I choose to.

- I am not recovered, I'm not even weight-restored yet. But my recovery goal is to be able to spend a full day thinking about my family, my neighbors, my research, my colleagues, my friends, and the events in the world around me. And not, for even 15 minutes, *miss it* because of panic about food, exercise, or my body. I am so excited for this imagined day and working hard to get there.

- My definition of what recovery will look like for me and what I am almost to the point of is being able to go to a restaurant and order whatever I want, not counting calories every minute of the day, exercising enough to feel good but never overdoing it, sitting around with friends and eating cookies and not thinking about how fat I will be the next day, drinking more than water even if it has calories in it, looking at myself in the mirror and loving the person both inside and out that is staring back at me. Accepting what was and moving on to what could be—a life of fulfillment, happiness, and love.

- I considered myself recovered from my ED ... yet, this is still a question I have a hard time answering because there are so many different levels to it. There have been times I have thought I was recovered, and then months later I progressed further in life/recovery, and then realized that maybe I wasn't recovered before. It's a hard question. I have even had times recently when I will be faced with a food that I haven't had in a while, and my immediate reaction is still anxiety/fear. I can work through it now without much pain or effort, but it still shocks me when it happens.

These qualitative descriptions of recovery—quickly gathered from my own personal blog—are actually just about as rigorous as many formal studies on eating disorder recovery. An extensive search through the literature showed that most quantitative research evaluating anorexia recovery was based on the Morgan-Russell scale. This scale was developed in 1975 by two British psychologists (H.G. Morgan and Gerald Russell) to provide non-specialists with an easy-to-use tool to evaluate their patient's progress. The Morgan-Russell scale assesses 14 different factors, from employment to psychosocial functioning, to body weight and menstrual status. The Morgan-Russell scale also provides a general outcome measure based on weight and menstruation, which is the most commonly used criterion in most research studies. Patients with a good outcome have a body weight that is at least 85 percent of ideal body weight (IBW) and menstruate regularly. Fair or intermediate outcome consists of patients with 75 to 85 percent IBW or irregular menstruation. Poor outcome means the patient's body weight is less than 75 percent of ideal (Morgan and Russell, 1975).

Russell and his colleagues at the Maudsley hospital in London followed a group of 41 patients for approximately 20 years after they were discharged from inpatient anorexia treatment. The 1991 study publishing their results makes for a pretty grim read. Their findings give rise to the "Rule of Thirds" in anorexia recovery: one-third of patients had a good outcome, one-third remained chronically ill, and the remaining third was somewhere in the middle. Six of the 41 patients (15 percent) had died as a direct or indirect result of anorexia (Ratnasuriya *et al.*, 1991).

Even the patients who achieved a good outcome on the Morgan-Russell scale still had substantial difficulties with recovery and reported significant abnormalities in eating habits. Write the authors:

> Even among those whose outcome was generally good, a third were regularly restricting their diet and a third reported eating irregularly. Among them some reported, for example, that they avoided eating regular meals unless pressured by their husbands, often restricting themselves to irregular "snacks." Others found that they were only able to maintain their weight if they kept to a very rigid diet. Excessive preoccupations with thoughts of food and weight also tended to persist, being reported by over half of the patients who were otherwise doing well.
>
> (p. 497)

Which doesn't seem like much of a "recovery" to me. Aside from the sobering reality of recovery after inpatient anorexia treatment, the Morgan-Russell scale tells me that weight and menstrual status alone don't indicate recovery. The women described in the above paragraph were still very much trapped by anorexia. Maybe their weight isn't life-threateningly low, but the brain disease or mental illness of anorexia likely rages in their heads and lives. I'm not saying my eating habits are perfect, or that I don't have my moments of food- and weight-induced freakouts, but you would never know of my eating disorder history by looking in my pantry or watching me eat. I'm probably less obsessed with food than many of my friends who have never had an eating disorder.

More recent studies (the women in the Russell paper were all hospitalized in the 1950s and 1960s [Morgan and Hayward, 1988]) indicate that many adolescents hospitalized for anorexia do actually make a full recovery, but that it can take five to seven years (Strober *et al.*, 1997). New family-based interventions appear to shorten time to recovery somewhat (Eisler *et al.*, 1997), but recovery still takes time—lots of time. The authors of these outcome studies acknowledge that their results may not be representative of everyone with anorexia. A 2011 study found that only one-quarter of people with eating disorders actually receive treatment, whereas a 2010 study indicated that some anorexia sufferers have a relatively brief and transient course of illness. So it's unclear exactly how the chances of recovery for individuals needing inpatient anorexia treatment compare to others with the illness.

More Than a Box You Can Check

No matter what these studies show in terms of recovery, this still doesn't define what exactly recovery is. The Morgan-Russell scale appears to capture only a small fraction of anorexia recovery. The comments from my blog readers are definitely descriptive, but it's hard to systematically study and define such things as "the number on the scale doesn't define me." When researchers asked recovered eating disorder patients and their therapists about the factors they believed were important to recovery, they cited everything from eating disorder-specific items (attitude towards weight, healthy eating habits, physical activity, and purging) to a range of other factors, like sexuality, co-morbid disorders, and social functioning (Noordenbos and Seubring, 2006). The former patients and therapists all essentially agreed on which factors were important, and believed that evaluating psychological and social measures, as well as physiological and behavioral criteria, should be included in assessments of recovery (Noordenbos, 2011b).

The task for researchers is to develop a series of questions that provide a meaningful portrait of eating disorder recovery that can be fairly easily obtained and quantitatively assessed. It's something Anna Bardone-Cone, a psychologist at the University of North Carolina at Chapel Hill, has been working on. "If you look at personal narratives of recovery and then you look at journal articles of recovery, there's this disconnect," she said. "There's certainly an agreement about the behavioral aspect of it, but what you tend to see in qualitative analyses of eating disorder recovery is that people talk about having a different attitude toward food. And this isn't captured in behaviors or weight."

Bardone-Cone noticed the same problem with the Morgan-Russell scale as

I did. The data derived from two simple questions (How much do you weigh? Do you get regular periods?) is also pretty simplistic. Which isn't to say that information on weight and menstrual status isn't important, just that it doesn't tell the whole story—not even close. "Recovery was treated just like a box you could check," she said. As anyone with any familiarity with eating disorders will say, recovery is a whole hell of a lot more complicated than that.

By talking to women and men who considered themselves recovering or recovered from their eating disorder, as well as combing through the research literature, Bardone-Cone divided recovery into three different areas. The first was physical recovery. Is the person maintaining an appropriate weight? Are their periods regular? Do they have electrolyte imbalances? Are they fainting or having seizures? Have hormone levels normalized? It is these types of questions that the Morgan-Russell scale is grasping at. Many of the people I talked to reported similar experiences to mine, in that their weight normalized long before their thinking did.

"I fulfilled the weight criteria of recovery even while I was still very symptomatic, and no therapist worth their salt would have said I was recovered," I said.

"We do know that, when you start thinking of the things that start falling back into place, we know that the mindset stuff is some of the last stuff to happen," Bardone-Cone replied. "To an outsider, you might look recovered but not have this match the internal things."

Part of the mindset stuff that Bardone-Cone mentioned is part of behavioral recovery. This means eating normal meals and not fasting. It means not purging. It means binge eating is infrequent or non-existent. Exercise isn't abused, nor are diet pills or other supplements. It means the regular consumption of meals and snacks. All of these things have to exist for a minimum of three months as well.

Partial recovery, according to Bardone-Cone, means both physical and behavioral recovery. "If you check the weight box and the behavior box, you're left with a very heterogeneous group of people," she said. "Some people are essentially 'over it' and fit the definition of full recovery, while others look recovered on the outside, but on the inside they're still thinking about this all the time."

This is the hardest part of recovery, I told her, where you look normal but no longer have the low weight of anorexia or the constant medical emergencies to validate your suffering. Just when you need help the most, you feel you deserve it the least.

Lastly, Bardone-Cone spoke of psychological recovery. This, perhaps, is the hardest to measure because it contains the most qualitative answers. It means not constantly stepping on and off the scale or always looking up nutrition information. It means minimal fear foods. The easiest way to behavioral recovery is by the standard Eating Disorders Examination. If a person scores within the general range of others of their age and gender, then they are considered to have behavioral recovery.

Psychological recovery also means your relationships with your partner, parents, and/or friends are healing. It means you have developed self-compassion: you don't beat yourself up over every little mistake. Perfectionism has decreased. Anxiety, depression, and other co-morbid conditions are being addressed or managed. Body image has become less important. To get this sort of information, Bardone-Cone asked study participants a variety of questions about depression, anxiety, perfectionism, and psychosocial functioning (Bardone-Cone, Harney *et al.*, 2010).

Full recovery from an eating disorder means not just that the eating disorder-specific behaviors are under control, but also that the thinking styles common to eating disorders have also been resolved. You're not constantly fighting thoughts and behaviors. You've accepted your body and think of it in more holistic terms, even if you don't always look in the mirror and smile at that sexy beast staring back at you. "Recovery doesn't mean you love your body all the time," Bardone-Cone said.

Which is where I'm at in recovery, I told Bardone-Cone. My body is my body. I don't always like it, but I know that I don't have the build to be long and lean. I can even appreciate my Arnold Family Thighs™, especially when I'm riding my bike up the steep hill by my house. Mostly, though, I don't really give it much thought, positive or negative. This is ultimately the goal, Bardone-Cone said.

"It would be great if all women could love their bodies," she said, "but the goal is to have a realism about it and an acceptance of it that's not overshadowed by thoughts of *gotta be thin, gotta be thin*." Our bodies aren't just objects to be looked at. They enable us to do many meaningful things with our life: to hug a friend, run after a playful dog, and produce works of art. Shifting the focus of our bodies from what they look like to what they can do appears to be crucial to recovery. When Bardone-Cone looked at fully recovered women, she found that they didn't have much shame about their bodies, nor did they compare their size and shape to everyone they saw (Fitzsimmons-Craft *et al.*, 2011).

Full recovery is a hard, complicated task, Bardone-Cone says. "It's not just about the absence of things, but about the presence of things," she said. "It's not just the absence of obsessive thoughts about food and weight, but the presence of a great variety of things that come from being in the moment." I experienced this when I went snorkeling in the Caribbean right as I was writing this chapter. I wasn't obsessing over the calories in the rice and beans I had for lunch, nor was I thinking about my round tummy that everyone could see in my bathing suit. Instead, I was feeling the warm water on my skin and watching the colorful fish. Without recovery, my mind would have been focused on lunch and spandex at the expense of the dramatic coral reef.

"Do these aspects of recovery—the physical, behavioral, and psychological—generally normalize in that order?" I asked Bardone-Cone. They did for me, I explained, and she agreed that, for anorexia, that is generally the case. A malnourished brain isn't working properly, she said, which means it's hard for sufferers to actually make use of therapy and engage in significant psychological change until weight and nutritional status are more normalized.

One question about recovery that researchers still haven't really answered is whether eating disorder thoughts are non-existent, infrequent, or they just aren't obsessive. One woman who declared herself totally recovered from bulimia told Bardone-Cone that she never thinks about turning to binge eating to cope. For me, I still have the thoughts, but they're pretty infrequent and they don't really stick around. When I had the stomach flu, I did think about purging because I was horribly nauseous and knew that throwing up would make me feel better. Or if I had a big chunk of time free, I might think that I could, in theory, use this to exercise. I won't really want to, I won't have an urge to drop everything and put on my running shoes, but I am aware of the possibilities. It's as much a remembrance of things past as it is an eating disorder-specific thought.

"There haven't been many efforts to capture this in empirical work," Bardone-Cone said. She told me she just got a research grant funded by the National Institute of Mental Health to collect longitudinal data on eating disorder recovery. Her goal is to follow eating disorder patients through recovery to find out exactly how people do and don't proceed through this process. A new measure she wants to validate is the Eating Disorder Recovery Self-Efficacy scale, which asks people how confident they are about their ability to maintain a realistic recovery.

With this information, Bardone-Cone also wants to identify what aspects of recovery are the most important in predicting final outcome. "Maybe all that really matters in psychological recovery is weight concern and shape concern," Bardone-Cone said. Maybe, she said, it's something else entirely. Right now, no one knows (Noordenbos, 2011a).

Knowing what parts of recovery are the most crucial will give therapists helpful information. They can then focus more on these areas with their clients because they have the largest impact on whether they will ultimately recover. Preliminary studies seem to indicate that managing body image distortion is a key factor. A 2005 study by psychologist Pamela Keel at the University of Florida and her colleagues found that the strongest predictor of relapse after full symptom remission of an eating disorder is body image distress (Keel *et al.*, 2005). These results, the authors wrote, "suggest that focused body image work during relapse prevention may enhance long-term recovery from eating disorders" (p. 2263).

Less likely to relapse, however, doesn't mean that relapse will never happen. No therapist, no matter how skilled, has that kind of Magic 8 ball. Some people, like my friend and author Jenni Schaefer, as well as well-known eating disorders therapist Carolyn Costin, say they are fully recovered from their eating disorder and don't believe they will ever relapse. The eating disorder is banished from their lives and won't return because they've dealt with the issues that caused the eating disorder in the first place.

I have no doubt that Jenni and Carolyn are at very low risk of relapse, not just because they've "dealt with" the underlying issues, but also because they know to practice good self-care and have enough awareness to catch any small slips long before they become something significant. Although I have a good understanding of what triggered my eating disorder, I have a different understanding about what caused my anorexia. No amount of therapy will eliminate my biological predisposition to anorexia. I might have absolutely no behavioral or psychological signs of an eating disorder (I consider my eating disorder to be in remission), but I also know that improper eating can set off the cycle all over again.

Bardone-Cone said that some of the people she's interviewed in her research prefer to say that they are in recovery. This mindset gives them less pressure to be perfect, she said. The women she spoke with also said that saying they are in recovery empowers them to take early action if they do start to slip. They don't feel they have to hide their struggles from loved ones. For a long time, I thought that saying I was "in recovery" meant that I was condemning myself to constantly fighting off eating-disordered thoughts. Although this is usually a factor in early recovery, it's not as much an issue in lasting recovery.

"So what do you think about 'in recovery' or 'recovered'?" Bardone-Cone asked me.

I told her I had done a lot of thinking about the issue, and framed the question differently. "Maybe it's just me being a writer nerd, but I like to think of recovery in terms of verb tenses," I said. My goal wasn't to think of recovering or recovered, but to put my eating disorder in the past tense. I don't want to obsess about food and weight and exercise. That's not recovery by any name.

However, I need to keep my recovery in the present tense. So many of the things I did in recovery I will have to continue doing for the rest of my life in order to stay healthy. I can't skip meals or snacks. I can't call a candy bar "dinner" just because I can't be bothered to turn on the stove. Nor can I let myself get sleep deprived or overly stressed. They can set off the eating disorder, directly or indirectly, by making me more depressed and anxious. I need to have adequate "me" time, have a job or hobby that gives me a sense of purpose, and have good relationships with friends and family. If I want to stay well, I can't neglect these things. No amount of time, therapy, or self-discovery will eliminate my biological predisposition to anorexia. "So, to me, it's not really about recovering or recovered," I concluded.

Permanently Perfectionistic?

Without anorexia, I found, I was the same person I was before I got sick: obsessive, perfectionistic, and moody. All of the traits that made me so vulnerable to an eating disorder still exist. No amount of recovery or therapy can change who I am and how I tend to function best. Recovery, in a sense, has meant learning how to use these predisposing traits for good instead of evil. Take an obsessive attention to detail. It might mean that I can't summarize a short story very well or see the forest for the trees, but it also means that, when I sent out my resume, I could be absolutely sure it didn't have any typos. My impeccably spell-checked cover letter and resume actually got me a job—my employer told me I was chosen immediately because I was the only person without any editing errors.

Learning to live with your own unique temperament is one of the final and perhaps most important tasks of recovery. It's something that writer Aimee Liu knows a lot about. In 1979, Aimee published the first popular memoir about anorexia. After suffering a mid-life relapse of her illness, Aimee wrote the book *Gaining* to address the full spectrum of illness and recovery in eating disorders.

Like me, and many people with anorexia, Aimee describes herself as anxious, driven, and perfectionistic. Also like me, Aimee had to figure out how to live with her temperament in a healthy way. "I am up against these traits every day," she said.

These traits come out full-force in Aimee's work as a novelist. "If I don't produce three or four pages a day, I very quickly start to feel like a failure. So I have to step in and step back," she said. Working on a novel doesn't always mean writing. Sometimes it means thinking about the story and trying out different plot lines in your head. At other times, it means walking away from your desk and just letting the ideas marinate for a while.

"I realized there was a way to apply my perfectionism in my work as a writer and as a novelist, but there were also times when I had to consciously break that perfectionistic need and force myself to take chances artistically," Aimee said. She credits much of this realization to the study of mindfulness, or of being fully aware of the present moment. By focusing more on the here-and-now, rather than the past or what might be, she developed a better awareness of what her options were.

I often find myself falling into the same traps, even while working on this book. I assigned myself a daily quota of words I had to write, and not meeting that quota meant I was lazy and worthless. Never mind, of course, that I might be reading articles, doing interviews, organizing notes, or plotting out structure. Without these things, I would be producing page after page of meaningless drivel—hardly an accomplishment. Hardest for me was to actually step away from my computer and focus on something else for a while, to let my brain regenerate and recharge so I could write when I returned. Assessing my true progress meant dropping the perfectionistic rules and gaining a more holistic understanding of what writing a book meant.

It's not simple. The upside of rules and concrete standards is that I always knew exactly how I was faring. If I let my progress get too nebulous, I feared I would start slacking off. If I let go of my rigid eating habits, I might Velcro myself to the couch and shove Twinkies in my mouth all day. I realized several things. First, I don't have the personality to be a slacker. I would get bored and find something to do. Second, Twinkies aren't very good, so I needn't worry about eating too many of them. My fears were totally disconnected from reality, and I was hiding from a boogeyman that didn't even exist.

Making these connections requires a level of self-awareness that often requires the help of a therapist. Talking about my day-to-day problems with my therapist not only gave me an emotional release but also started me connecting the dots between my ingrained ways of thinking and my present problems. "You start to realize that your patterns of thinking can be completely counter-productive and even counter-intuitive," Aimee said.

These ways of thinking tend to exist before the eating disorder actually begins and generally persist even after food, eating, and weight have ceased to become issues. In 1995, Walter Kaye and his colleagues compared perfectionism and obsessive-compulsive behaviors in a group of 20 women who had been recovered from anorexia for more than a year with 16 control women. The women recovered from anorexia had significantly higher levels of perfectionism than the control women, as well as a higher need for exactness and ordered surroundings (Srinivasagam *et al.*, 1995).

A more recent study done on women who had recovered from eating disorders (not just anorexia) by Bardone-Cone and colleagues found that women who had fully recovered from their eating disorder had similar levels of perfectionism as women who had never had an eating disorder. When the researchers compared fully recovered individuals with those in partial recovery or an active eating disorder, however, they found much higher levels of perfectionism. These results seem to imply that fully recovering from your eating disorder means tackling perfectionism and, likely, other personality traits that make a person vulnerable to an eating disorder in the first place (Bardone-Cone, Sturm *et al.*, 2010). It's a stage that can sometimes take years to achieve.

As well, when Bardone-Cone compared the coping skills of women in various stages of eating disorder recovery to women who had never had an eating disorder, she found that, similar to her study on perfectionism, fully recovered women were indistinguishable from healthy controls. When both groups were faced with difficult situations, these women could distract themselves by taking specific steps to deal with the problem. The women that were partially recovered or still active in their eating disorder had much more emotional coping skills and tended to over-think the situation or avoid it completely. Although I don't think an eating disorder is a coping skill per se, developing a full arsenal of coping skills also helps the individual leave their eating disorder behind (Fitz simmons and Bardone-Cone, 2010).

After Aimee published her memoir, she entered what she describes as the "half-life" of recovery from anorexia. Although her weight normalized, her attitudes towards food and even life didn't. "For close to 30 years, I was recovered physically from an eating disorder," she said, "but I still had these traits of persistence and beating myself up and feeling constantly apologetic if I made any kind of error in anything. I had this sense that there were all these rules about things I was supposed to do."

It wasn't until she started to write *Gaining* that she began to put the pieces together. These traits that seemed to have nothing to do with food were actually an inherent part of the eating disorder. They were part of what made Aimee vulnerable to anorexia in the first place, and what prevented her from shaking her eating disorder completely. Part of the healing process for Aimee meant going back to school and getting her Master's degree in creative writing. "It was the best thing I ever did in my life," she said.

I made a similar decision in my own life, to go back to school and get my Master's in science writing, and I came to the same conclusion as Aimee: it was the best thing I ever did. Since I was 12, I had planned on being a research scientist and getting my Ph.D. The onset of anorexia in college changed the field in which I was interested (biochemistry to epidemiology), but not the overall career path. Still, I remained vaguely unsatisfied but too tied to my plans to consider something different. A chance Internet search while trying to write a website for my current job led me to a program in science writing at Johns Hopkins University. It was almost as if angels started singing hymns in my head. For the first time, I realized I didn't have to decide between my love of science and my love of writing. So with just a few weeks until the application deadline, I worked furiously and sent an envelope to Baltimore. Two months later, I got the phone call asking me to come to Hopkins.

This wasn't some miracle cure-all. My eating disorder was alive and well, and I continued to struggle and relapse for several years after this decision. But I felt a tremendous sense of freedom from breaking the self-imposed "rule" that I was going to become a researcher myself. Breaking the rules, whether or not they were directly related to eating and exercise, became a huge part of my recovery. Aimee found the same to be true. "Sometimes the rule is that you need to break the rules," she said.

A Life Worth Living

One of the rules I had to break was the belief that recovery was going to be a relatively straightforward task. It would be something I could check off on my life's to do list: go to college, buy a house, recover from anorexia. *Check, check, check.* I never realized just how much I had to learn about myself and my disorder before I could create a meaningful, lasting recovery. Then, I had to expand my recovery work to include creating a meaningful life, of which my eating disorder history was only one part. As my recovery became more and more about my actual life, I found my focus shifting away from the eating disorder to include a wide variety of things that had nothing to do with anorexia. I help run a local knitting and crochet group. I write about topics that have nothing to do with food and body image. I meet friends for coffee.

I noticed a parallel expansion in one of my fellow eating disorder bloggers, Sarah. "My life has expanded a lot. My energy these days isn't focused as much on recovery, or maintaining recovery, or getting further in recovery. Those kinds of things are not what occupy my energy anymore. So it felt strange to keep writing about something that wasn't occupying my energy or my headspace," she said. "I don't want to dwell on my history, but I want to remember that it was there." So Sarah shifted the focus of her blog from eating disorder recovery to her journey through life as a whole person—one that loves Starbucks and dogs and family.

Sarah started over-exercising and worrying about food while in high school, but it wasn't until she started college that things got out of hand. Eventually, Sarah was sent to an eating disorders program near her house, where she spent the day in group therapy and eating meals but went home in the evenings. Slowly, over many months, Sarah returned to a healthy weight. During this process, she began reading and looking for support online, and ran across some eating disorder blogs. In need of an outlet, and in search of support for her own recovery, Sarah started her own blog. I started reading Sarah's blog shortly after that.

In the years I've known Sarah, I've watched her move through many of the stages of recovery that Bardone-Cone talked about. At first, much of Sarah's writing focused on eating what she needed to and conquering any slips. As the years passed, however, Sarah spent less time dealing with behavioral issues and more time addressing her psychological recovery. This, too, slowly drifted to the background as she was able to place her life front and center. Recently, she started a job at a non-profit organization where she teaches emotional coping skills to adolescent girls. "I can actually concentrate on work stuff for an entire day. I'm really passionate about what I do, and it's a big thing I focus on. I wouldn't be able to do that if I was still sick," Sarah said. "Finding a job that I really care about and being able to help other girls every day, it feels like I'm being a role model for them. I can't really do that and have headspace for other things."

Recovery has impacted more than just Sarah's career. It also helped repair family dynamics with her parents and siblings, and has enabled her to become a better and more confident wife. "I'm fully present now. Before, in our relationship, I felt I was only half there. My husband could see the full me, but I couldn't bring him the full me. He deserved the full me, and now I can bring him all of my energy, my love, my attention. He used to only get half of this, because the other half was reserved for the eating disorder," Sarah said.

I asked Sarah what advice she had for other people who were still in the trenches and fighting their eating disorder. "I remember a quote that I read from Alcoholics Anonymous that says you're only as sick as your secrets. I needed to open up to somebody and let them know what my secrets were. That was a huge part of my healing," she said. Blogging, for her, became a safe place for her to share her secrets and get feedback. "I thought that maybe I could have something to say, and maybe this could be good for me. I didn't really know where I was going to take it at first, but it was one of the most helpful things I did in recovery," Sarah said.

She also said that it was helpful to break down recovery into a series of small but manageable steps. "I remember looking at the entire day and thinking how much I had to eat before bed. But if I told myself that I just have to eat breakfast, and I didn't think ahead, I could usually motivate myself to do that. Then I told myself that I had an hour break, and then I had a snack," Sarah said.

These small steps enabled Sarah to reclaim her life from anorexia. "I feel like my life still has all the same elements to it that it did before I got sick, I just enjoy them more," Sarah concluded.

Maybe this is why it's so hard to quantify recovery—how do you measure the creation of a life worth living? All of us, whether we have an eating disorder or not, use different threads to weave our lives. For Sarah, a huge part of her life is her husband, her job, and her faith. For me, it's yarn, cats, and writing. No two people are identical, which means no two recoveries will be, either.

This life I've created for myself is one of my biggest buffers against relapse. It has made the costs of the eating disorder much more apparent and in my face. When the anorexia started, I didn't have much of a social life anyway, so isolating myself hardly made a difference. Nor did I have any hobbies or a particular attachment to my career. So the loss of friends, free time, and jobs only made me shrug my shoulders. The benefits of the eating disorder—the reduction in anxiety, the sense of accomplishment—far outweighed any of the costs.

A substantial amount of time in recovery, however, gave me the chance to cultivate new friendships and hobbies. It allowed me to become interested in things that weren't school- or work-related. It gave me time to spend with family. Relapsing would cost me all of this, and it's not a bill I want to pay. These things give me a reason to hold on and fight back against anorexia. If I were to resume marathon exercise sessions, I wouldn't have as much time to read or crochet. If I started restricting, I wouldn't be able to spend time with friends and family, nor would I have the energy and concentration to work on my writing.

My recovery isn't finished. It's still a work in progress because *I'm* still a work in progress. My food and exercise issues might be mostly a thing of the past, but I still have plenty of things to work on. I never forget that I am one of the lucky ones. I could access treatment. I finally found a competent therapist who stopped buying my bullshit. My parents continued to support me for years. Anorexia damaged my health, but it's not severely compromised. My weight is healthy. I have the confidence (most of the time) to tackle the day. Simply, I am alive. Too many people who have struggled with eating disorders aren't. Many more are still firmly ensnared in their disorder, alive in the technical sense but feeling dead on the inside.

I am trying to think of how to end this book with the right combination of hope and seriousness. I don't like clichés or want to give the impression that recovery is all unicorns and rainbows. It's not. Who you are and how you operate don't really change. In a world that values multi-tasking, risk-taking, and über-drivenness, I have had to make peace with both who I am and who I'm not. I've had to learn how to respect my limits and my history without letting them define me.

I can't tell someone how to recover from anorexia. I don't have a guide book or road map. What I can say is this: find support, get good, evidence-based treatment, and start eating. Don't settle, either. Create the life you want to live. Eventually, anorexia will just become a small speck in your rearview mirror.

References

Chapter 1

Bennett, D., Sharpe, M., Freeman, C., and Carson, A. (2004). Anorexia nervosa among female secondary school students in Ghana. *British Journal of Psychiatry, 185,* 312–317.

Brumberg, J. (2000). *Fasting Girls: The History of Anorexia Nervosa.* New York, NY: Vintage Books.

Crisafulli, M.A., Von Holle, A., and Bulik, C.M. (2008). Attitudes towards anorexia nervosa: the impact of framing on blame and stigma. *International Journal of Eating Disorders, 41,* 333–319.

Dailey, A.H. (1894). *Mollie Fancher, The Brooklyn Enigma.* New York, NY: Eagle Book Printing Department.

Goulston, M. (2010, February 23). Anorexia: starving for love. *The Huffington Post.* Retrieved from www.huffingtonpost.com/mark-goulston-md/anorexia-starving-for-lov_b_472540.html.

Greenblatt, J. (2010). *Answers to Anorexia: A Breakthrough Nutritional Treatment That Is Saving Lives.* North Branch, MN: Sunrise River Press.

Herpertz-Dahlmann, B., Seitz, J., and Konrad, K. (2011). Aetiology of anorexia nervosa: from a "psychosomatic family model" to a neuropsychiatric disorder? *European Archives of Psychiatry and Clinical Neuroscience, 261,* S177–181.

Husni, M., Koye, N., and Haggarty, J. (2001). Severe anorexia in an Amish Mennonite teenager. *Canadian Journal of Psychiatry, 46,* 183.

Latham, J. and Wilson, A. (2010, December 8). The great DNA data deficit: are genes for disease a mirage? *Independent Science News.* Retrieved from http://independentsciencenews.org/health/the-great-dna-data-deficit/.

Lee, S., Ho, T.P., and Hsu, L.K. (1993). Fat phobic and non-fat phobic anorexia nervosa: a comparative study of 70 Chinese patients in Hong Kong. *Psychological Medicine, 23,* 999–1017.

Lyster-Mensh, L. (2011, June 12). Letting parents off the hook? Not hardly. *Laura's Soap Box.* Retrieved from www.laurassoapbox.net/2011/06/letting-parents-off-hook-not-hardly.html.

Mayer, L.E., Roberto, C.A., Glasofer, D.R., Etu, S.F., Gallagher, D., Wang, J., Heymsfield, S.B., Pierson, R.N., Attia, E., Devlin, M.J., and Walsh, B.T. (2007). Does percent body fat predict outcome in anorexia nervosa? *American Journal of Psychiatry, 164,* 970–972.

Paquette, V., Lévesque, J., Mensour, B., Leroux, J.M., Beaudoin, G., Bourgouin, P., and Beauregard, M. (2003). "Change the mind and you change the brain": effects of cognitive-behavioral therapy on the neural correlates of spider phobia. *Neuroimage, 18*, 401–409.

Ravin, S. (2009). Clinician faces old ideas as she pursues new career. *Special to FEAST.* Retrieved from: http://feast-ed.org/TheFacts/RavinEssay.aspx.

Ravin, S. (2011, June 2). Blame it on the brain. *Dr Sarah Ravin blog.* Retrieved from: www.blog.drsarahravin.com/psychotherapy/blame-it-on-the-brain/.

Reda, M. and Sacco, G. (2001). Anorexia and the holiness of Saint Catherine of Siena. *Journal of Criminal Justice and Popular Culture, 8*, 37–47.

Schwartz, J.M., Stoessel, P.W., Baxter, L.R., Martin, K.M., and Phelps, M.E. (1996). Systematic changes in cerebral glucose metabolic rate after successful behavior modification treatment of obsessive-compulsive disorder. *Archives of General Psychiatry, 53*, 109–113.

Stacey, M. (2002). *The Fasting Girl: A True Victorian Medical Mystery.* New York, NY: Penguin Putnam.

Strober, M. (2004). Pathologic fear conditioning and anorexia nervosa: on the search for novel paradigms. *International Journal of Eating Disorders, 35*, 504–508.

Chapter 2

Aharoni, R. and Hertz, M.M. (2012). Disgust sensitivity and anorexia nervosa. *European Eating Disorders Review, 20*, 106–110.

American Medical Association. (2011). AMA adopts new policies at annual meeting. *American Medical Association website.* Retrieved from: www.ama-assn.org/ama/pub/news/news/a11-new-policies.page.

Antonova, E., Parslow, D., Brammer, M., Simmons, A., Williams, S., Dawson, G.R., and Morris, R. (2011). Scopolamine disrupts hippocampal activity during allocentric spatial memory in humans: an fMRI study using a virtual reality analogue of the Morris Water Maze. *Journal of Psychopharmacology, 25*, 1256–1265.

Arnold, C. (2012). Inside the wrong body. *Scientific American Mind*, May/June, 32–37.

Becker, A.E., Thomas, J.J., and Pike, K.M. (2009). Should non-fat-phobic anorexia nervosa be included in DSM-V? *International Journal of Eating Disorders, 42*, 620–635.

Blakeslee, S. (2007, February 6). A small part of the brain, and its profound effects. *The New York Times.* Retrieved from: www.nytimes.com/2007/02/06/health/psychology/06brain.html?pagewanted=all.

Botvinick, M. and Cohen, J. (1998). Rubber hands 'feel' touch that eyes see. *Nature, 391*, 756.

Bourke, M.P., Taylor, G.J., Parker, J.D., and Bagby, R.M. (1992). Alexithymia in women with anorexia nervosa. A preliminary investigation. *British Journal of Psychiatry, 161*, 240–243.

Calogero, R.M., Davis, W.N., and Thompson, J.K. (2005). The role of self-objectification in the experience of women with eating disorders. *Sex Roles, 52*, 43–50.

Carei, T.R., Fyfe-Johnson, A.L., Breuner, C.C., and Brown, M.A. (2010). Randomized controlled clinical trial of yoga in the treatment of eating disorders. *Journal of Adolescent Health, 346*, 346–351.

Carter, J.C. and Bewell-Weiss, C.V. (2011). Nonfat phobic anorexia nervosa: clinical characteristics and response to inpatient treatment. *International Journal of Eating Disorders, 44*, 220–224.

Chowdhury, U., Gordon, I., Lask, B., Watkins, B., Watt, H., and Christie, D. (2003).

Early-onset anorexia nervosa: is there evidence of limbic system imbalance? *International Journal of Eating Disorders, 33,* 388–396.

Critchley, H.D., Wiens, S., Rotshtein, P., Ohman, A., and Dolan, R.J. (2004). Neural systems supporting interoceptive awareness. *Nature Neuroscience, 7,* 189–195.

Damasio, A. (2003). *Looking for Spinoza: Joy, Sorrow, and the Feeling Brain.* New York, NY: Mariner Books.

Dittmann, K.A. and Freedman, M.R. (2009). Body awareness, eating attitudes, and spiritual beliefs of women practicing yoga. *Eating Disorders, 17,* 273–292.

Dunn, B.D., Stefanovitch, I., Evans, D., Oliver, C., Hawkins, A., and Dalgleish, T. (2010). Can you feel the beat? Interoceptive awareness is an interactive function of anxiety- and depression-specific symptom dimensions. *Behaviour Research and Therapy, 48,* 1133–1138.

Fredrickson, B.L. and Roberts, T.-A. (1997). Objectification theory. *Psychology of Women Quarterly, 21,* 173–206.

Fredrickson, B.L., Roberts, T.-A., Noll, S.M., Quinn, D.M., and Twenge, J.M. (1998). That swimsuit becomes you: sex differences in self-objectification, restrained eating, and math performance. *Journal of Personality and Social Psychology, 75,* 269–284.

Gazalle, F.K., Frey, B.N., Hallal, P.C., Andreazza, A.C., Cunha, A.B.M., Santin, A., and Kapczinski, F. (2007). Mismatch between self-reported quality of life and functional assessment in acute mania: a matter of unawareness of illness? *Journal of Affective Disorders, 103,* 247–252.

Greenberg, S.J. (1997). Alexithymia in an anorexic population: prevalence and predictive variables. (Doctoral dissertation). Retrieved from Digital Commons at Pace University (AAI9801921).

Harrison, A., Tchanturia, K., and Treasure, J. (2010). Attentional bias, emotion recognition, and emotion regulation in anorexia: state or trait? *Biological Psychiatry, 68,* 755–761.

Herbert, B.M., Herbert, C., and Pollatos, O. (2011). On the relationship between interoceptive awareness and alexithymia: is interoceptive awareness related to emotional awareness? *Journal of Personality, 79,* 1149–1175.

Herz, R. (2012). *That's Disgusting: Unraveling the Mysteries of Repulsion.* New York, NY: W. W. Norton & Company.

Hoek, H.W. and van Hoeken, D. (2003). Review of the prevalence and incidence of eating disorders. *International Journal of Eating Disorders, 34,* 383–396.

Jenkinson, P.M., Preston, C., and Ellis, S.J. (2011). Unawareness after stroke: a review and practical guide to understanding, assessing, and managing anosognosia for hemiplegia. *Journal of Clinical and Experimental Neuropsychiatry, 33,* 1079–1093.

Kaye, W.H., Bulik, C.M., Thornton, L., Barbarich, N., and Masters, K. (2004). Comorbidity of anxiety disorders with anorexia and bulimia nervosa. *American Journal of Psychiatry, 161,* 2215–2221.

Khalsa, S.S., Rudrauf, D., Damasio, A.R., Davidson, R.J., Lutz, A., and Tranel, D. (2008). Interoceptive awareness in experienced meditators. *Psychophysiology, 45,* 671–677.

Lask, B., Gordon, I., Christie, D., Frampton, I., Chowdhury, U., and Watkins, B. (2005). Functional neuroimaging in early-onset anorexia nervosa. *International Journal of Eating Disorders, 37,* supplement SW49–S51; discussion S87–S89.

Mussap, A.J. and Salton, N. (2006). A 'rubber-hand' illusion reveals a relationship between perceptual body image and unhealthy body change. *Journal of Health Psychology, 11,* 627–639.

Ng, V.W., Bullmore, E.T., de Zubicaray, G.I., Cooper, A., Suckling, J., and Williams,

S.C. (2001). Identifying rate-limiting nodes in large-scale cortical networks for visuo-spatial processing: an illustration using fMRI. *Journal of Cognitive Neuroscience, 13*, 537–545.

Noll, S.M. and Fredrickson, B.L. (1998). A mediational model linking self-objectification body shame, and disordered eating. *Psychology of Women Quarterly, 22*, 623–636.

Nunn, K., Hanstock, T., and Lask, B. (2008). *Who's Who of the Brain: A Guide to Its Inhabitants, Where They Live and What They Do*. London: Jessica Kingsley Books.

Nunn, K., Frampton, I., Gordon, I., and Lask, B. (2008). The fault is not in her parents but in her insula—a neurobiological hypothesis of anorexia nervosa. *European Eating Disorders Review, 16*, 355–360.

Osman, S., Cooper, M., Hackmann, A., and Veale, D. (2004). Spontaneously occurring images and early memories in people with body dysmorphic disorder. *Memory, 12*, 428–436.

Pia, L. and Tamietto, M. (2006). Unawareness in schizophrenia: neuropsychological and neuroanatomical findings. *Psychiatry and Clinical Neurosciences, 60*, 531–537.

Pollatos, O., Kurz, A.L., Albrecht, J., Schreder, T., Kleemann, A.M., Schöpf, V., Kopietz, R., Wiesmann, M., and Schandry, R. (2008). Reduced perception of bodily signals in anorexia nervosa. *Eating Behaviors, 9*, 381–388.

Råstam, M., Bjure, J., Vestergren, E., Uvebrant, P., Gillberg, I.C., Wentz, E., and Gillberg, C. (2001). Regional cerebral blood flow in weight-restored anorexia nervosa: a preliminary study. *Developmental Medicine and Child Neurology, 43*, 239–242.

Riva, G. (2011). The key to unlocking the virtual body: virtual reality in the treatment of obesity and eating disorders. *Journal of Diabetes Science and Technology, 5*, 283–292.

Riva, G. (2012). Neuroscience and eating disorders: the allocentric lock hypothesis. *Medical Hypotheses, 78*, 254–257.

Rolls, E.T. (2005). Taste, olfactory, and food texture processing in the brain, and the control of food intake. *Physiology and Behavior, 85*, 45–56.

Sachdev, P., Mondraty, N., Wen, W., and Gulliford, K. (2008). Brains of anorexia nervosa patients process self-images differently from non-self-images: an fMRI study. *Neuropsychologia, 46*, 2161–2168.

Sherman, B.J., Savage, C.R., Eddy, K.T., Blais, M.A., Deckersbach, T., Jackson, S.C., Franko, D.L., Rauch, S.L., and Herzog, D.B. (2006). Strategic memory in adults with anorexia nervosa: are there similarities to obsessive compulsive spectrum disorders? *International Journal of Eating Disorders, 39*, 468–476.

Speranza, M., Loas, G., Wallier, J., and Corcos, M. (2007). Predictive value of alexithymia in patients with eating disorders: a 3-year prospective study. *Journal of Psychosomatic Research, 63*, 365–371.

Troop, N.A., Murphy, F., Bramon, E., and Treasure, J.L. (2000). Disgust sensitivity in eating disorders: a preliminary investigation. *International Journal of Eating Disorders, 27*, 446–451.

Tsakiris, M., Tajadura-Jiménez, A., and Costantini, M. (2010). Just a heartbeat away from one's body: interoceptive sensitivity predicts malleability of body-representations. *Proceedings of the Royal Society B, 278*, 2470–2476.

Uher, R., Treasure, J., and Campbell, I.C. (2003). Neuroanatomical bases of eating disorders, in *Biological Psychiatry* (eds H. D'Haenen, J.A. den Boer and P. Willner), Chichester: John Wiley & Sons, Ltd.

Wagner, A., Ruf, M., Braus, D.F., and Schmidt, M.H. (2003). Neuronal activity changes and body image distortion in anorexia nervosa. *Neuroreport, 14*, 2193–2197.

Wagner, A., Aizenstein, H., Mazurkewicz, L., Fudge, J., Frank, G.K., Putnam, K., Bailer,

U.F., Fischer, L., and Kaye, W.H. (2008). Altered insula response to taste stimuli in individuals recovered from restricting-type anorexia nervosa. *Neuropsychopharmacology, 33,* 513–523.

Zigman, J.M. and Elmquist, J.K. (2003). Minireview: From anorexia to obesity—the yin and yang of body weight control. *Endocrinology, 144,* 3749–3756.

Chapter 3

Bell, R.M. (1987). *Holy Anorexia.* Chicago, IL: University of Chicago Press.

Binitie, A., Osaghae, and Akenzua, O.A. (2000). A case report of anorexia nervosa. *African Journal of Medicine and Medical Sciences, 29,* 175–177.

Bloss, C.S., Berrettini, W., Bergen, A.W., Magistretti, P., Duvvuri, V., Strober, M., Brandt, H., Crawford, S., Crow, S., Fichter, M.M., Halmi, K.A., Johnson, C., Kaplan, A.S., Keel, P., Klump, K.L., Mitchell, J., Treasure, J., Woodside, D.B., Marzola, E., Schork, N.J., and Kaye, W.H. (2011). Genetic association of recovery from eating disorders: the role of GABA receptor SNPs. *Neuropsychopharmacology, 36,* 2222–2232.

Bruch, H. (1979). *Eating Disorders: Obesity, Anorexia Nervosa, and the Person Within.* New York, NY: Basic Books.

Bulik, C.M., Sullivan, P.F., Wade, T.D., and Kendler, K.S. (2000). Twin studies of eating disorders: a review. *International Journal of Eating Disorders, 27,* 1–20.

Bulik, C.M., Tozzi, F., Anderson, C., Mazzeo, S.E., Aggen, S., and Sullivan, P.F. (2003). The relation between eating disorders and components of perfectionism. *American Journal of Psychiatry, 160,* 366–368.

Bulik, C.M., Sullivan, P.F., Tozzi, F., Furberg, H., Lichtenstein, P., and Pedersen, N.L. (2006). Prevalence, heritability, and prospective risk factors for anorexia nervosa. *Archives of General Psychiatry, 63,* 305–312.

Clarke, T.K., Weiss, A.R., and Berrettini, W.H. (2012). The genetics of anorexia nervosa. *Clinical Pharmacology and Therapeutics, 91,* 181–188.

Culbert, K.M., Breedlove, S.M., Burt, S.A., and Klump, K.L. (2008). Prenatal hormone exposure and risk for eating disorders: a comparison of opposite-sex and same-sex twins. *Archives of General Psychiatry, 65,* 329–336.

Dellava, J.E., Kendler, K.S., and Neale, M.C. (2011). Generalized anxiety disorder and anorexia nervosa: evidence of shared genetic variation. *Depression and Anxiety, 28,* 728–733.

Dobbs, D. (December 2009). The science of success. *The Atlantic.* Retrieved from: www.theatlantic.com/magazine/archive/2009/12/the-science-of-success/7761/.

Durant, C., Christmas, D., and Nutt, D. (2010). The pharmacology of anxiety. *Current Topics in Behavioral Neuroscience, 2,* 303–330.

Frieling, H., Römer, K.D., Scholz, S., Mittelbach, F., Wilhelm, J., De Zwaan, M., Jacoby, G.E., Kornhuber, J., Hillemacher, T., and Bleich, S. (2010). Epigenetic dysregulation of dopaminergic genes in eating disorders. *International Journal of Eating Disorders, 43,* 577–583.

Fumagalli, F., Molteni, R., Racagni, G., and Riva, M.A. (2007). Stress during development: impact on neuroplasticity and relevance to psychopathology. *Progress in Neurobiology, 81,* 197–217.

Garner, D.M. and Garfinkel, P.E. (1980). Socio-cultural factors in the development of anorexia nervosa. *Psychological Medicine, 10,* 647–656.

Grice, D.E., Halmi, K.A., Fichter, M.M., Strober, M., Woodside, D.B., Treasure, J.T., Kaplan, A.S., Magistretti, P.J., Goldman, D., Bulik, C.M., Kaye, W.H., and Berrettini,

W.H. (2002). Evidence for a susceptibility gene for anorexia nervosa on chromosome 1. *American Journal of Human Genetics, 70,* 787–792.

Habermas, T. (1989). The psychiatric history of anorexia nervosa and bulimia nervosa: weight concerns and bulimic symptoms in early case reports. *International Journal of Eating Disorders, 8,* 259–273.

Helder, S.G. and Collier, D.A. (2011). The genetics of eating disorders. *Current Topics in Behavioral Neuroscience, 6,* 157–175.

Holland, A.J., Sicotte, N., and Treasure, J. (1988). Anorexia nervosa: evidence for a genetic basis. *Journal of Psychosomatic Research, 32,* 561–571.

Husni, M., Koye, N., and Haggarty, J. (2001). Severe anorexia in an Amish Mennonite teenager. *Canadian Journal of Psychiatry, 46,* 183.

Kaye, W.H., Gwirtsman, H.E., George, D.T., and Ebert, M.H. (1991). Altered serotonin activity in anorexia nervosa after long-term weight restoration. *Archives of General Psychiatry, 48,* 556–562.

Kaye, W.H., Lilenfeld, L.R., Berrettini, W.H., Strober, M., Devlin, B., Klump, K.L., Goldman, D., Bulik, C.M., Halmi, K.A., Fichter, M.M., Kaplan, A., Woodside, D.B., Treasure, J., Plotnicov, K.H., Pollice, C., Rao, R., and McConaha, C.W. (2000). A search for susceptibility loci for anorexia nervosa: methods and sample description. *Biological Psychiatry, 47,* 794–803.

Kaye, W.H., Bulik, C.M., Thornton, L., Barbarich, N., and Masters, K. (2004). Comorbidity of anxiety disorders with anorexia and bulimia nervosa. *American Journal of Psychiatry, 161,* 2215–2221.

Keel, P.K. and Klump, K.L. (2003). Are eating disorders culture-bound syndromes? Implications for conceptualizing their etiology. *Psychological Bulletin, 129,* 747–769.

Klump, K.L. and Gobrogge, K.L. (2005). A review and primer of molecular genetic studies of anorexia nervosa. *International Journal of Eating Disorders, 37,* S43–S48.

Klump, K. L., McGue, M., and Iacono, W. G. (2003). Differential heritability of eating attitudes and behaviors in prepubertal versus pubertal twins. *International Journal of Eating Disorders, 33,* 287–292.

Klump, K.L., Burt, S.A., McGue, M., and Iacono, W.G. (2007). Changes in genetic and environmental influences on disordered eating across adolescence: a longitudinal twin study. *Archives of General Psychiatry, 64,* 1409–1415.

Kupfer, D.J., Frank, E., and Phillips, M.L. (2012). Major depressive disorder: new clinical, neurobiological, and treatment perspectives. *Lancet, 379,* 1045–1055.

Leibowitz, S.F. and Alexander, J.T. (1998). Hypothalamic serotonin in control of eating behavior, meal size, and body weight. *Biological Psychiatry, 44,* 851–864.

Lilenfeld, L.R., Kaye, W.H., Greeno, C.G., Merikangas, K.R., Plotnicov, K., Pollice, C., Rao, R., Strober, M., Bulik, C.M., and Nagy, L. (1998). A controlled family study of anorexia nervosa and bulimia nervosa: psychiatric disorders in first-degree relatives and effects of proband comorbidity. *Archives of General Psychiatry, 55,* 603–610.

Lydecker, J.A., Pisetsky, E.M., Mitchell, K.S., Thornton, L.M., Kendler, K.S., Reichborn-Kjennerud, T., Lichtenstein, P., Bulik, C.M., and Mazzeo, S.E. (2012). Association between co-twin sex and eating disorders in opposite sex twin pairs: evaluations in North American, Norwegian, and Swedish samples. *Journal of Psychosomatic Research, 72,* 73–77.

Lydiard, R.B. (2003). The role of GABA in anxiety disorders. *Journal of Clinical Psychiatry, 64,* 21–27.

McEwen, B.S. (2007). Physiology and neurobiology of stress and adaptation: central role of the brain. *Physiological Reviews, 87,* 873–904.

McLaren, L., Gauvin, L., and White, D. (2001). The role of perfectionism and excessive commitment to exercise in explaining dietary restraint: replication and extension. *International Journal of Eating Disorders, 29*, 307–313.

Martinowich, K., Manji, H., and Lu, B. (2007). New insights into BDNF function in depression and anxiety. *Nature Neuroscience, 10*, 1089–1093.

Matsushita, S., Suzuki, K., Murayama, M., Nishiguchi, N., Hishimoto, A., Takeda, A., Shirakawa, O., and Higuchi, S. (2004). Serotonin transporter regulatory region polymorphism is associated with anorexia nervosa. *American Journal of Medical Genetics Part B: Neuropsychiatric Genetics, 128B*, 114–117.

Minuchin, S., Rosman, B.L., and Baker, L. (1978). *Psychosomatic Families: Anorexia Nervosa in Context.* Cambridge, MA: Harvard University Press.

Owen, P.R. and Laurel-Seller, E. (2000). Weight and shape ideals: thin is dangerously in. *Journal of Applied Sociology, 30*, 979–990.

Ozaki, N., Goldman, D., Kaye, W.H., Plotnicov, K., Greenberg, B.D., Lappalainen, J., Rudnick, G., and Murphy, D.L. (2003). Serotonin transporter missense mutation associated with a complex neuropsychiatric phenotype. *Molecular Psychiatry, 8*, 933–936.

Pinker, S. (2003). *The Blank Slate: The Modern Denial of Human Nature.* New York, NY: Penguin Books.

Rieger, E., Touyz, S.W., Swain, T., and Beumont, P.J. (2001). Cross-cultural research on anorexia nervosa: assumptions regarding the role of body weight. *International Journal of Eating Disorders, 29*, 205–215.

Roth, T.L., Lubin, F.D., Funk, A.J., and Sweatt, J.D. (2009). Lasting epigenetic influence of early life adversity on the BDNF gene. *Biological Psychiatry, 65*, 760–769.

Rubinstein, S. and Caballero, B. (2000). Is Miss America an undernourished role model? *Journal of the American Medical Association, 283*, 1569.

Strober, M., Morrell, W., Burroughs, J., Salkin, B., and Jacobs, C. (1985). A controlled family study of anorexia nervosa. *Journal of Psychiatric Research, 19*, 239–246.

Tsankova, N., Renthal, W., Kumar, A., and Nestler, E.J. (2007). Epigenetic regulation in psychiatric disorders. *Nature Reviews Neuroscience, 8*, 355–367.

Tsuang, M.T., Bar, J.L., Stone, W.S., and Faraone, S.V. (2004). Gene-environment interactions in mental disorders. *World Psychiatry, 3*, 73–83.

Wade, T.D., Bulik, C.M., Neale, M., and Kendler, K.S. (2000). Anorexia nervosa and major depression: shared genetic and environmental risk factors. *American Journal of Psychiatry, 157*, 469–471.

Walters, E.E. and Kendler, K.S. (1995). Anorexia nervosa and anorexic-like syndromes in a population-based female twin sample. *American Journal of Psychiatry, 152*, 64–71.

Woodside, D.B., Bulik, C.M., Halmi, K.A., Fichter, M.M., Kaplan, A., Berrettini, W.H., Strober, M., Treasure, J., Lilenfeld, L., Klump, K., and Kaye, W. H. (2002). Personality, perfectionism, and attitudes toward eating in parents of individuals with eating disorders. *International Journal of Eating Disorders, 31*, 290–299.

Chapter 4

American Psychiatric Association. (2000). *Diagnostic and Statistical Manual of Mental Disorders, Fourth Edition, Text Revision.* American Psychiatric Association: Washington, DC.

Anderluh, M.B., Tchanturia, K., Rabe-Hesketh, S., and Treasure, J. (2003). Childhood obsessive-compulsive personality traits in adult women with eating disorders: defining a broader eating disorder phenotype. *American Journal of Psychiatry, 160*, 242–247.

Bellodi, L., Cavallini, M. C., Bertelli, S., Chiapparino, D., Riboldi, C., and Smeraldi, E. (2001). Morbidity risk for obsessive-compulsive spectrum disorders in first-degree relatives of patients with eating disorders. *American Journal of Psychiatry, 158*(4), 563–569.

Bulik, C.M., Tozzi, F., Anderson, C., Mazzeo, S.E., Aggen, S., and Sullivan, P.F. (2003). The relation between eating disorders and components of perfectionism. *American Journal of Psychiatry, 160*, 366–368.

Cassin, S.E. and von Ranson, K.M. (2005). Personality and eating disorders: a decade in review. *Clinical Psychology Review, 25*, 895–916.

Castro-Fornieles, J., Gual, P., Lahortiga, F., Gila, A., Casulà, V., Fuhrmann, C., Imirizaldu, M., Saura, B., Martínez, E., and Toro, J. (2007). Self-oriented perfectionism in eating disorders. *International Journal of Eating Disorders, 40*(6), 562–568.

Fassino, S., Abbate-Daga, G., Amianto, F., Leombruni, P., Boggio, S., and Rovera, G.G. (2002). Temperament and character profile of eating disorders: a controlled study with the Temperament and Character Inventory. *International Journal of Eating Disorders, 32*(4), 412–425.

Flett, G.L. and Hewitt, P.L. (2002). Perfectionism and maladjustment: an overview of theoretical, definitional, and treatment issues, in *Perfectionism: theory, research, and treatment* (eds G.L. Flett and P.L. Hewitt), Washington, D.C.: American Psychological Association.

Forbush, K., Heatherton, T.F., and Keel, P.K. (2007). Relationships between perfectionism and specific disordered eating behaviors. *International Journal of Eating Disorders, 40*(1), 37–41.

Halmi, K.A., Sunday, S.R., Strober, M., Kaplan, A., Woodside, D.B., Fichter, M., Treasure, J., Berrettini, W.H., and Kaye, W.H. (2000). Perfectionism in anorexia nervosa: variation by clinical subtype, obsessionality, and pathological eating behavior. *American Journal of Psychiatry, 157*, 1799–1805.

Holtkamp, K., Müller, B., Heussen, N., Remschmidt, H., and Herpertz-Dahlmann, B. (2005). Depression, anxiety, and obsessionality in long-term recovered patients with adolescent-onset anorexia nervosa. *European Child and Adolescent Psychiatry, 14*, 106–110.

LeDoux, J. (2003). The emotional brain, fear, and the amygdala. *Cellular and Molecular Neurobiology, 23*, 727–738.

Ribases, M., Gratacos, M., Badia, A., Jimenez, L., Solano, R., Vallejo, J., Fernandez-Aranda, F., and Estivill, X. (2005). Contribution of NTRK2 to the genetic susceptibility to anorexia nervosa, harm avoidance and minimum body mass index. *Molecular Psychiatry, 10*, 851–860.

Shin, L.M. and Liberzon, I. (2010). The neurocircuitry of fear, stress, and anxiety disorders. *Neuropsychopharmacology, 35*, 165–191.

Steinglass, J.E., Walsh, B.T., and Stern, Y. (2006). Set shifting deficit in anorexia nervosa. *Journal of the International Neuropsychological Society, 12*, 431–435.

Tchanturia, K., Davies, H., Roberts, M., Harrison, A., Nakazato, M., Schmidt, U., Treasure, J., and Morris R. (2012). Poor cognitive flexibility in eating disorders: examining the evidence using the Wisconsin card sorting task. *PLoS ONE, 7*, e28331.

Tenconi, E., Santonastaso, P., Degortes, D., Bosello, R., Titton, F., Mapelli, D., and Favaro, A. (2010). Set-shifting abilities, central coherence, and handedness in anorexia nervosa patients, their unaffected siblings and healthy controls: exploring putative endophenotypes. *World Journal of Biological Psychiatry, 11*, 813–823.

Thompson-Brenner, H. and Westen, D. (2005). Personality subtypes in eating disorders: validation of a classification in a naturalistic sample. *British Journal of Psychiatry,* *186,* 516–524.

Treasure, J. (2007). Getting beneath the phenotype of anorexia nervosa: the search for viable endophenotypes and genotypes. *Canadian Journal of Psychiatry, 52,* 212–219.

WebMD Health News. (2003). Perfectionism linked to eating disorders. *WebMD.* Retrieved from: www.webmd.com/news/20030205/perfectionism-linked-to-eating-disorders.

Westen, D. and Harnden-Fischer, J. (2001). Personality profiles in eating disorders: rethinking the distinction between axis I and axis II. *American Journal of Psychiatry,* *158,* 547–562.

Chapter 5

Bellodi, L., Cavallini, M.C., Bertelli, S., Chiapparino, D., Riboldi, C., and Smeraldi, E. (2001). Morbidity risk for obsessive-compulsive spectrum disorders in first-degree relatives of patients with eating disorders. *American Journal of Psychiatry, 158,* 563–569.

Bulik, C.M., Klump, K.L., Thornton, L., Kaplan, A.S., Devlin, B., Fichter, M.M., Halmi, K.A., Strober, M., Woodside, D.B., Crow, S., Mitchell, J.E., Rotondo, A., Mauri, M., Cassano, G.B., Keel, P.K., Berrettini, W.H., and Kaye, W.H. (2004). Alcohol use disorder comorbidity in eating disorders: a multicenter study. *Journal of Clinical Psychiatry, 65,* 1000–1006.

Cassin, S.E. and von Ranson, K.M. (2005). Personality and eating disorders: a decade in review. *Clinical Psychology Review, 25,* 895–916.

Drummond, L. (2009). *Study Reveals Prevalence Of Disordered Eating In Patients With Anxiety.* Annual Meeting of the Royal College of Psychiatrists, BT Convention Centre, Liverpool, June 2–5, 2009.

Fornaro, M., Perugi, G., Gabrielli, F., Prestia, D., Mattei, C., Vinciguerra, V., and Fornaro, P. (2010). Lifetime co-morbidity with different subtypes of eating disorders in 148 females with bipolar disorders. *Journal of Affective Disorders, 121,* 147–151.

Gillberg, C. and Billstedt, E. (2000). Autism and Asperger syndrome: coexistence with other clinical disorders. *Acta Psychiatrica Scandinavica, 102,* 321–330.

Giovanni, A.D., Carla, G., Enrica, M., Federico, A., Maria, Z., and Secondo, F. (2011). Eating disorders and major depression: role of anger and personality. *Depression Research and Treatment, 2011,* Article ID 194732, doi: 10.1155/2011/194732.

Hambrook, D., Tchanturia, K., Schmidt, U., Russell, T., and Treasure, J. (2008). Empathy, systemizing, and autistic traits in anorexia nervosa: a pilot study. *British Journal of Clinical Psychology, 47,* 335–339.

Harris, J. (2000). Self-harm: cutting the bad out of me. *Qualitative Health Research, 10,* 164–173.

Herzog, D.B., Nussbaum, K.M., and Marmor, A.K. (1996). Comorbidity and outcome in eating disorders. *Psychiatric Clinics of North America, 19,* 843–859.

Keys, A., Brozek, J., Henschel, A., Mickelsen, O., and Taylor, H.L. (1950). *The Biology of Human Starvation.* Minneapolis: University of Minnesota Press.

Krug, I., Pinheiro, A. P., Bulik, C., Jiménez-Murcia, S., Granero, R., Penelo, E., Masuet, C., Agüera, Z., and Fernández-Aranda, F. (2009). Lifetime substance abuse, family history of alcohol abuse/dependence and novelty seeking in eating disorders: comparison study of eating disorder subgroups. *Psychiatry and Clinical Neurosciences, 63,* 82–87.

Liang, K.Y. and Meg Tseng, M.C. (2011). Impulsive behaviors in female patients with eating disorders in a university hospital in northern Taiwan. *Journal of the Formosan Medical Association, 110*, 607–610.

Nock, M.K. and Mendes, W.B. (2008). Physiological arousal, distress tolerance, and social problem-solving deficits among adolescent self-injurers. *Journal of Consulting and Clinical Psychology, 76*, 28–38.

Nock, M.K. and Prinstein, M.J. (2004). A functional approach to the assessment of self-mutilative behavior. *Journal of Consulting and Clinical Psychology, 72*, 885–890.

Nock, M.K., and Prinstein, M.J. (2005). Contextual features and behavioral functions of self-mutilation among adolescents. *Journal of Abnormal Psychology, 114*, 140–146.

Oldershaw, A., Treasure, J., Hambrook, D., Tchanturia, K., and Schmidt, U. (2011). Is anorexia nervosa a version of autism spectrum disorders? *European Eating Disorders Review, 19*(6), 462–474.

Peebles, R., Wilson, J.L., and Lock, J.D. (2011). Self-injury in adolescents with eating disorders: correlates and provider bias. *Journal of Adolescent Health, 48*, 310–313.

Reyes-Rodríguez, M.L., Von Holle, A., Ulman, T.F., Thornton, L.M., Klump, K.L., Brandt, H., Crawford, S., Fichter, M.M., Halmi, K.A., Huber, T., Johnson, C., Jones, I., Kaplan, A.S., Mitchel, J.E., Strober, M., Treasure, J., Woodside, D.B., Berrettini, W.H., Kaye, W.H., and Bulik, C.M. (2011). Posttraumatic stress disorder in anorexia nervosa. *Psychosomatic Medicine, 73*, 491–497.

Rothenberg, A. (1990). Adolescence and eating disorder: the obsessive-compulsive syndrome. *Psychiatric Clinics of North America, 13*, 469–488.

Royal College of Psychiatrists. (2009). Study reveals prevalence of disordered eating in patients with anxiety. *Royal College of Psychiatrists press release*. Retrieved from: www. rcpsych.ac.uk/press/pressreleases2009/disorderedeating.aspx.

Sansone, R.A. and Levitt, J.L. (2002). Self-harm behaviors among those with eating disorders: an overview. *Eating Disorders, 10*, 205–213.

Schulze, U.M., Calame, S., Keller, F., and Mehler-Wex, C. (2009). Trait anxiety in children and adolescents with anorexia nervosa. *Eating and Weight Disorders, 14*, e163–168.

Selby, E.A., Anestis, M.D., and Joiner, T.E. (2008). Understanding the relationship between emotional and behavioral dysregulation: emotional cascades. *Behavior Research and Therapy, 46*, 593–611.

Stein, D., Lilenfeld, L.R., Wildman, P.C., and Marcus, M.D. (2004). Attempted suicide and self-injury in patients diagnosed with eating disorders. *Comprehensive Psychiatry, 45*, 447–451.

Zucker, N.L., Losh, M., Bulik, C.M., LaBar, K.S., Piven, J., and Pelphrey, K.A. (2007). Anorexia nervosa and autism spectrum disorders: guided investigation of social cognitive endophenotypes. *Psychological Bulletin, 133*, 976–1006.

Chapter 6

Bailer, U.F., Price, J.C., Meltzer, C.C., Mathis, C.A., Frank, G.K., Weissfeld, L., McConaha, C.W., Henry, S.E., Brooks-Achenbach, S., Barbarich, N.C., and Kaye, W.H. (2004). Altered 5-HT(2A) receptor binding after recovery from bulimia-type anorexia nervosa: relationships to harm avoidance and drive for thinness. *Neuropsychopharmacology, 29*, 1143–1155.

Bailer, U.F., Frank, G.K., Henry, S.E., Price, J.C., Meltzer, C.C., Weissfeld, L., Mathis, C.A., Drevets, W.C., Wagner, A., Hoge, J., Ziolko, S.K., McConaha, C.W., and

Kaye, W.H. (2005). Altered brain serotonin 5-HT1A receptor binding after recovery from anorexia nervosa measured by positron emission tomography and [carbonyl11C]WAY-100635. *Archives of General Psychiatry, 62*, 1032–1041.

Bailer, U.F., Frank, G.K., Henry, S.E., Price, J.C., Meltzer, C.C., Mathis, C.A., Wagner, A., Thorton, L., Hoge, J., Ziolko, S.K., Becker, C.R., McConaha, C.W., and Kaye, W.H. (2007). Exaggerated 5-HT1A but normal 5-HT2A receptor activity in individuals ill with anorexia nervosa. *Biological Psychiatry, 61*, 1090–1099.

Baker, D., Roberts, R., and Towell, T. (2000). Factors predictive of bone mineral density in eating-disordered women: a longitudinal study. *International Journal of Eating Disorders, 27*, 29–35.

Beckmann, N., Turkalj, I., Seelig, J., and Keller, U. (1991). 13C NMR for the assessment of human brain glucose metabolism in vivo. *Biochemistry, 30*, 6362–6366.

Broglio, F., Gianotti, L., Destefanis, S., Fassino, S., Abbate Daga, G., Mondelli, V., Lanfranco, F., Gottero, C., Hofland, L., Van der Lely, A.J., and Ghigo, E. (2004). The endocrine response to acute ghrelin administration is blunted in patients with anorexia nervosa, a ghrelin hypersecretory state. *Clinical Endocrinology, 60*, 592–599.

Cason, J., Ainley, C.C., Wolstencroft, R.A., Norton, K.R., and Thompson, R.P. (1986). Cell-mediated immunity in anorexia nervosa. *Clinical & Experimental Immunology, 64*(2), 370–375.

Chin-Chance, C., Polonsky, K., and Schoeller, D. (2000). Twenty-four-hour leptin levels respond to cumulative short-term energy imbalance and predict subsequent intake. *Journal of Clinical and Endocrinological Metabolism, 85*, 2685–2691.

Cramer, T. (2008, January 20). Anorexia nearly killed my wife. *Glamour*. Retrieved from: www.msnbc.msn.com/id/22688706/.

Dezaki, K., Sone, H., Koizumi, M., Nakata, M., Kakei, M., Nagai, H., Hosoda, H., Kangawa, K., and Yada, T. (2006). Blockade of pancreatic islet-derived ghrelin enhances insulin secretion to prevent high-fat diet-induced glucose intolerance. *Diabetes, 55*, 3486–3493.

Dubuc, G., Phinney, S., Stern, J., and Havel, P. (1998). Changes of serum leptin and endocrine and metabolic parameters after 7 days of energy restriction in men and women. *Metabolism: Clinical and Experimental, 47*, 429–434.

Exner, C., Hebebrand, J., Remschmidt, H., Wewetzer, C., Ziegler, A., Herpertz, S., Schweiger, U., Blum, W.F., Preibisch, G., Heldmaier, G., and Klingenspor, M. (2000). Leptin suppresses semi-starvation induced hyperactivity in rats: implications for anorexia nervosa. *Molecular Psychiatry, 5*, 476–481.

Frank, G.K., Kaye, W.H., Meltzer, C.C., Price, J.C., Greer, P., McConaha, C., and Skovira, K. (2002). Reduced 5-HT2A receptor binding after recovery from anorexia nervosa. *Biological Psychiatry, 52*, 896–906.

Frederich, R., Hu, S., Raymond, N., and Pomeroy, C. (2002). Leptin in anorexia nervosa and bulimia nervosa: importance of assay technique and method of interpretation. *Journal of Laboratory and Clinical Medicine, 139*, 72–79.

Gaudio, S., Nocchi, F., Franchin, T., Genovese, E., Cannatà, V., Longo, D., and Fariello, G. (2011). Gray matter decrease distribution in the early stages of anorexia nervosa restrictive type in adolescents. *Psychiatry Research, 191*, 24–30.

Germain, N., Galusca, B., Le Roux, C.W., Bossu, C., Ghatei, M.A., Lang, F., Bloom, S.R., and Estour, B. (2007). Constitutional thinness and lean anorexia nervosa display opposite concentrations of peptide YY, glucagon-like peptide 1, ghrelin, and leptin. *American Journal of Clinical Nutrition, 85*, 967–971.

Golden, N.H., Ashtari, M., Kohn, M.R., Patel, M., Jacobson, M.S., Fletcher, A., and

Shenker, I.R. (1996). Reversibility of cerebral ventricular enlargement in anorexia nervosa, demonstrated by quantitative magnetic resonance imaging. *Journal of Pediatrics, 128,* 296–301.

Golla, J.A., Larson, L.A., Anderson, C.F., Lucas, A.R., Wilson, W.R., and Tomasi, T.B., Jr. (1981). An immunological assessment of patients with anorexia nervosa. *American Journal of Clinical Nutrition, 34,* 2756–2762.

Hebebrand, J., Exner, C., Hebebrand, K., Holtkamp, C., Casper, R.C., Remschmidt, H., Herpertz-Dahlmann, B., and Klingenspor, M. (2003). Hyperactivity in patients with anorexia nervosa and in semistarved rats: evidence for a pivotal role of hypoleptinemia. *Physiology and Behavior, 79,* 25–37.

Hettema, J.M., Neale, M.C., Myers, J.M., Prescott, C.A., and Kendler, K.S. (2006). A population-based twin study of the relationship between neuroticism and internalizing disorders. *American Journal of Psychiatry, 163,* 857–864.

Hillebrand, J.J., van Elburg, A.A., Kas, M.J., van Engeland, H., and Adan, R.A. (2005). Olanzapine reduces physical activity in rats exposed to activity-based anorexia: possible implications for treatment of anorexia nervosa? *Biological Psychiatry, 58,* 651–657.

Himmerich, H., Schönknecht, P., Heitmann, S., and Sheldrick, A.J. (2010). Laboratory parameters and appetite regulators in patients with anorexia nervosa. *Journal of Psychiatric Practice, 16,* 82–92.

Inui, A., Asakawa, A., Bowers, C.Y., Mantovani, G., Laviano, A., Meguid, M.M., and Fujimiya, M. (2004). Ghrelin, appetite, and gastric motility: the emerging role of the stomach as an endocrine organ. *FASEB Journal, 18,* 439–456.

Karczewska-Kupczewska, M., Straczkowski, M., Adamska, A., Nikolajuk, A., Otziomek, E., Górska, M., and Kowalska, I. (2010). Increased suppression of serum ghrelin concentration by hyperinsulinemia in women with anorexia nervosa. *European Journal of Endocrinology, 162,* 235–239.

Kaye, W.H. and Weltzin, T.E. (1991). Serotonin activity in anorexia and bulimia nervosa: relationship to the modulation of feeding and mood. *Journal of Clinical Psychiatry, 52S,* 41–48.

Kaye, W.H., Bailer, U.F., Frank, G.K., Wagner, A., and Henry, S.E. (2005). Brain imaging of serotonin after recovery from anorexia and bulimia nervosa. *Physiology and Behavior, 86,* 15–17.

Kojima, M., Hosoda, H., Date, Y., Nakazato, M., Matsuo, H., and Kangawa, K. (1999). Ghrelin is a growth-hormone-releasing acylated peptide from stomach. *Nature, 402,* 656–660.

Kolata, G. (2007). *Rethinking Thin: The New Science of Weight Loss—and the Myths and Realities of Dieting.* New York, NY: Farrar, Straus and Giroux.

Lawson, E.A., Donoho, D., Miller, K.K., Misra, M., Meenaghan, E., Lydecker, J., Wexler, T., Herzog, D.B., and Klibanski, A. (2009). Hypercortisolemia is associated with severity of bone loss and depression in hypothalamic amenorrhea and anorexia nervosa. *Journal of Clinical Endocrinology and Metabolism, 94,* 4710–4716.

Lawson, E.A., Miller, K.K., Bredella, M.A., Phan, C., Misra, M., Meenaghan, E., Rosenblum, L., Donoho, D., Gupta, R., and Klibanski, A. (2010). Hormone predictors of abnormal bone microarchitecture in women with anorexia nervosa. *Bone, 46,* 456–463.

Lohr, A. (2008, June 16). Hormone disorder may contribute to lack of menstruation in teenage athletes. *The Endocrine Society.* Retrieved from: www.eurekalert.org/pub_releases/2008-06/tes-hdm061408.php.

Margetic, S., Gazzola, C., Pegg, G.G., and Hill, R.A. (2002). Leptin: a review of its peripheral actions and interactions. *International Journal of Obesity and Related Metabolic Disorders, 26*, 1407–1433.

Miller, A.K.H and Corsellis, J.A.N. (1977). Evidence for a secular increase in human brain weight during the past century. *Annals of Human Biology, 4*, 253–257.

Misra, M., Miller, K.K., Tsai, P., Gallagher, K., Lin, A., Lee, N., Herzog, D.B., and Klibanski, A. (2006). Elevated peptide YY levels in adolescent girls with anorexia nervosa. *Journal of Clinical Endocrinology and Metabolism, 91*, 1027–1033.

Misra, M., Katzman, D., Miller, K.K., Mendes, N., Snelgrove, D., Russell, M., Goldstein, M.A., Ebrahimi, S., Clauss, L., Weigel, T., Mickley, D., Schoenfield, D.A., Herzog, D.B., and Klibanski, A. (2011). Physiologic estrogen replacement increases bone density in adolescent girls with anorexia nervosa. *Journal of Bone and Mineral Research, 26*, 2430–2438.

Müller, T.D., Föcker, M., Holtkamp, K., Herpertz-Dahlmann, B., and Hebebrand, J. (2009). Leptin-mediated neuroendocrine alterations in anorexia nervosa: somatic and behavioral implications. *Child and Adolescent Psychiatric Clinics of North America, 18*, 117–129.

Murphy, K.G. and Bloom, S.R. (2006). Gut hormones and the regulation of energy homeostasis. *Nature, 444*, 854–859.

Nova, E., Samartín, S., Gómez, S., Morandé, G., and Marcos, A. (2002). The adaptive response of the immune system to the particular malnutrition of eating disorders. *European Journal of Clinical Nutrition, 56*, S34–S37.

Page, A., Slattery, J., Milte, C., Laker, R., O'Donnell, T., Dorian, C., Brierley, S.M., and Blackshaw, L.A. (2007). Ghrelin selectively reduces mechanosensitivity of upper gastrointestinal vagal afferents. *American Journal of Physiological and Gastrointestinal Liver Physiology, 292*, 1376–1384.

Scheid, J.L., Toombs, R.J., Ducher, G., Gibbs, J.C., Williams, N.I., and De Souza, M.J. (2011). Estrogen and peptide YY are associated with bone mineral density in premenopausal exercising women. *Bone, 49*, 194–201.

Teng, K. (2011). Premenopausal osteoporosis, an overlooked consequence of anorexia nervosa. *Cleveland Clinic Journal of Medicine, 78*, 50–58.

Tolle, V., Kadem, M., Bluet-Pajot, M.T., Frere, D., Foulon, C., Bossu, C., Dardennes, R., Mounier, C., Zizzari, P., Lang, F., Epelbaum, J., and Estour, B. (2003). Balance in ghrelin and leptin plasma levels in anorexia nervosa patients and constitutionally thin women. *Journal of Clinical Endocrinology and Metabolism, 88*, 109–116.

Tschöp, M., Smiley, D.L., and Heiman, M.L. (2000). Ghrelin induces adiposity in rodents. *Nature, 407*, 908–913.

Tucker, T. (2008). *The Great Starvation Experiment: Ancel Keys and the Men Who Starved for Science.* Minneapolis, MN: University of Minnesota Press.

Utz, A.L., Lawson, E.A., Misra, M., Mickley, D., Gleysteen, S., Herzog, D.B., Klibanski, A., and Miller, K.K. (2008). Peptide YY (PYY) levels and bone mineral density (BMD) in women with anorexia nervosa. *Bone, 43*, 135–139.

Wong, J.C., Lewindon, P., Mortimer, R., and Shepherd, R. (2001). Bone mineral density in adolescent females with recently diagnosed anorexia nervosa. *International Journal of Eating Disorders, 29*, 11–16.

Zandian, M., Ioakimidis, I., Bergh, C., and Södersten, P. (2007). Cause and treatment of anorexia nervosa. *Physiology and Behavior, 92*, 283–290.

Zhang, Y., Proenca, R., Maffei, M., Barone, M., Leopold, L., and Friedman, J.M. (1994). Positional cloning of the mouse obese gene and its human homologue. *Nature, 372*, 425–432.

Chapter 7

Adan, R.A.H. and Vink, T. (2001). Drug target discovery by pharmacogenetics: mutations in the melanocortin system and eating disorders. *European Neuropsychopharmacology, 11,* 483–490.

Ananth, J., Burgoyne, K.S., Gadasalli, R., and Aquino, S. (2001). How do the atypical antipsychotics work? *Journal of Psychiatry and Neuroscience, 26,* 385–394.

Bergh, C. and Sodersten, P. (1996). Anorexia nervosa, self-starvation and the reward of stress. *Nature Medicine, 2,* 21–22.

Bingle, C.D. and Gowan, S. (1996). Molecular cloning of the forkhead transcription factor HNF-3 alpha from a human pulmonary adenocarcinoma cell line. *Biochimica et Biophysica Acta, 1307,* 17–20.

Birmingham, C.L. and Gritzner, S. (2006). How does zinc supplementation benefit anorexia nervosa? *Eating and Weight Disorders, 11,* e109–111.

Bissada, H., Tasca, G.A., Barber, A.M., and Bradwejn, J. (2008). Olanzapine in the treatment of low body weight and obsessive thinking in women with anorexia nervosa: a randomized, double-blind, placebo-controlled trial. *American Journal of Psychiatry, 165,* 1281–1288.

Brick, D.J., Gerweck, A.V., Meenaghan, E., Lawson, E.A., Misra, M., Fazeli, P., Johnson, W., Klibanski, A., and Miller, K.K. (2010). Determinants of IGF-1 and GH across the weight spectrum: from anorexia nervosa to obesity. *European Journal of Endocrinology, 163,* 185–191.

Coates, J.C. and de Bono, M. (2002). Antagonistic pathways in neurons exposed to body fluid regulate social feeding in Caenorhabditis elegans. *Nature, 419,* 925–929.

Cryan, P.M., Meteyer, C.U., Boyles, J.G., and Blehert, D.S. (2010). Wing pathology of white-nose syndrome in bats suggests life-threatening disruption of physiology. *BMC Biology, 8,* 1–8.

Davis, W.L., Goodman, D.B.P., Crawford, L.A., Cooper, O.J., and Matthews, J.L. (1990). Hibernation activates glyoxylate cycle and gluconeogenesis in black bear brown adipose tissue. *Biochimica et Biophysica Acta, 1051,* 276–278.

de Bono, M., Tobin, D.M., Davis, M.W., Avery, L., and Bargmann, C.I. (2002). Social feeding in Caenorhabditis elegans is induced by neurons that detect aversive stimuli. *Nature, 419,* 899–903.

Demitrack, M.A., Lesem, M.D., Listwak, B.S., Brandt, H.A., Jimerson, D.C., and Gold, R.W. (1990). CSF oxytocin in anorexia nervosa and bulimia nervosa: clinical and pathophysiologic considerations. *American Journal of Psychiatry, 147,* 882–886.

Denou, E., Jackson, W., Lu, J., Blennerhassett, P., McCoy, K., Verdu, E.F., Collins, S.M., and Bercik, P. (2011). The intestinal microbiota determines mouse behavior and brain BDNF levels. *Gastroenterology, 140,* S-57.

Diamond, J. (2000, March 24). Blitzkrieg against the moas. *Science, 287,* 2170–2171.

Dobzhansky, T. (1973). Nothing in biology makes sense except in the light of evolution. *American Biology Teacher, 35,* 125–129.

Donohoe, D.R., Phan, T., Weeks, K., Aamodt, E.J., and Dwyer, D.S. (2008). Antipsychotic drugs up-regulate tryptophan hydroxylase in ADF neurons of Caenorhabditis elegans: role of calcium-calmodulin dependent protein kinase II and transient receptor potential vanilloid channel. *Journal of Neuroscience Research, 86,* 2553–2563.

Dwyer, D.S., Horton, R.Y., and Aamodt, E.J. (2011). Role of the evolutionarily conserved starvation response in anorexia nervosa. *Molecular Psychiatry, 16,* 595–603.

Engelmann, M., Wotjak, C.T., Neumann, I., Ludwig, M., and Landgraf, R. (1996).

Behavioral consequences of intracerebral vasopressin and oxytocin: focus on learning and memory. *Neuroscience and Biobehavioral Reviews, 20*, 341–358.

Favaro, A., Caregaro, L., Burlina, A.B., and Santonastaso, P. (2000). Tryptophan levels, excessive exercise, and nutritional status in anorexia nervosa. *Psychosomatic Medicine, 62*, 535–538.

Groscolas, R. and Leloup, J. (1989). The effect of severe starvation and captivity stress on plasma thyroxine and triiodothyronine concentrations in an antarctic bird (emperor penguin). *General and Comparative Endocrinology, 73*, 108–117.

Guisinger, S. (2003). Adapted to flee famine: adding an evolutionary perspective on anorexia nervosa. *Psychological Review, 110*, 745–761.

Guisinger, S. (2008). Competing paradigms for anorexia nervosa. *American Psychologist, 63*, 199–204.

Hebebrand, J., van der Heyden, J., Devos, R., Kopp, W., Herpertz, S., Remschmidt, H., and Herzog, W. (1995). Plasma concentrations of obese protein in anorexia nervosa. *Lancet, 346*, 1624–1625.

Helm, B. and Gwinner, E. (2006). Migratory restlessness in an equatorial non-migratory bird. *PLoS Biology, 4*, e110, doi:10.1371/journal.pbio.0040110.

Johnson, C. and Flach, A. (1985). Family characteristics of 105 patients with bulimia. *American Journal of Psychiatry, 142*, 1321–1324.

Jumpertz, R., Le, D.S., Turnbaugh, P.J., Trinidad, C., Bogardus, C., Gordon, J.I., and Krakoff, J. (2011). Energy-balance studies reveal associations between gut microbes, caloric load, and nutrient absorption in humans. *American Journal of Clinical Nutrition, 94*, 58–65.

Kaye, W.H. (1996). Neuropeptide abnormalities in anorexia nervosa. *Psychiatry Research, 62*, 65–74.

Kaye, W. H., Gendall, K., and Strober, M. (1998). Serotonin neuronal function and selective serotonin reuptake inhibitor treatment in anorexia and bulimia nervosa. *Biological Psychiatry, 44*, 825–838.

Keys, A., Brozek, J., Henschel, A., Mickelsen, O., and Taylor, H.L. (1950). *The Biology of Human Starvation*. Minneapolis: University of Minnesota Press.

Komatsu, M., Waguri, S., Ueno, T., Iwata, J., Murata, S., Tanida, I., Ezaki, J., Mizushima, N., Ohsumi, Y., Uchiyama, Y., Kominami, E., Tanaka, K., and Chiba, T. (2007). Impairment of starvation-induced and constitutive autophagy in Atg7-deficient mice. *Journal of Cell Biology, 169*, 425–434.

Kramer, J.M., Davidge, J.T., Lockyer, J.M., and Staveley, B.E. (2003). Expression of Drosophila FOXO regulates growth and can phenocopy starvation. *BMC Developmental Biology, 3*, 1–14.

Lask, B., Fosson, A., Rolfe, U., and Thomas, S. (1993). Zinc deficiency and childhood-onset anorexia nervosa. *Journal of Clinical Psychiatry, 54*, 63–66.

Lee, H.J., Macbeth, A.H., Pagani, J.H., and Young, W.S. (2009). Oxytocin: the great facilitator of life. *Progress in Neurobiology, 88*, 127–151.

Ley, R.E., Turnbaugh, P.J., Klein, S., and Gordon, J.I. (2006). Microbial ecology: human gut microbes associated with obesity. *Nature, 444*, 1022–1023.

Liang, B., Moussaif, M., Kuan, C., Gargus, J.J., and Sze, J.Y. (2006). Serotonin targets the DAF-16/FOXO signaling pathway to modulate stress responses. *Cell Metabolism, 4*, 429–440.

Lock, J. and Fitzpatrick, K.K. (2009). Anorexia nervosa. *Clinical Evidence (Online), 3*, 1011–1029.

Lockwood, S. (2006). *Polar Bears*. Chanhassen, MN: The Child's World.

McKnight, R.F. and Park, R.J. (2010). Atypical antipsychotics and anorexia nervosa: a review. *European Eating Disorders Review, 18,* 10–21.

Mehler-Wex, C., Romanos, M., Kirchheiner, J., and Schulze, U.M. (2008). Atypical antipsychotics in severe anorexia nervosa in children and adolescents—review and case reports. *European Eating Disorders Review, 16,* 100–108.

Messaoudi, M., Lalonde, R., Violle, N., Javelot, H., Desor, D., Nejdi, A., Bisson, J.F., Rougeot, C., Pichelin, M., Cazaubiel, M., and Cazaubiel J.M. (2011). Assessment of psychotropic-like properties of a probiotic formulation (Lactobacillus helveticus R0052 and Bifidobacterium longum R0175) in rats and human subjects. *British Journal of Nutrition, 105,* 755–764.

Mondraty, N., Birmingham, C.L., Toyuz, S., Sundakov, V., Chapman, L., and Beumont, P. (2005). Randomized controlled trial of olanzapine in the treatment of cognitions in anorexia nervosa. *Australasian Psychiatry, 13,* 72–75.

National Institutes of Health. (n.d.). Zinc. *Dietary Supplement Fact Sheets, Office of Dietary Supplements, National Institutes of Health.* Retrieved from: http://ods.od.nih.gov/factsheets/Zinc-HealthProfessional/.

Philbrick, N. (2001). *In the Heart of the Sea: The Tragedy of the Whaleship Essex.* New York: Penguin Books.

Powers, P.S., Santana, C.A., and Bannon, Y.S. (2002). Olanzapine in the treatment of anorexia nervosa: an open label trial. *International Journal of Eating Disorders, 32,* 146–154.

Sachdev, P., Mondraty, N., Wen, W., and Gulliford, K. (2008). Brains of anorexia nervosa patients process self-images differently from non-self-images: an fMRI study. *Neuropsychologia, 46,* 2161–2168.

Scarth, J.P. (2006). Modulation of the growth hormone-insulin-like growth factor (GH-IGF) axis by pharmaceutical, nutraceutical and environmental xenobiotics: an emerging role for xenobiotic-metabolizing enzymes and the transcription factors regulating their expression. A review. *Xenobiotica, 36,* 119–218.

Scott, R.C., Schuldiner, O., and Neufeld, T.P. (2004). Role and regulation of starvation-induced autophagy in the drosophila fat body. *Developmental Cell, 7,* 167–178.

Strober, M. (1995). Family-genetic perspectives on anorexia nervosa and bulimia nervosa, in *Eating Disorders and Obesity* (eds K.D. Brownell and C.G. Fairburn), pp. 212–218, New York: Guilford Press.

Tuteja, G. and Kaestner, K.H. (2007). SnapShot: forkhead transcription factors I. *Cell, 130,* 1160.

van der Horst, A. and Burgering, B.M. (2007). Stressing the role of FoxO proteins in lifespan and disease. *Nature Reviews Molecular and Cell Biology, 8,* 440–450.

Vazquez, A., Beg, Q.K., deMenezes, M.A., Ernst, J., Bar-Joseph, Z., Barabási, A.L., Boros, L.G., and Oltvai, Z.N. (2008). Impact of the solvent capacity constraint on *E. coli* metabolism. *BMC Systems Biology, 2, 7.*

Weinberger, D.R. and Zink, C.F. (2010). Cracking the moody brain: the rewards of self-starvation. *Nature Medicine, 16,* 1382–1383.

You, Y., Kim, J., Raizen, D.M., and Avery, L. (2008). Insulin, cGMP, and TGF-b signals regulate food intake and quiescence in C. elegans: a model for satiety. *Cell Metabolism, 7,* 249–257.

Zhou, Q.Y. and Palmiter, R.D. (1995). Dopamine-deficient mice are severely hypoactive, adipsic and aphagic. *Cell, 83,* 1197–1209.

Zhu, G., Spellman, P.T., Volpe, T., Brown, P.O., Botstein, D., Davis, T.N., and Futcher, B. (2000). Two yeast forkhead genes regulate the cell cycle and pseudohyphal growth. *Nature, 406,* 90–94.

Chapter 8

Anderluh, M.B., Tchanturia, K., Rabe-Hesketh, S., and Treasure, J. (2003). Childhood obsessive-compulsive personality traits in adult women with eating disorders: defining a broader eating disorder phenotype. *American Journal of Psychiatry, 160,* 242–247.

Bamber, D.J., Cockerill, I.M., Rodgers, S., and Carroll, D. (2003). Diagnostic criteria for exercise dependence in women. *British Journal of Sports Medicine, 37,* 393–400.

Bean, P., Maddocks, M.B., Timmel, P., and Weltzin, T. (2005). Gender differences in the progression of co-morbid psychopathology symptoms of eating disordered patients. *Eating and Weight Disorders, 10,* 168–174.

Beumont, P.J.V., Arthur, B., Russell, J.D., and Touyz, S.W. (1994). Excessive physical activity in dieting disorder patients: proposals for a supervised exercise program. *International Journal of Eating Disorders, 15,* 21–36.

Blumenthal, J.A., O'Toole, L.C., and Chang, J.L. (1984). Is running an analogue of anorexia nervosa? An empirical study of obligatory running and anorexia nervosa. *Journal of the American Medical Association, 252,* 520–523.

Bratland-Sanda, S., Martinsen, E.W., Rosenvinge, J.H., Rø, Ø., Hoffart, A., and Sundgot-Borgen, J. (2011). Exercise dependence score in patients with longstanding eating disorders and controls: the importance of affect regulation and physical activity intensity. *European Eating Disorders Review, 19,* 249–255.

Dalle Grave, R., Calugi, S., and Marchesini, G. (2008). Compulsive exercise to control shape or weight in eating disorders: prevalence, associated features, and treatment outcome. *Comprehensive Psychiatry, 49,* 346–352.

Davis, C. and Kaptein, S. (2006). Anorexia nervosa with excessive exercise: a phenotype with close links to obsessive-compulsive disorder. *Psychiatry Research, 142,* 209–217.

Davis, C., Kennedy, S.H., Ralevski, E., Dionne, M., Brewer, H., Neitzert, C., and Ratusny, D. (1995). Obsessive compulsiveness and physical activity in anorexia nervosa and high-level exercising. *Journal of Psychosomatic Research, 39,* 967–976.

Davis, C., Kaptein, S., Kaplan, A.S., Olmsted, M.P., and Woodside, D.B. (1998). Obsessionality in anorexia nervosa: the moderating influence of exercise. *Psychosomatic Medicine, 60,* 192–197.

Davis, C., Blackmore, E., Katzman, D.K., and Fox, J. (2005). Female adolescents with anorexia nervosa and their parents: a case-control study of exercise attitudes and behaviours. *Psychological Medicine, 35,* 377–386.

Dietrich, M.O. and Horvath, T.L. (2009, October 27). Wired for hunger: the brain and obesity. *Dana Foundation Cerebrum.* Retrieved from: www.dana.org/NEWS/CEREBRUM/detail.aspx?id=23672.

Goldfarb, A.H. and Jamurtas, A.Z. (1997). Beta-endorphin response to exercise. An update. *Sports Medicine, 24,* 8–16.

Greenleaf, C., Petrie, T.A., Carter, J., and Reel, J.J. (2009). Female collegiate athletes: prevalence of eating disorders and disordered eating behaviors. *American Journal of College Health, 57,* 489–495.

Greenwood, B.N. and Fleshner, M. (2008). Exercise, learned helplessness, and the stress-resistant brain. *Neuromolecular Medicine, 10,* 81–98.

Hausenblas, H.A. and Downs, D.S. (2002). How much is too much? The development and validation of the Exercise Dependence Scale. *Psychology and Health, 17,* 387–404.

Hausenblas, H.A. and Fallon, E.A. (2002). Relationship among body image, exercise behavior, and exercise dependence symptoms. *International Journal of Eating Disorders, 32,* 179–185.

Kanarek, R.B., D'Anci, K.E., Jurdak, N., and Mathes, W.F. (2009). Running and addiction: precipitated withdrawal in a rat model of activity-based anorexia. *Behavioural Neuroscience, 123,* 905–912.

Kaye, W.H. and Weltzin, T.E. (1991). Serotonin activity in anorexia and bulimia nervosa: relationship to the modulation of feeding and mood. *Journal of Clinical Psychiatry, 52S,* 41–48.

Kaye, W.H., Bulik, C.M., Thornton, L., Barbarich, N., and Masters, K. (2004). Comorbidity of anxiety disorders with anorexia and bulimia nervosa. *American Journal of Psychiatry, 161,* 2215–2221.

Naylor, H., Mountford, V., and Brown, G. (2011). Beliefs about excessive exercise in eating disorders: the role of obsessions and compulsions. *European Eating Disorders Review, 19,* 226–236.

O'Dea, J.A. and Abraham, S. (2002). Eating and exercise disorders in young college men. *Journal of American College Health, 50,* 273–278.

Ogden, J., Veale, D., and Summers, Z. (1997). The development and validation of the Exercise Dependence Questionnaire. *Addiction Research, 5,* 343–355.

Reynolds, G. (2009, November 18). Phys ed: why exercise makes you less anxious. *New York Times,* Well Blog. Retrieved from: http://well.blogs.nytimes.com/2009/11/18/phys-ed-why-exercise-makes-you-less-anxious.

Schorow, S. (2009, May 20). Going for broke. *MIT News Office.* Retrieved from: http://web.mit.edu/newsoffice/2009/vegas-tt0520.html.

Schultz, W. (2007). Behavioral dopamine signals. *Trends in Neurosciences, 30,* 203–210.

Shroff, H., Reba, L., Thornton, L.M., Tozzi, F., Klump, K.L., Berrettini, W.H., Brandt, H., Crawford, S., Crow, S., Fichter, M.M., Goldman, D., Halmi, K.A., Johnson, C., Kaplan, A.S., Keel, P., LaVia, M., Mitchell, J., Rotondo, A., Strober, M., Treasure, J., Woodside, D.B., Kaye, W.H., and Bulik, C. M. (2006). Features associated with excessive exercise in women with eating disorders. *International Journal of Eating Disorders, 39,* 454–461.

Spear, N.E. and Hill, W.F. (1962). Methodological note: weight loss in rats living in running wheel cages. *Psychological Reports, 11,* 437–438.

Terry, A., Szabo, A., and Griffiths, M. (2004). The Exercise Addiction Inventory: a new brief screening tool. *Addiction Research and Theory, 12,* 489–499.

Van Dijk, K.R.A., Sabuncu, M.R., and Buckner, R.L. (2012). The influence of head motion on intrinsic functional connectivity MRI. *Neuroimage, 59,* 431–438.

Veale, D. (1987). Exercise dependence. *British Journal of Addiction, 82,* 735–740.

Wagner, A., Aizenstein, H., Venkatraman, V.K., Fudge, J., May, J.C., Mazurkewicz, L., Frank, G.K., Bailer, U.F., Fischer, L., Nquyen, V., Carter, C., Putnam, K., and Kaye, W.H. (2007). Altered reward processing in women recovered from anorexia nervosa. *American Journal of Psychiatry, 164,* 1842–1849.

Weight, L.M. and Noakes, T.D. (1987). Is running an analog of anorexia? A survey of the incidence of eating disorders in female distance runners. *Medicine and Science in Sports and Exercise, 19,* 213–217.

Weltzin, T.E., Weisensel, N., Franczyk, D., Burnett, K., Klitz, C., and Bean, P. (2005). Eating disorders in men: update. *Journal of Men's Health, 2,* 186–193.

Yates, A., Leehey, K., and Shisslak, C.M. (1983). Running—an analogue of anorexia? *New England Journal of Medicine, 308,* 251–255.

Chapter 9

Arnold, C. (2011, July 3). Diagnosis: play games, treat anorexia. *Psychology Today*. Retrieved from: www.psychologytoday.com/articles/201108/diagnosis-play-games-treat-anorexia.

Bulik, C.M., Baucom, D.H., Kirby, J.S., and Pisetsky, E. (2011). Uniting Couples (in the treatment of) Anorexia Nervosa (UCAN). *International Journal of Eating Disorders, 44*, 19–28.

Chen, E.Y., le Grange, D., Celio Doyle, A., Zaitsoff, S., Doyle, P., Roehrig, J.P., and Washington, B. (2010). A case series of family-based therapy for weight restoration in young adults with anorexia nervosa. *Journal of Contemporary Psychotherapy, 40*, 219–224.

Dare, C., Eisler, I., Russell, G.F.M. and Szmukler, G.I. (1990). The clinical and theoretical impact of a controlled trial of family therapy in anorexia nervosa. *Journal of Marital and Family Therapy, 16*, 39–57.

Eisler, I., Dare, C., Russell, G.F., Szmukler, G., le Grange, D., and Dodge, E. (1997). Family and individual therapy in anorexia nervosa. A 5-year follow-up. *Archives of General Psychiatry, 54*, 1025–1030.

Epstein, R.H. (2009, July 13). When eating disorders strike in midlife. *New York Times*. Retrieved from: www.nytimes.com/ref/health/healthguide/esn-eating-disorders-ess.html.

Genders, R. and Tchanturia, K. (2010). Cognitive remediation therapy (CRT) for anorexia in group format: a pilot study. *Eating and Weight Disorders, 15*, e234–239.

Goldner, E.M., Birmingham, C.L., and Smye, V. (1997). *Addressing Treatment Refusal in Anorexia Nervosa: Clinical, Ethical, and Legal Considerations*. New York, NY: Guilford Press.

Griffiths, R.A., Beumont, P.J., Russell, J., Touyz, S.W., and Moore, G. (1997). The use of guardianship legislation for anorexia nervosa: a report of 15 cases. *Australia and New Zealand Journal of Psychiatry, 31*, 525–531.

Guarda, A.S., Pinto, A.M., Coughlin, J.W., Hussain, S., Haug, N.A., and Heinberg, L.J. (2007). Perceived coercion and change in perceived need for admission in patients hospitalized for eating disorders. *American Journal of Psychiatry, 164*, 108–114.

Gura, T. (2007). *Lying in Weight: The Hidden Epidemic of Eating Disorders in Adult Women*. New York, NY: HarperCollins.

Halmi, K.A., Agras, W.S., Crow, S., Mitchell, J., Wilson, G.T., Bryson, S.W., and Kraemer, H.C. (2005). Predictors of treatment acceptance and completion in anorexia nervosa: implications for future study designs. *Archives of General Psychiatry, 62*, 776–781.

Laurin, K., Kay, A., and Fitzsimons, G. (2012). Reactance versus rationalization: divergent responses to policies that constrain freedom. *Psychological Science, 23*, 205–209.

le Grange, D., Crosby, R.D., Rathouz, P.J., and Leventhal, B.L. (2007). A randomized controlled comparison of family-based treatment and supportive psychotherapy for adolescent bulimia nervosa. *Archives of General Psychiatry, 64*, 1049–1056.

le Grange, D., Lock, J., Loeb, K., and Nicholls, D. (2010). Academy for eating disorders position paper: the role of the family in eating disorders. *International Journal of Eating Disorders, 43*, 1–5.

Liu, A. (2011). *Restoring Our Bodies, Reclaiming Our Lives: Guidance and Reflections on Recovery from Eating Disorders*. Boston, MA: Trumpeter Books.

Lock, J., Le Grange, D., Agras, W.S., Moye, A., Bryson, S.W., and Jo, B. (2010). Randomized clinical trial comparing family-based treatment with adolescent-focused individual therapy for adolescents with anorexia nervosa. *Archives of General Psychiatry,* 67, 1025–1032.

McCormick, L.M., Keel, P.K., Brumm, M.C., Bowers, W., Swayze, V., Andersen, A., and Andreasen, N. (2008). Implications of starvation-induced change in right dorsal anterior cingulate volume in anorexia nervosa. *International Journal of Eating Disorders,* 41, 602–610.

Menon, D. (2011, November 1). People rationalize situations they're stuck with, but rebel when they think there's an out. *Association for Psychological Science press release.* Retrieved from: www.psychologicalscience.org/index.php/news/releases/people-rationalize-situations-theyre-stuck-with-but-rebel-when-they-think-theres-an-out.html.

Mitchum, R. (2010). Family-based treatment found most effective for anorexia nervosa patients. *University of Chicago press release.* Retrieved from: www.eurekalert.org/pub_releases/2010-10/uocm-fbt093010.php.

Nilsson, K. and Hagglof, B. (2006). Patient perspectives of recovery in adolescent onset anorexia nervosa. *Eating Disorders,* 14, 305–311.

Pitt, S., Lewis, R., Morgan, S., and Woodward, D. (2010). Cognitive remediation therapy in an outpatient setting: a case series. *Eating and Weight Disorders,* 15, e281–286.

Russell, G.F., Szmukler, G.I., Dare, C., and Eisler, I. (1987). An evaluation of family therapy in anorexia nervosa and bulimia nervosa. *Archives of General Psychiatry,* 44, 1047–1056.

Tchanturia, K., Davies, H., and Campbell, I.C. (2007). Cognitive remediation therapy for patients with anorexia nervosa: preliminary findings. *Annals of General Psychiatry,* 6, 14.

Timini, S. and Robinson, P. (1996). Disturbances in children of patients with eating disorders. *European Eating Disorders Review,* 4, 183–188.

Tozzi, F., Sullivan, P.F., Fear, J.L., McKenzie, J., and Bulik, C.M. (2003). Causes and recovery in anorexia nervosa: the patient's perspective. *International Journal of Eating Disorders,* 33, 143–154.

Watson, T.L., Bowers, W.A., and Andersen, A.E. (2000). Involuntary treatment of eating disorders. *American Journal of Psychiatry,* 157, 1806–1810.

Whitney, J., Easter, A., and Tchanturia, K. (2008). Service users' feedback on cognitive training in the treatment of anorexia nervosa: a qualitative study. *International Journal of Eating Disorders,* 41, 542–550.

Wood, L., Al-Khairulla, H., and Lask, B. (2011). Group cognitive remediation therapy for adolescents with anorexia nervosa. *Clinical Child Psychology and Psychiatry,* 16, 225–231.

Woodside, D. and Shekter-Wolfson, L. (1990). Parenting by patients with anorexia nervosa and bulimia nervosa. *International Journal of Eating Disorders,* 9, 303–309.

Chapter 10

Baran, S.A., Weltzin, T.E., and Kaye, W.H. (1995). Low discharge weight and outcome in anorexia nervosa. *American Journal of Psychiatry,* 152, 1070–1072.

Barton, J. and Pretty, J. (2010). What is the best dose of nature and green exercise for improving mental health? A multi-study analysis. *Environmental Science and Technology,* 44, 3947–3955.

Carter, J.C., Blackmore, E., Sutandar-Pinnock, K., and Woodside, D.B. (2004). Relapse in anorexia nervosa: a survival analysis. *Psychological Medicine,* 34, 671–679.

Carter, J.C., McFarlane, T.L., Bewell, C., Olmsted, M.P., Woodside, D.B., Kaplan, A.S. and Crosby, R.D. (2009). Maintenance treatment for anorexia nervosa: a comparison of cognitive behavior therapy and treatment as usual. *International Journal of Eating Disorders, 42,* 202–207.

Castro, J., Gila, A., Puig, J., Rodriguez, S., and Toro, J. (2004). Predictors of rehospitalization after total weight recovery in adolescents with anorexia nervosa. *International Journal of Eating Disorders, 36,* 22–30.

Castro-Fornieles, J., Casulà, V., Saura, B., Martínez, E., Lazaro, L., Vila, M., Plana, M.T., and Toro, J. (2007). Predictors of weight maintenance after hospital discharge in adolescent anorexia nervosa. *International Journal of Eating Disorders, 40,* 129–145.

Cloninger, C.S. (1993). A psychobiological model of temperament and character. *Archives of General Psychiatry, 50,* 975–990.

Davis, C. and Kaptein, S. (2006). Anorexia nervosa with excessive exercise: a phenotype with close links to obsessive-compulsive disorder. *Psychiatry Research, 142,* 209–217.

Devlin, B., Bacanu, S.A., Klump, K.L., Bulik, C.M., Fichter, M.M., Halmi, K.A., Kaplan, A.S., Strober, M., Treasure, J., Woodside, D.B., Berrettini, W.H., and Kaye, W.H. (2002). Linkage analysis of anorexia nervosa incorporating behavioral covariates. *Human Molecular Genetics, 11,* 689–696.

Doidge, N. (2007). *The Brain That Changes Itself: Stories of Personal Triumph from the Frontiers of Brain Science.* New York, NY: Penguin Books.

Eddy, K.T., Keel, P.K., Dorer, D.J., Delinsky, S.S., Franko, D.L., and Herzog, D.B. (2002). Longitudinal comparison of anorexia nervosa subtypes. *International Journal of Eating Disorders, 31,* 191–201.

Gowers, S.G., Weetman, J., Shore, A., Hossain, F., and Elvins, R. (2000). Impact of hospitalisation on the outcome of adolescent anorexia nervosa. *British Journal of Psychiatry, 176,* 138–141.

Halmi, K.A., Agras, W.S., Crow, S., Mitchell, J., Wilson, G.T., Bryson, S.W., and Kraemer, H.C. (2005). Predictors of treatment acceptance and completion in anorexia nervosa: implications for future study designs. *Archives of General Psychiatry, 62,* 776–781.

Hildebrandt, T., Bacow, T., Markella, M., and Loeb, K. L. (2012). Anxiety in anorexia nervosa and its management using family-based treatment. *European Eating Disorders Review, 20,* e1–e16.

Lund, B.C., Hernandez, E.R., Yates, W.R., Mitchell, J.R., McKee, P.A., and Johnson, C.L. (2009). Rate of inpatient weight restoration predicts outcome in anorexia nervosa. *International Journal of Eating Disorders, 42,* 301–305.

McGaugh, J.L., Cahill, L., and Roozendaal, B. (1996). Involvement of the amygdala in memory storage: interaction with other brain systems. *Proceedings of the National Academy of Sciences, 93,* 13508–13514.

Pike, K.M., Walsh, B.T., Vitousek, K., Wilson, G.T., and Bauer, J. (2003). Cognitive behavior therapy in the posthospitalization treatment of anorexia nervosa. *American Journal of Psychiatry, 160,* 2046–2049.

Reyes-Rodríguez, M.L., Von Holle, A., Ulman, T.F., Thornton, L.M., Klump, K.L., Brandt, H., Crawford, S., Fichter, M.M., Halmi, K.A., Huber, T., Johnson, C., Jones, I., Kaplan, A.S., Mitchell, J.E., Strober, M., Treasure, J., Woodside, D.B., Berrettini, W.H., Kaye, W.H., and Bulik, C.M. (2011). Posttraumatic stress disorder in anorexia nervosa. *Psychosomatic Medicine, 73,* 491–497.

Robergeau, K., Joseph, J., and Silber, T.J. (2006). Hospitalization of children and adolescents for eating disorders in the State of New York. *Journal of Adolescent Health,* *39,* 806–810.

Schebendach, J.E., Mayer, L.E., Devlin, M.J., Attia, E., Contento, I.R., Wolf, R.L., and Walsh, B.T. (2008). Dietary energy density and diet variety as predictors of outcome in anorexia nervosa. *American Journal of Clinical Nutrition, 87,* 810–816.

Schebendach, J., Mayer, L.E., Devlin, M.J., Attia, E., and Walsh, B.T. (2012). Dietary energy density and diet variety as risk factors for relapse in anorexia nervosa: a replication. *International Journal of Eating Disorders, 45,* 79–84.

Steinglass, J. and Walsh, B.T. (2006). Habit learning and anorexia nervosa: a cognitive neuroscience hypothesis. *International Journal of Eating Disorders, 39,* 267–275.

Steinglass, J., Albano, A.M., Simpson, H.B., Carpenter, K., Schebendach, J., and Attia, E. (2011). Fear of food as a treatment target: exposure and response prevention for anorexia nervosa in an open series. *International Journal of Eating Disorders, 45,* 615–621.

Steinhausen, H.C., Grigoroiu-Serbanescu, M., Boyadjieva, S., Neumärker, K.J., and Winkler Metzke, C. (2008). Course and predictors of rehospitalization in adolescent anorexia nervosa in a multisite study. *International Journal of Eating Disorders, 41,* 29–36.

Syed, M. (2010). *Bounce: Mozart, Federer, Picasso, Beckham, and the Science of Success.* New York, NY: HarperCollins.

Tozzi, F., Thornton, L.M., Klump, K.L., Fichter, M.M., Halmi, K.A., Kaplan, A.S., Strober, M., Woodside, D.B., Crow, S., Mitchell, J., Rotondo, A., Mauri, M., Cassano, G., Keel, P., Plotnicov, K.H., Pollice, C., Lilenfeld, L.R., Berrettini, W.H., Bulik, C.M., and Kaye, W.H. (2005). Symptom fluctuation in eating disorders: correlates of diagnostic crossover. *American Journal of Psychiatry, 162,* 732–740.

Walsh, B.T., Kaplan, A.S., Attia, E., Olmsted, M., Parides, M., Carter, J.C., Pike, K.M., Devlin, M.J., Woodside, B., Roberto, C.A., and Rockert, W. (2006). Fluoxetine after weight restoration in anorexia nervosa: a randomized controlled trial. *Journal of the American Medical Association, 295,* 2605–2612.

Willer, M.G., Thuras, P., and Crow, S.J. (2005). Implications of the changing use of hospitalization to treat anorexia nervosa. *American Journal of Psychiatry, 162,* 2374–2376.

Wiseman, C.V., Sunday, S.R., Klapper, F., Harris, W.A., and Halmi, K.A. (2001). Changing patterns of hospitalization in eating disorder patients. *International Journal of Eating Disorders, 30,* 69–74.

Chapter 11

Bardone-Cone, A.M., Harney, M.B., Maldonado, C.R., Lawson, M.A., Robinson, D.P., Smith, R., and Tosh, A. (2010). Defining recovery from an eating disorder: conceptualization, validation, and examination of psychosocial functioning and psychiatric comorbidity. *Behaviour Research and Therapy, 48,* 194–202.

Bardone-Cone, A.M., Sturm, K., Lawson, M.A., Robinson, D.P., and Smith, R. (2010). Perfectionism across stages of recovery from eating disorders. *International Journal of Eating Disorders, 43,* 139–148.

Eisler, I., Dare, C., Russell, G.F., Szmukler, G., le Grange, D., and Dodge, E. (1997). Family and individual therapy in anorexia nervosa. A 5-year follow-up. *Archives of General Psychiatry, 54,* 1025–1030.

Fitzsimmons, E.E. and Bardone-Cone, A.M. (2010). Differences in coping across stages of recovery from an eating disorder. *International Journal of Eating Disorders, 43,* 689–693.

Fitzsimmons-Craft, E.E., Bardone-Cone, A.M., and Kelly, K.A. (2011). Objectified body consciousness in relation to recovery from an eating disorder. *Eating Behaviors, 12,* 302–308.

Keel, P.K., Dorer, D.J., Franko, D.L., Jackson, S.C., and Herzog, D.B. (2005). Postremission predictors of relapse in women with eating disorders. *American Journal of Psychiatry, 162,* 2263–2268.

Morgan, H.G. and Russell, G.F.M. (1975). Value of family background and clinical features as predictors of long-term outcome in anorexia nervosa: four year follow-up study of 41 patients. *Psychological Medicine, 5,* 355–371.

Morgan, H.G. and Hayward, A.E. (1988). Clinical assessment of anorexia nervosa. The Morgan-Russell outcome assessment schedule. *British Journal of Psychiatry, 152,* 367–371.

Noordenbos, G. (2011a). When have eating disordered patients recovered and what do the DSM-IV criteria tell about recovery? *Eating Disorders, 19,* 234–245.

Noordenbos, G. (2011b). Which criteria for recovery are relevant according to eating disorder patients and therapists? *Eating Disorders, 19,* 441–451.

Noordenbos, G. and Seubring, A. (2006). Criteria for recovery from eating disorders according to patients and therapists. *Eating Disorders, 14,* 41–54.

Ratnasuriya, R.H., Eisler, I., Szmukler, G.I., and Russell, G.F. (1991). Anorexia nervosa: outcome and prognostic factors after 20 years. *British Journal of Psychiatry, 158,* 495–502.

Srinivasagam, N.M., Kaye, W.H., Plotnicov, K.H., Greeno, C., Weltzin, T.E., and Rao, R. (1995). Persistent perfectionism, symmetry, and exactness after long-term recovery from anorexia nervosa. *American Journal of Psychiatry, 152,* 1630–1634.

Strober, M., Freeman, R., and Morrell, W. (1997). The long-term course of severe anorexia nervosa in adolescents: Survival analysis of recovery, relapse, and outcome predictors over 10–15 years in a prospective study. *International Journal of Eating Disorders, 22,* 339–360.

Index